£1.00p

DUPLICATE

THE NORTH-EAST ENGINEERS' STRIKES OF 1871
THE NINE HOURS' LEAGUE

The North-East Engineers' Strikes of 1871

THE NINE HOURS' LEAGUE

E. ALLEN   J. F. CLARKE
N. McCORD   D. J. ROWE

FRANK GRAHAM

6 Queen's Terrace, Newcastle upon Tyne 2

Published 1971

SBN 902833 61 8

Printed in Great Britain by
Northumberland Press Limited
Gateshead

CONTENTS

5

PREFACE

This book originated in discussion in the North-East Group for the Study of Labour History, where it was decided to arrange for the appearance of a study of the 1871 strikes to coincide with their centenary. In order to set the strikes in their proper context, it was decided that the account of the strikes themselves should be preceded by introductory chapters dealing with the regional economy, the previous history of industrial relations in the area, and the background to the movement for reduction of hours of work.

The chapters were drafted by individual writers, Chapter 1 by E. Allen, Chapters 2 and 3 by D. J. Rowe, Chapters 4 and 5 by N. McCord, Chapter 6 by E. Allen and N. McCord. For the latter part of Chapter 3 and Chapters 4 and 5, J. F. Clarke's thesis was an important source. These drafts have, however, been considered by all four authors, and revised in the light of decisions reached during these discussions.

CHAPTER ONE

An Introduction to Industrial Tyneside

THE numerous accounts of varying length and quality of the economic development of Tyneside have a great deal in common: they tend to draw on much the same stock of facts and, invariably, they find their basic explanation of its industrial and commercial evolution in the coal resources of the Great Northern Coalfield and a river, which, for some fourteen miles or so from its entry into the sea is tidal. Two quotations selected almost at random provide some indication of this common emphasis.[1] But clearly there is something more to the explanation than reference simply to coal and a tidal river. That there is indeed something more to be explained is brought out sharply if we reflect that the Nine Hours' Movement which it is the purpose of this book to explore was a movement amongst Tyneside engineers and that by the early part of the present century the percentage of metal workers on Tyneside was nearly double the percentage of coal-miners.

Undoubtedly coal and a tidal river provide a basis for the growth of economic activity on Tyneside: if it were not so, it would be difficult to explain why the tag about the foolishness of carrying coals to Newcastle passed so early and remained so firmly and for so long in the folk-speech of the British people. But somewhere in the explanation a place must be found for the warships of Palmer's Iron & Shipbuilding Company at Jarrow, the warships and guns of the Armstrong enterprises at Elswick and Walker, and, eventually, the Mauretania, built for the Cunard Shipping Company by Swan, Hunter and Wigham Richardson at Wallsend, and the steam turbines produced by Sir Charles Parsons for the propelling of ships and the driving of generators in the production of electricity. Somewhere, too, in the explanation there must be a place for all those improvements to the river itself, without which the industrial and technological achievements mentioned would not have been possible. When R. W. Johnson entitled his study of these improvements 'The Making of the Tyne', he was justifiably putting the emphasis on what man

9

had done rather than nature. The clue of course to the basic importance of coal as a factor in stimulating economic growth in the North-
East coast area as a whole let alone that part of it we designate 'Industrial Tyneside'[2] is provided by the quantity of coal which lay
underground to be exploited and the varying classes of coal within
the total deposits which were capable of meeting the needs of diverse
markets. Coal is not homogeneous: it can vary in composition and
therefore in potential use enormously: and different classes of user
have vastly different needs. The Northern Coalfield had not only a
great deal of coal: it also had a great deal of the different classes of
coal which the various markets required. The extraction of coal from
pits in the north-east and its shipment from the Tyne, though not
exclusively from this river, began at an early date, as J. U. Nef has
shown.[3] But the massive totals of the last 150 years or so, particularly since the middle of the nineteenth century, were a product of the
industrial and technological changes of the nineteenth century. In
1816 the tonnage of coal raised in the whole of the coalfield was
approximately $4\frac{1}{2}$ million tons. In 1871 the total was over 27 million
tons and by 1911 it had reached approximately $56\frac{1}{2}$ million tons.
The biggest decennial percentage changes in production occurred
between 1826 and 1836 (+62%), 1851 and 1861 (+85%), 1861
and 1871 (+43%) and 1871 and 1881 (+28%). Between 1851
and 1871, the percentage increase is about 165%: between 1851
and 1881, the percentage increase is about 240%.[4]

A map of the coalfield, with labels showing the different classes
of coal produced in different parts of the coalfield would show a
division between House Coal, Steam Coal, Gas Coal and Coking
Coal.[5] Markets for all these classes of coal expanded considerably
during the nineteenth century, and the Tyneside area, as indeed other
parts of the north-east region, was admirably endowed by nature
to serve them. The House Coal met the needs of households both
in the north-east and in the briskly growing London market with
which, for centuries, the Tyne had had a profitable connection. Gas
Coal, more a product of that part of the field in the south-east of
Durham and therefore more easily shippable from ports other than
the Tyne, nevertheless served the needs of the region as well as those
of the London area in a similar fashion. Steam Coal became the
indispensable fuel of factories, brickworks, steam locomotives and,
as steam engines replaced sail for the propelling of ships, a market
was developed for the use of ships all over the world. Coking Coal
was an indispensible element in the making of iron and steel: Durham
coking coals were often described by the fuel and metallurgical

experts as amongst the best in Western Europe.

It is perhaps a commonplace of Economic History that the great expansion of population and output in Great Britain from 1750 or so onwards may be largely explained in terms of coal, steam and technology. This is an explanation which may be applied to the regional economy of Tyneside with enhanced relevance and force. The period from 1750 or so to 1914 has been described in a phrase of apt felicity as 'the era of carboniferous capitalism'. Nature gave Tyneside an endowment in the shape of accessible coal and a tidal river which fitted the economic and technological changes of the nineteenth century with providential precision. The economic and technological conjunction was as near to being perfect as human experience is ever likely to encounter. But one additional element, implied perhaps in the technological changes which were part of the total situation, needs to be related, and related very firmly and explicitly to the forces making for economic growth. This is the element of business enterprise. Given an economic system which is operated on the basis of economic freedom and private enterprise, the element or agency without which the system cannot function, at any rate function effectively, is that of entrepreneurship.

If it is a commonplace of Economic History that the growth of the British economy from the late eighteenth century onwards may be explained in terms of coal, steam and technology, it is equally a commonplace of the economics of a private enterprise system that production, whether in the shape of consumable goods or capital goods, depends upon the availability of natural resources, labour and capital, with business enterprise and organisation as the dynamic agency which makes the decisions as to how the available resources shall be most effectively used. Natural resources, labour and capital, while necessary for the production of output on which the livelihoods of the people will depend, do not arrange and organize themselves any more than the essential elements of sand, cement and water will spontaneously arrange themselves in the right quantities for the making of concrete. They have to be arranged and organized and, in the sort of system indicated, it is the entrepreneur who must take on this function. Typically, production, based on the principles of division of labour and the use of the device of the business firm, whether one-man business or public company, as its decision-making agency has involved anticipation of the market's requirements and has therefore necessarily involved the carrying of risks against which no insurance policy can provide a safeguard. In this system of private enterprise and private ownership, the entrepreneur may be thought of both as one who not only manages and steers a business along already settled lines, but also initiates changes in products, in methods of production, in scale of capital investment and in all the other respects where key decisions in the economic field have to be made. Tyneside's natural endowments needed to be managed. The coal needed to be mined and brought to the places of shipment or use: the river needed to be made serviceable for the needs of industry and commerce to an extent far beyond the limit at which nature alone left it. In the business world of the nineteenth century, men with the required entrepreneurial attitudes and energies came forward to provide the dynamic element which was needed. It is in this context of economic growth resulting from the purposeful actions of business-men who understood not only the conventions of competitive business but also, in varying degree, the new scientific technologies which were being harnessed to the productive process that the confrontation of employers and workmen in the Nine Hours' Movement on Tyneside needs to be set.

This confrontation is possibly as much a product of the evolutionary process which was taking place as the iron ship, and later the steel ship, in superseding wood, or the steam engine in superseding sail. Men tend to be caught up in a process of decision-making, whether in relation to production and its methods, or to industrial relations, where what they do is partly the outcome of their own free will and partly the outcome of the context in which they find themselves, to the creation of which they have, of course, made some contribution by reason of their decisions within the context of earlier and related situations. The economic development of Industrial Tyneside may thus be seen as the regional expression of an interplay between human purposes and a condition of technology which induced the greatest rate of economic growth of the last two and a half centuries. We may remind ourselves again of the apt phrase in which Dr Bowden[6] described the process—'carboniferous capitalism'—a particular form of capitalism, nowadays as outmoded as is a Galsworthy play. In the outcome, the growth rate of the region and Tyneside in particular was, not accidentally, greater at times than that of the economy as a whole.

Support for this interpretation of what has happened on and to Tyneside could be sought in various ways. In the first place, we could examine the growth of population in Industrial Tyneside as a whole and in the various towns and villages that make it up. In the second place, we could look at the lives and activities of individual business-men who became prominent in regional life. In the third place, we might consider the way in which, with the creation of the Tyne Improvement Commission in 1850, the river Tyne was eventually transformed from being a wayward and undependable, even though inescapably necessary co-operant with man in his commercial life, to being a splendidly tamed and predictably usable river capable of providing services which, at the beginning of the nineteenth century, would have been impossible.

As regards the first consideration, that of population and its distribution, the great growth in the Tyneside area may be seen at once by comparing the percentage increase of total population in Great Britain as a whole between 1801 and the beginning of the twentieth century and the percentage increase of population on Tyneside for the same period.[7] The population of Great Britain in 1801 is generally accepted as being a little over 10 million persons: the census of 1901 shows the figure to be about 37 millions, a rise of rather more than three and a half times. The population of Industrial Tyneside was about 80,000 persons at the beginning of the century and about 800,000 persons at the end, a rise of tenfold over the period. The dramatic changes in population may be seen even more vividly if we consider the changes in population for particular towns within the Tyneside economy.

Newcastle upon Tyne grew from approximately 15,000 at the beginning of the century to roughly 215,000 at the end. Some part of the change in the totals is due, of course, particularly in the case of Newcastle, to boundary extensions which brought within the city townships which had previously been outside. In 1835 the city took in Westgate, Elswick, Jesmond, Heaton and Byker. The city population which had been roughly 54,000 in 1831 was roughly 71,000 in 1841. Even so the operation of powerful forces making for increase in the city's population, quite apart from boundary changes, is revealed by an increase from a total of about 35,000 persons in 1821 to about 54,000 in 1831. These figures are for the same civic area and are therefore comparable directly. The demographic surges which were taking place, largely, though not necessarily exclusively, as a result of the growth of industry and commerce can be plainly seen from the figures for various separately identifiable and registerable districts within the city area. Between 1851 and 1901 the population of Elswick rose from about 3,500 persons to about 59,000: the rise between 1851 and 1881 was from 3,539 persons to 34,642 persons. The population of Heaton rose from less than half of a thousand to about 16,000 and of this rise about half took place in the period up to 1891 and the other half in the decade 1891-1901. Changes, similarly large-scale, occurred in other parts of Industrial Tyneside as may be readily seen from Table 1:—

Table 1

POPULATION IN VARIOUS PARTS OF TYNESIDE ooo's

Place	c.1801	1851	1871	1881	1891	1901
Newcastle upon Tyne . .	28	88	128	145	186	215
Gateshead	8	25	48	65	86	110
Wallsend	1	6	7	14	20	31
Jarrow	—	4	24	25	34	34
Tynemouth	—	29	39	44	47	51
South Shields . . .	—	29	45	57	78	101
Felling	—	9	14	16	17	22
Walker	—	4				
Blaydon	—	7	9	11	14	20

There were boundary changes during the century but none of them were of sufficient significance to invalidate the comparisons made here.

Clearly different parts of Tyneside experienced their population surges in differing intensities and at differing times, but the changes can be easily identified as changes occurring in the places in which industrial enterprises of eventually world-wide fame were establishing themselves. Further insight into the nature and significance of these changes could possibly be gained by drawing on the views expressed about the relation between population and employment by Dr H. A. Mess in 1928 for County Durham.[8] His calculations, based on census data, covered and compared the periods 1851-81 and 1881-1921. His conclusion is expressed in these terms: 'The figures seem to indicate that whereas formerly industry was expanding more rapidly than the growth of population, of recent years (he wrote in 1928) the natural growth of population has been more rapid than the growth of industry.' The inward movement of people in the period 1851-81 in County Durham, and the rather later inward movement in south-east Northumberland, have been seen to be due to the migration of people from nearby counties such as Yorkshire, from distant counties as far off as Norfolk, Cornwall and Staffordshire and from various parts of Scotland and Ireland. If today the facts compel us to think of vacua in the north-east because of the massive decline of basic industries, the facts of the period from 1851 onwards may perhaps be thought to justify us in thinking of the region as exerting a powerful magnetic force on people elsewhere, even though strict accuracy in the interpretation of the statistical data makes it necessary to indicate that the magnetic field varied in intensity over the period mentioned and that towards the closing years of the period there is already evidence that the inward movement of people is being replaced by an outward movement.

This picture of a massive increase in population accompanied by large surges in growth within narrow periods of time can be reinforced from studies of population change in North-East England which have been made by Professor J. W. House of the University of Newcastle upon Tyne.[9] For the area as a whole it is evident that especially powerful forces were at work making for increase in the decade 1831-41 and then again in the two decades 1851-61 and 1861-71. Some of the figures are set out in more detail in Appendix A. These changes imposed a particularly heavy strain upon the building resources of the region in this period. An inward migration of people would be likely to include a number of younger adults, particularly males, possibly a high proportion of the total of people in movement. There could also be, dependent on the economic circumstances of the areas from which they came, a number of people moving as families. Whatever the nature of the movement there would be bound to be abnormally severe pressure on existing accommodation and on the resources of the building industry in the provision of additional accommodation. This pressure is possibly reflected accurately enough, so far as its social implications are concerned, in the higher than average degree of overcrowding which was constantly made a subject of comment in housing studies from the end of the century right through to the present time and in the type of house structure for working men and their families which became standard in the rapidly extending areas in which houses for working people were being built. If a particular type of house construction—the free colliery house—became a standard feature of the mining village it could be said with equal truth that the rows of closely-packed two-storey structures, divided into two self-contained flats, one up, one down, became a standard feature of the working-class areas of the rapidly growing Tyneside towns. The question to be asked is whether this close packing of a type of housing not in any case lending itself to attractiveness of layout and appearance may be regarded as a consequence of the population surge of the middle part of the century. It is a more complicated issue than, at first sight, it might seem to be and it would be superficial to conclude that it was a direct outcome of the obvious need to provide additional housing at an unprecedented rate of house-building. There seems to be evidence that in the coalmining areas, and even in rural parts of Northumberland, no less than in the communities of Industrial Tyneside, an abnormally high percentage of overcrowding existed, and indeed had existed before the beginning of rapid population growth. 'The Health of Towns Commission in 1845', wrote H. A. Mess[10] in 1928, 'gave a very bad account of the Tyneside towns.' G. Culley and J. Bailey in their 'General View of the Agriculture of the County of Northumberland' in 1797 are inclined to explain the poorness of housing in rural areas as 'part of a backwardness which has its roots deep in the conditions of life of past centuries'. One indisputable fact about house construction on Tyneside is the very small area of land which was allowed as the site on which to build the typical 'Tyneside Flats' already mentioned: 'Row after row of flats can be found', wrote H. A. Mess, 'each pair of flats occupying with its yard a total site of from 150 square yards to 200 square yards'. The surge in numbers in mid-century did not create this standard; the standard existed when the need for additional working-class accommodation began to press on the available building resources: the existing standard was accepted uncritically and comprehensively as the standard to which to work, and the damage to human welfare ultimately brought about was largely due to the fact that they built so many and packed them so close.

As regards the businessmen who took on the function of entrepreneurship and by their energy and drive built up the growing industrial and trading complex of Tyneside, the most significant, particularly in relation to the organizing by the workmen of the Nine Hours' Movement in 1871, are those who belonged to the metal, shipbuilding and engineering industries. Not everybody who made a contribution, possibly substantial, to the development and growth of the firms which made up these industries can be mentioned: it will be considered to be enough to select those men who, in one field or another, and in the case of some of those who must be mentioned in several fields of enterprise and endeavour at one and the same time, put an indisputable stamp upon the pattern of Industrial Tyneside. The purpose will be to select such detail and such persons as will serve to support the view that the growth of Industrial Tyneside cannot be satisfactorily explained nor the confrontation between engineering employers and their workmen in 1871 adequately presented without them. It is perhaps not inappropriate to begin with shipbuilding and to enter at that point in the history of shipbuilding on the Tyne when Charles M. Palmer launched and put into service for the conveyance of coals between the Tyne and London the iron screw collier *John Bowes*. That it is not inappropriate may perhaps be acknowledged, even though there were already in existence engineering firms of earlier dates of establishment, if we reflect that this is the effective start of iron shipbuilding on the river and that the putting into service of the *John Bowes* helped the Tyne to retain a large share of the valuable London market for coal in the face of new and potentially extremely damaging competition in the supplying of the London market with coal.[11] Hitherto the London market had drawn the bulk of its coal supply from the north-east, for it was from the ports of the north-east that the coal of the Northern Coalfield could most effectively be conveyed, by water. By the 1840's, however, the arrival of a more efficient steam locomotive and the creation of a railway network between London, the midlands and the north-west meant that coal could be transported by rail from the collieries in these areas more dependably and, in time, more cheaply than from the north-east. The coal from the north-east pits for the London area was conveyed on railways from the pits to convenient points on a river where it could be loaded on to keels which would take the coal down the river to be reloaded into collier brigs or, where geographical circumstances permitted, it could be loaded from staiths directly into the holds of the collier brigs themselves. The collier brigs would then sail from the Tyne, or whatever river was the most convenient, generally in 'fleets', bound for the Thames. Having discharged their cargo of coal in the Thames they would then return to the north-east in ballast. If it was an advantageous way of carrying coals in large quantities to London, it was not without its drawbacks. The collier brigs were small, slow, dependent on favourable conditions of wind and weather and involved in the awkward additional chore of having to take on ballast in the Thames—mostly chalk—and discharge their ballast on the Tyne or whatever river it might be, before they could make themselves ready to receive their next cargo of coal. Their deliveries in the London market tended to be irregular: for some periods the market might find itself short of coal because of the late arrival of the collier fleet, held up through unfavourable conditions of wind and weather: or, at other periods, the market tended to be over-supplied as a mass of collier brigs arrived in the Thames estuary in a more than normal size of fleet. With the arrival of the steam locomotive and the creation of a railway network an opportunity was clearly provided to inland pits to cut into the London market, to the possibly considerable trading discomfiture of those organizing the sale and transport of coal by ship from the north-east.

Charles Palmer was quick to recognize the threat and equally quick to come forward with a remedy—the iron screw collier, which was wholly independent of wind and largely independent of weather through its use of steam. In addition he released the carriage of coal by ship from its previous time- and cost-absorbing dependence upon solid ballast. Though not the originator of a system of water ballast, he successfully incorporated an effective design for using water ballast in his ship, the *John Bowes*: water taken into tanks as ballast while the vessel was in the water could equally easily be discharged without the vessel having to interrupt its steaming. The *John Bowes* was followed very shortly by another vessel using the same principles, but larger and more economical. This vessel was the not-so-well-known *James Dixon*. In a paper to the British Association when it met in Newcastle in 1863, Palmer pointed out that on its first voyage the *John Bowes* had done the same amount of work in five days as would have taken two sailing colliers one month. His second steam collier, the *James Dixon*, proved even more efficient. This is what we would not hesitate to describe nowadays as a gain in productivity. The inland collieries with a rail connection with London continued, of course, to build up an increasing trade with the London market. What had, in earlier days, been very largely a north-east monopoly had now to be shared; if it had not been for the prompt introduction of the screw collier and its rapid effective improvement the share which might very easily have been captured by the inland pits could have been very large indeed.

Charles Palmer showed his qualities of enterprise and initiative in other ways. At his own expense he produced 'rolled' iron armour plates for warships.[12] Eventually, he convinced an unbelieving and un-co-operative Admiralty that not only were the Palmer-style rolled plates cheaper than the forged plates hitherto regarded as essential, but that they were also every bit as resistant, even more so, to heavy shells fired at them. Palmer's of Jarrow became a name known all over the world for iron-making, later steel-making, shipbuilding and ship-repairing. Their warships were bought not only by the British Government but also by governments over a wide area of the world, from Japan on the one hand to Greece on the other. Over the period from 1852 to 1933 the firm built 110 ships for the British Admiralty with a total displacement of approximately 280,000 tons. Included in this number were 12 gunboats, 57 torpedo boat destroyers, 10 cruisers, 3 monitors, 7 battleships and 2 submarines. The firm built merchant ships of various kinds for the leading shipping companies of many countries. It made a big contribution to the Tyne's output of oil tankers: by the date of its closure in 1933 it had built 94 vessels of this sort with a gross registered tonnage of well over half a million tons. The story may begin with a close connection with coal and the urge to introduce improvements which would safeguard the coal export trade of the Tyne, but it ends with a pattern of activity so far removed from a concern with coal that to have predicted at an earlier date that such a development would be likely to take place on Tyneside would have seemed no more than a foolish flight of fancy. The growth of Palmer's and the continuing diversification of its output contributed to Tyneside's increasing significance in the newly developing world of engineering and shipbuilding.[13]

Tyneside contained another diversified firm of great size which not only achieved a world-wide reputation in shipbuilding but also a similarly world-wide reputation in the making and sale of armaments. Like Palmer's, it did not begin as a shipbuilder, but unlike Palmer's it did not make its first connection with coal. This is the firm which began in 1847 to manufacture, in a small way, the hydraulic cranes which had just been invented by a young solicitor in Newcastle, William George Armstrong,[14] eventually to become Lord Armstrong. He was born in 1810, son of a corn merchant in Cowgate, Newcastle, and he died in 1900: he packed his life with an astonishing variety of technical achievement and business success and, with the highly qualified associates he attracted to his service, he succeeded in converting an enterprise which began by making hydraulic cranes on part of a $5\frac{1}{2}$-acre site, with a total capital of £40,000 and an initial labour force of no more than 30 men, into one which, by the turn of the century, had a 312-acre property, six to seven millions of pounds sterling in nominal capital and a labour force of over 25,000. If its pattern of output at the start was simple and limited, chiefly the hydraulic cranes, it ended by becoming massively sophisticated and diverse—guns, light and heavy, for use on land or sea, warships, bridges, with the world as their market. W. G. Armstrong was an accepted leader of men: if he was an 'indifferent' lawyer—and 'indifferent' might seem to be very much the appropriate word here, for it has been said that he was keener on scientific experiment than on legal matters—he was undoubtedly an acknowledged leader in business and technology, on Tyneside, in London, and in circles ranging even wider. That his leadership was recognized, by himself no less than by others, may perhaps have some part in explaining his attitude to the engineers on strike in 1871. If there were uncertainties and anxieties in the early days of his crane-building venture, there were certainly none in the later days or if there were they were certainly not connected with the possible failure of his enterprises. The status and prestige he enjoyed in this way, as inventor, man of science and as an outstanding industrialist, were undoubtedly factors in enabling him to command his massive and diversified enterprises. The growth and success of his business concerns were, equally undoubtedly, a boon to Tyneside because of the increased employment they created and the contribution they made to the building up of the occupational skill-structure of the workforce on Tyneside.

This assessment of Armstrong and his relation to the industrial economy of Tyneside is perhaps supported by examining the development of his work in the making and selling of armaments.[15] The story starts with Armstrong's urge to try to discover some means of constructing field guns which would be an improvement on existing field-pieces of artillery both in their fire-power and ease of handling. It is a familiar story, no doubt, but what it brings out is the quickness with which his mind could define an issue and the tenacity with which he would wrestle with the finding of a solution once his interests were engaged. The stimulus came from reading about the decisive part which field guns had played in producing a British victory at the Battle of Inkerman in the Crimea in November 1854 and the difficulty which the soldiers had had in moving these cumbrous pieces into position. There is a simple but graphic and illuminating account in Cochrane's *Early History of Elswick* (1909) which prints in book form a lecture given by him to the Elswick Foremen and Draughtsmen's Association in the same year. According to Cochrane, Armstrong set his mind to solving the problem of how to produce a more efficient and manoeuvrable gun and, by the end of the year, having found, as he thought, a satisfactory solution in the shape of a rifled barrel and an easier arrangement of the gun's mountings, sought and obtained an interview, in December 1854, with the Secretary of State for War. He carried a measure of conviction at the War Office and received authority to make a small number of guns. From this moment his relations with the War Office were almost unbelievably successful. He received orders for the manufacture of guns in much larger quantity and entered into special relation with the Government as Engineer of Rifled Ordnance with an official salary and the task of superintending the manufacture of the guns at Elswick. 'I do not suppose', said Cochrane, 'that any inventor ever occupied such a commanding station as Mr Armstrong did at that moment.' He made over his patents in the manufacture of the guns to the

Crown and he was knighted. Negotiations of this sort took Armstrong to London a great deal and there, inevitably, he moved in high governmental and military circles. He made contacts there which were important, both then and later, to the development of the work at Elswick on armaments. In August 1860, there is a reference to the appointment on the staff at Elswick of Captain Andrew Noble. Captain Noble was an artillery officer and an expert on explosives. There can be no doubt of the importance of his work at Elswick in consolidating its position in the world of armament making. He was a scientist as well as business executive, and his researches into fixed explosives are regarded as laying down the basic standard principles of scientific gunnery. Captain Noble was secretary to the 'Committee on Rifled Guns', which had been set up in August 1858 to examine the capabilities of all rifled guns extant and to report upon their possible usefulness for garrison and naval work. Although, as this implies, there were other types of gun which might be held to be possible rivals to the Armstrong gun, particularly those constructed on the principles laid down by Whitworth of Manchester, official approval was, after examination of the position, which some have thought to be not as thorough as it might have been, given to the Armstrong principle.

The story of the adoption by the Government of the Armstrong gun is a good deal more complicated than is traditionally and commonly supposed; but the consequences of its adoption for Tyneside are both simple and clear: it provided a basis for the increase of employment and the acquiring of greater and higher working skills for the labour force. Armstrong also built up a notable record in the construction and fitting-out of warships.[16] Before 1867 the Elswick Company had been occupied almost exclusively in the production of cranes, bridges and guns. About that date a decision was made to extend the operations of the firm by developing warship building. For this purpose arrangements were made with Mr Charles Mitchell to build the warships at his shipyard at Walker, where a number of warships of various types and sizes had already been constructed.

In 1882 the two firms entered into a formal amalgamation and shortly afterwards a yard for the construction of naval vessels was laid down at Elswick. Its first vessel was a cruiser built for the Austrian Government, launched in 1885. Between the date at which warships began to be built in Mitchell's yard at Walker in 1854 and 1914, Armstrong & Mitchell, whether independently, or in the looser arrangement obtaining before 1882, or as a single company after the amalgamation, built 136 vessels. Nine were built by Mitchell before

1867: 127 were built or were under construction by 1914. Of this total 41 had been built for the British Government, 22 for China, 13 for Japan, 10 for Chile, 9 for Brazil, 5 for Argentina, 5 for Italy, 6 for Norway and others were for Portugal, the U.S.A., Austria, Hungary, Spain, Rumania and Holland. The Tyne built not only for Britain but for the world. The engines for many of the vessels were supplied by Tyneside marine engineering concerns. Prominent amongst the firms supplying engines were Hawthorn Leslie and Company, the North-East Marine Engineering Company, the Wallsend Slipway and Engineering Company, and after 1901, when Sir Charles Parsons' marine steam turbine was beginning to command attention, if not, as yet, complete confidence, Parsons' Marine Steam Turbine Company. Of the 127 vessels recorded as built or building, no fewer than 55 were equipped with engines supplied by Hawthorn Leslie and Company: no more than approximately 50 engine sets were supplied by marine engineering firms situated away from the Tyne. The construction of a ship is a work of assembly: it is possible for quite important and expensive components to be bought by the builder from other, possibly distant, places: such purchases may be regarded as 'imports' to the building centre which call for a payment outwards. If the components are made by firms on the same river, then the local economy enjoys the value, in terms of receipts and employment, of whatever the local multiplier effect may be.

Another striking feature of the activities of the Armstrong concern in the building of warships is the frequency with which men in high positions in the British Admiralty took up key managerial and executive positions within Armstrong's, and men, previously in the employ of Armstrong's, passed from the firm to positions of prestige and responsibility in the Admiralty. This is a continuation of relationships which could be noted earlier in the days when Sir William was discussing gun contracts with the War Office. Reference was made earlier to the entry into the firm's top managerial structure of Captain (later Sir Andrew) Noble. Names of similar distinction occur in the record of warship building, and more frequently. George Rendel, for example, who initiated and managed the shipbuilding department, left the firm in 1882 for the Board of Admiralty, but returned later to the service of the firm and was a leading figure in the organization and management of the works and yard which later Armstrong's developed at Pozzuoli, in Italy. Another name of high distinction is that of Sir William E. Smith. He was, at one time, Superintendent of Admiralty Shipbuilding Work: he was closely concerned in negotiating the design and construction of one of the famous line of

'Elswick Cruisers'.[17] These cruisers set the style for a type of warship which gained a high reputation for speed, fire-power and protection. It was as notable in its own particular field of use as, earlier, the Armstrong gun had been in connection with artillery. Smith became a director of Armstrong's. Another name is that of Sir William Henry White.[18] He was born at Devonport in 1845. His first important appointment was to serve Sir Edward Reed, Chief of the Design Staff at the Admiralty, as private secretary. He rose through a series of important posts at the Admiralty to become, in 1881, Chief Constructor. In 1883 Armstrong invited him to assist in the laying down of the Elswick Naval Yard and White accepted the invitation. He remained with Armstrong's for two years, only leaving them to become, in 1885, Director of Naval Construction at the British Admiralty and Assistant Naval Controller.

Other names too could be mentioned: they would give added force to the implication which reference to them introduces: it is that Sir William Armstrong had powerful and influential connections in high places and that he would be no doubt in a position to benefit from his contacts both at the Admiralty and in his works. This is not to imply that there is anything necessarily sinister or deplorable in these relationships: they were at one and the same time a source of strength to the Armstrong enterprises and a sign of the high technical esteem in which the firm came to be held: they enabled the firm to grow in size and in its command of a very special market: in so doing the firm promoted the growth of employment and income on Tyneside. They may, however, have involved Armstrong and a part of the senior executive staff of the firm in a pattern of relationships the influence of which on the working of the firm it may be most difficult to assess. This interchange of high management between the works, and the Admiralty or War Office, together with the frequency with which interchanges seem to have taken place and the relatively short duration of some of the spells which Admiralty personalities had with the firm may have given a character to the top management of the firm which was significantly different from that normally to be observed. It is possible that both the personnel at the top and the frequent reshuffle of their number may have contributed to making the management more aloof from other personnel within the firm, particularly from the mass of shop floor labour. In so far as any such aloofness may have developed, it would be likely to be strengthened by the frequency with which the higher executives would be engaged in negotiations, in London, or elsewhere, with the representatives of governments and government departments. It is not difficult to conjecture that executives, including Armstrong, involved for possibly a good deal of their time in such activities, far removed from contact with day-to-day problems of shop floor relationships, may have found a gulf developing between themselves and their labour force. Impatience with shop floor aspirations which might threaten at times to bring production to a stop could easily be engendered: and discussions between working men and management conducted in a context of impatience and aloofness might more readily ensue in mutual estrangement than co-operation.

The account given so far of the growth and the size, and the technological leadership of the Armstrong enterprises is by no means a complete record of all that was done. They achieved notable pioneering successes in the construction of special types of ships, the Lake Baikal train ferry, for example, and the oil tanker, in the development of which they were, if not the first in framing the idea, the first at any rate under the leadership of Col. H. F. Swan in introducing an effective oil tanker which established the standard design for such vessels. Nor does the account so far given move forward to the period when Charles Parsons was introducing his steam turbine principle and establishing a new branch of engineering on Tyneside in the making of generating equipment for use in power stations on land or of steam turbine sets for the propulsion of ships. Details of these developments would carry the narrative too far away from those most immediately relevant changes in engineering and shipbuilding which lie close to the events of the Nine Hours' Movement of 1871. The only reason for mentioning them is that they are part of a continuous story of innovation in engineering technology and the formation of businesses which established an international reputation and created new employment possibilities for the people of Tyneside. Men like Sir William Armstrong, Charles Palmer, B. G. Hunter,[19] J. Wigham Richardson[20] are not only important to the growth of the Tyneside economy because of what they were and did themselves: their qualities attracted men of similar high quality in technology and business enterprise to join their firms: there is thus a cumulative contribution to industrial growth. They were additionally significant in the evolution of the local economy because of their power to attract high skills to live and work in it. If it had not been for the vast improvement in the river itself, however, these achievements would not have been possible. The vessels launched at Elswick, Walker, Hebburn, Jarrow and Wallsend would not have found water or riverway to take them to the sea.

Here we touch upon the last of those considerations that were

mentioned at the beginning of this chapter, namely the improvement
of the river itself.[21] Until 1850, the control of the river was exercised
by the Corporation of Newcastle upon Tyne. It had done little or
nothing to improve the river or even maintain it in a minimally useful
condition for the small craft which, alone, could navigate its tortuous
channels and shallow reaches. In 1850, a decisive and much-needed
change in administrative control was introduced. A Tyne Improvement Commission was established by Act of Parliament on which
the elected representatives of other major towns along the Tyne could
sit. It took time for the Commission to assemble and be furnished
with all those powers and functions which would make it a truly
collective and representative body and it took time also for the members of the Commission to determine their policy and frame their
plans for the improvement of the river. By 1858, they had clarified
their minds a good deal as to the collective purpose and a sign of this
is their appointment, in that year, of John Francis Ure, to be their
Resident Engineer.[22] J. R. Ure came to this post on Tyneside from
a similar appointment on Clydeside where he had been Resident
Engineer to the Clyde Navigation Trustees. In 1859, he presented
the first of a series of important reports on the necessary improvements and the Commissioners incorporated his proposals in a Parliamentary Bill which became the 'Tyne Improvement Act' of 1861.
Part of the work of improvement consisted in the construction of a
north pier and a south pier to protect the entrance to the river from
the sea. Other improvements consisted in the deepening and straight-
ening of channels and the maintenance of a reliable depth of water
for larger vessels by continuous dredging. Whereas in the earlier
period before improvement began it was not uncommon for small
vessels drawing no more than three feet or four feet of water to be
grounded, vessels drawing as much as thirty feet of water could find
safe anchorage in Shields' harbour even at low spring tides and even
for three miles above Newcastle there was a minimum depth at low
water of eighteen feet. The construction of the piers was supervised
by Philip John Messent,[23] a civil engineer born at Dover in 1830.
When J. F. Ure[24] retired from his post as Resident Engineer to the
Tyne Improvement Commissioners in 1873 Philip Messent succeeded him in the post which he retained until his death in 1897.[25]
To these two men more than to anybody else—both, it may be
noted, 'incomers' to the Tyneside area—must be attributed the praise
for the conversion of the Tyne from a miserable water-course, even
though tidal, to a reliable waterway capable of providing regular
dependable service to the largest vessels afloat. The usefulness of

the river to large vessels was, of course, considerably enhanced by the construction by Armstrong's of the low swing bridge. Even so, as vessels, particularly warships, grew bigger, the river authorities experienced a welcome relief when, subsequent to the amalgamation of W. G. Armstrong's with C. S. Mitchell's, it was decided that the largest vessels they were commissioned to build should be built at Walker and so escape the increasingly tight squeeze which passage through the swing bridge came to involve. The making of the Tyne contributed vitally to the making of an Industrial Tyneside in which engineering, shipbuilding and armament making had become major means in the provision of livelihoods.

In 1862, when Gladstone, then Chancellor of the Exchequer, visited Newcastle, he said 'I know not where to seek even in this busy country, a spot or district in which we perceive so extraordinary and multifarious a combination of the various great branches of mining, manufacturing, trading and shipbuilding industry, and I greatly doubt whether the like can be shown, not only within the limits of this land, but upon the whole surface of the globe'. We may smile a little at his eloquence in relation to a date as early as 1862 but the lines of engineering and shipbuilding development were plainly enough to be seen.

NOTES TO CHAPTER 1

1. Mess, H. A., *Industrial Tyneside* (1928). 'Coal and a tidal river are the *raison d'être* of urban Tyneside, but the uses to which the advantages have been put have differed very much at different times. The vicissitudes have been striking: quite a number of industries have risen and have decayed afterwards.'

Smailes, A. E., *North England* (1960). 'The economic core of North England is the mining and industrial area known as the North East coast ... where the coalfield is widest, in South West Durham, its western border is only about 3 miles from the sea and thanks to the penetration of tide water up the re-entrant estuaries, the most distant collieries are little more than 20 miles from shipping points.'

2. 'Industrial Tyneside', according to H. A. Mess, was made up of Newburn, Gosforth, Newcastle upon Tyne, Wallsend, Whitley and Monkseaton and Tynemouth, constituting the north bank of the river, with Blaydon, Whickham, Gateshead, Felling, Hebburn, Jarrow and South Shields constituting the south bank. This is a wider designation than that used by Professor J. W. House in his *North Eastern England: Population Movements and the Landscape since the early 19th century* (first issued 1954, re-issued 1959: Research Series No. 1, Department of Geography in what is now the University of Newcastle upon Tyne). Professor House constructs two groupings, namely, Upper Tyneside and Lower Tyneside; Newburn, Gosforth, Whitley and Monkseaton and Blaydon are not included.

3. Nef, J. U., *The Rise of the British Coal Trade* 2 vols. (1932).

4. Source: House, J. W., op. cit., Table 9, p. 61.

5. See Smailes, A. E., op. cit., Fig. 41, p. 190.

6. Bowden, P. J., and Gibb, A. A., in a so far unpublished report for the Department of Economic Affairs in 1967 entitled 'Economic Growth in the North East'.

7. Sources for the description of population changes are:—
   (a) Decennial Census Returns.
   (b) Mess, H. A., op. cit.
   (c) Middlebrook, S., *Newcastle upon Tyne: Its growth and achievement* (1950): pp. 150, 175, 202, 206 and 258: Appendix A, p. 321 and Appendix B, p. 322.
   (d) House, J. W., op. cit., Table 1, p. 56 and Table 3 (inset folding page pp. 56/57).

8. Mess, H. A., op. cit., Chapter II: pp. 28/38.

9. House, J. W., op. cit.: Table I, p. 56, Table III, inset to follow p. 56.

10. Mess, H. A., op. cit.: Chapter VI, pp. 75/99.

11. Palmer, Charles M., 'The Construction of Iron Ships and the progress of Iron Shipbuilding on the Tyne, the Wear and the Tees' in *The Industrial Resources of the Tyne, Wear and Tees*, eds. Sir W. G. Armstrong, I. Lowthian Bell, John Taylor and Dr Richardson (1864). These are reports and papers read before the British Association on the occasion of its visit to Newcastle in 1863: pp. 237/48.

12. Palmer, Charles M., op cit., p. 244.

13. Dougan, David, *The History of North East Shipbuilding* (1968), pp. 31/2 and 57/8.

14. Cochrane, A., *The Early History of Elswick* (1909). Wigham Richardson (ed.), *Handbook to the Industries of Newcastle & District* (British Association, 1889). Chapter on Sir W. G. Armstrong Mitchell & Company Limited, pp. 93/6. Chapter on 'Shipbuilding' by John A. Rowe, pp. 83/92.

Dougan, David, op. cit., numerous references between pp. 31 and 93 (see index).

15. Tennent, Sir J. Emerson, *The Story of the Guns* (1864): Part II.

Noble, Sir Andrew: 'The rise and progress of Rifled Naval Artillery', *Transactions of the Institution of Naval Architects* (1899).

16. Perrett, J. R., 'Warships designed and constructed by the firm of Armstrongs 1867-1914', *Transactions of the N.E. Institution of Engineers and Shipbuilders*, Vol. XXX (1913/14).

17. Watts, Philip, 'Elswick Cruisers', *Transactions of the Institution of Naval Architects*, Vol. XLI (1899).

18. White, Sir William, 1845-1913: Obituary notice: *The Shipbuilder*, VIII, pp. 214/6.

19. Hunter, George Burton, Obituary notice, *The Shipbuilder*, I, pp. 91/2.

20. Richardson, John Wigham, 1837-1908, Obituary notice, *The Shipbuilder*, Vol. III. *Transactions of the Institution of Naval Architects*, Vol. L, pp. 323/4.

21. Johnson, R. W., *The Making of the Tyne* (1895).

22. Ure, J. F., 'On the improvements now being carried out in the River Tyne', in *Industrial Resources of Tyne, Wear and Tees*, eds. Sir William Armstrong *et al.* (1864).

23. Messent, Philip J., 'Description of the Improvements of the River Tyne', *Transactions of the Institute of Naval Architects* (1888).

24. Ure, J. F., 1820-83, Obituary notice, *Proceedings Institution of Civil Engineers,* Vol. LXXIII (1883) and *Engineering,* May 25, 1883.

25. Messent, Philip J., 1830-97, Obituary notice, *Proceedings Institution of Civil Engineers,* Vol. CXXIX, pp. 376/9.

26. Dougan, David, op. cit., p. 61.

27. Rowe, John, 'Shipbuilding' in *Handbook to Industries,* ed. J. Wigham Richardson (British Association, 1889).

28. Swan, H. F., 'Reminiscences of Tyne Shipbuilding', *Transactions N.E. Coast Institute of Engineers and Shipbuilders,* Vol. XIII (1896/7). Also, Swan, H. F., Obituary notice, *Transactions of the Institution of Naval Architects,* Vol. L, pp. 320/2.

CHAPTER TWO

Movements to Reduce Hours of Labour before 1871

BEFORE looking at the various attempts to reduce working hours before the engineering strike to obtain the nine hours' day, it is worth considering that the formal working day, regulated by the clock, was a fairly recent innovation in the early nineteenth century. The clock, other than in primitive sun-dial form, only dated to any general extent from the seventeenth century and it was not until the eighteenth century, with the growth of labour in textile factories, mines, iron-making, etc., that the clock came to regulate the hours of labour of any considerable proportion of the labour force. As Edward Thompson has recently shown,[1] however, it should not be thought that disciplined work-effort, with the hours of labour controlled, was an evil introduced during the period of the 'industrial revolution', which is so often, sometimes unfortunately, considered an age which saw the degradation of the working man. In two of the largest sources of employment, domestic service and agriculture, time-discipline had been prevalent for centuries. In agriculture it was limited by daylight and by weather conditions. The effect of time discipline was also mitigated by the fact that there were few workers who were purely agricultural labourers until the eighteenth century. Where the domestic textile worker was also a subsistence farmer and where the crafts-man had a small plot of land to cultivate, there was the opportunity to switch occupations to avoid tedium, quite apart from the greater economic stability provided by two occupations.[2] Where there was no fixed work-load, as in the cloth-making and small metal-working trades, the psychological effect of freedom to decide when to work may have prepared the worker for long hours when necessary. This free-dom did not mean that he worked a shorter week than his counterpart in a cotton factory in the early nineteenth century. The domestic worker might work very hard for days at a time when orders were heavy but might also take a day off, to go to a fair or wake, or when the weather was fine. Like the shoemakers of the Castle Garth in

29

Newcastle, or the Spitalfields and other weavers, he may have paid homage to Saint Monday,[3] yet worked late at night on Thursday or Friday to make up for this indulgence. Such a method of work organization may well have been seen as a better system by the workman who subsequently found himself involved in the time discipline of the factory.

As a rigid and widespread system, time discipline only began to develop from the mid-eighteenth century. It developed in those occupations where capital, in the form of machinery and other equipment such as blast furnaces, was more important than labour as a factor of production. It was the speed at which the machinery could work which dictated the maximum output and it was, therefore, realized that it was inefficient and wasteful for machinery to lie idle. From this it was a short step to the decision that the labour force should be available whenever the machinery could be worked. As a result, shift-working came to be adopted, along with a discipline aimed to ensure that the labour force worked to the dictates of machinery. In industries where the workforce was collected together in factories or industrial sites, artificial light could be used on a large scale to extend working hours. At first this took the form of the very poor light obtained from oil lamps but in 1798 the Soho factory of Boulton and Watt was illuminated by gas as a result of the inventive genius of William Murdock.[4] A further technological development which affected working hours was the invention by Watt of rotary motion for the steam engine in 1782-3. It speeded up machinery and gradually reduced the necessity to use the less reliable water power, although as late as 1850 water-powered mills were still being built. By 1800, therefore, technical conditions as well as entrepreneurial desire were making possible the working of regular long hours in manufacturing industry. In such industries as textiles it was necessary to enforce a system of discipline to ensure that regular hours were worked, more especially since the workmen had to be drafted from largely non-industrial occupations where they had been used to working to completely different rhythms. Thus we get the development of codes of organization. Among the earliest of these was the very long organizational and disciplinary code drawn up by Ambrose Crowley for the running of his Tyneside ironworks in the early eighteenth century.[5] Another eighteenth-century industrialist to try to combat the lack of discipline among his workers was Josiah Wedgewood. Of him it has been written:[6]

The life he designed for his workmen was not an indulgent one.

They were not to have the luxury of downing tools for a wake or a fair; nor of working for three days in order to drink for four. The cherished St Monday was to be unfrocked, and all the gods of idleness and mindless enjoyment similarly banished. Time was the new idol—together with care, regularity and obedience. There can be no doubt that the workmen lost much of their old liberty, and their lives much of its old variety.

This discipline was to be achieved by the ringing of a bell at 5.45 a.m. or a '¼ of an hour before [the men] can see to work', again at 8.30 a.m. for breakfast, at 9 a.m. to recall them and so on throughout the day until 'the last bell when they can no longer see'. There was also a primitive, and probably at the time unparalleled, clocking-in system and those consistently late were to have their wages stopped for the time they missed, while there was a long list of other misdemeanours for which workmen might be fined.

The extent of time discipline should not be exaggerated in the early years of industrialization up to the mid-nineteenth century. It was only in a few industries, including textiles, iron manufacture and some aspects of engineering that machinery was of much importance[7] and in not all factories was the management of a sufficiently high standard to realize the necessity for efficient working. Time discipline was certainly insufficiently all-pervasive to justify the widely accepted view of the 'industrial revolution', which has been recently expressed in the words, 'Harsh discipline, [and] excessive hours—[were among] the evils of the new industrial system'.[8] It is easy to adopt slipshod thinking about the past and assume that all industry became mechanized in the late eighteenth and early nineteenth centuries and that as a result all workmen were pushed from an era when they could work what hours they liked under pleasant conditions into one when they worked long, set hours in conditions of dirt and noise— slaves to machinery. Of course it was true of some but even in those trades where the need for discipline was greatest it was not completely achieved—British working men were not automata. Wedgewood failed to stop his men going to wakes. On one occasion he wrote, 'Our men have been at play 4 days this week, it being Burslem Wakes. I have rough'd and smoothed them over, and promised them a long Xmass [sic], but I know it is all in vain, for Wakes must be observed though the World was to end with them.'[9] Traditional forms of absenteeism, such as St Monday, continued into the mid-nineteenth century, even in industrial towns. As a result of this determination of their workmen not to be subdued, by the end of the eighteenth century, many industrialists were retreating from time discipline and instituting payment by results.[10] Piece-rate payment often proved a more successful method of obtaining industrial efficiency, since it enabled men by working harder to earn more and raise their living standards. In the first half of the nineteenth century, payment by results[11] was common in a number of industries, including the textile trades and coal-mining,[12] but was strongly opposed by the workmen and was relatively unsuccessful in the engineering trades.

In a different sense time discipline affected the domestic textile workers. As a result of the competition of machinery they were forced to work harder for longer hours in order to obtain subsistence wages. Possibly this is one of the worst examples of the effect of industrialization in leading to long hours, but it was not only the result of, but existed before, mechanization. There was over-competition in many domestic trades, such as nail-making[13] and hand-loom weaving; this was a consequence of the ease with which such occupations could be learned and the initial attraction of good wages which soon fell as the labour force became overstocked. Finally, one should remember the many trades which were only marginally affected by industrialization, where the need to subjugate the labour force to machinery did not exist to the same extent. In such occupations time discipline was less severe and indeed of one industrial town it has been written, 'The factory hooter was heard at St Helens for the first time in January 1869'.[14]

The corollary to a rising pressure of hours of work was inevitably to be found in attempts by working men to restrict their hours of labour. Doubtless this was no new activity. It is probable that there had for centuries been action among small groups of workmen to reduce their working hours. By the end of the eighteenth century, however, this action was apparent. For instance in 1786 the London bookbinders struck successfully for a reduction of one hour a day in their hours of 14 a day, which included one and a half hours for meals, thus bringing their actual working day to $11\frac{1}{2}$ hours or 69 a week.[15] The bookbinders obtained a further hour a day reduction in 1794. This, however, was almost certainly an example of individual action on a relatively small scale. From 1800 and more especially from the second quarter of the nineteenth century, by contrast, there was a widespread and growing demand among working men for a reduction of hours. It became an issue of sufficient importance for Nassau Senior, a leading economist of the 1830's, to formulate his 'last hours theory', that the whole of a manufacturer's profit came from the last two hours that his factory was worked and that it was therefore impossible to reduce the hours of labour without going bankrupt.[16]

It would be possible to trace at least four different strands in the general movement for shorter hours. There was action by some employers such as Robert Owen, who obviously springs to mind, but also the Cadburys, the Greggs and no doubt other unsung but equally philanthropic entrepreneurs. There was also a continuation of the traditional group/union action within a particular trade aimed at obtaining a reduction in the hours of labour from a small number of employers. From the 1820's there was a rapidly growing agitation by groups of workmen, especially in the Lancashire and Yorkshire textile districts, joined together in short time committees, who aimed at persuading Parliament to pass legislation restricting the working day at first for children, later for women and finally for men, in an attitude which harked back to earlier periods of paternalistic legislation. Finally, often merging into one or more of the previous three groups, there were philanthropists of varying levels of social importance, from those who offered financial assistance to the short time committees to Lord Ashley. The latter's is only the most frequently mentioned name among those of many people who felt that existing hours were excessive and who devoted much time and money to obtaining reductions in them, and in so doing showed that industrializing Britain was not the land of harsh class differentials and indifference to suffering which some commentators would have us believe.

Of the first and last of these strands in the movement little will be said separately. It is likely that those employers who adopted enlightened policies with regard to the hours they worked their employees, and also the conditions in which they employed them, the wages they paid them and the accommodation they provided for them, had little effect in encouraging the general run of employers to follow suit. The general view that profits would suffer was too strong to allow of this. Such employers were, of course, of some effect where they merged into one of the other strands, as where Owen gave evidence before parliamentary commissions. Of the philanthropists much the same may be said. During the first four decades of the century general opinion among employers was so strongly opposed to reduction of hours that no amount of emotive appeal or size of subscription list to support the agitation was likely to be effective. Here, again, the philanthropists were important, as in the case of Lord Ashley, where they were involved in the parliamentary campaign.

Much of the agitation in the early part of the century was aimed at obtaining parliamentary legislation to restrict the hours of particular groups. Almost invariably it began through the action of individuals leading through state control to the principle of the greatest happiness of the greatest number. It was one example of a growing concept which has come to be called the Victorian social conscience, partly arising from the fact that economic growth encouraged magnanimity. As one historian has aptly put it 'England was shifting uneasily and convulsively from an old to a new discipline, and the early stages were painful'.[17] In the first half of the century parliamentary interference with the hours of labour was limited to certain textile mills and factories, but this does not imply, as some historians have done, that conditions were worse and hours longer in the new factories than in traditional employments. Indeed in the debate on a factory bill in 1844 Sir Robert Peel pointed out that conditions in workshops in many trades were much worse than in the factories under discussion. The fact was that factories were new and therefore newsworthy, while because of their size and relatively small numbers it was considerably easier to notice their conditions and hours of work in them than it was in agriculture or the myriad small workshops of such towns as Birmingham and the surrounding region.

Even the limitation of hours in textile factories had begun in a very small way. So early as 1784 the Manchester magistrates, acting on a report of local medical men, had resolved not to allow parish apprentices to be indentured if they were 'obliged to work in the night or more than ten hours in the day'.[18] However, little was done and the evil of the overworking of pauper children, often sent to the textile districts by parishes in London anxious to be rid of the burden of providing for them, grew worse. Largely as a result of his knowledge of the way in which such apprentices were exploited in his own factories, the first Sir Robert Peel was instrumental in obtaining the passage in 1802 of the Health and Morals of Apprentices Act. It laid down that the hours of work of such apprentices were to be limited to twelve a day and that night work was to cease by June 1804, while justices of the peace were to be responsible for inspecting factories and ensuring that the Act was enforced. Partly as a result of the inefficiency of the provisions for inspection but mainly because parish apprentices were becoming less used as steam power made possible the erection of factories in towns and villages where there was a ready supply of free labour, the Act was of little importance. Although mainly an extension of existing poor law legislation and of little effect, the Act should not be dismissed since by it the legislature was breaking new ground and it provided the peg on which subsequent campaigners hung their demands for limitation of hours.

Robert Owen was instrumental in obtaining the next step in legislation on the subject. When Owen took over the running of the New Lanark cotton mills in 1800, he found that the hours of work of children there were $11\frac{1}{2}$ per day as compared with a minimum 12 hour day worked by most manufacturers and the much longer normal day, as at the Backbarrow mills, of 5 a.m.-8 p.m. with one hour allowed for meals. Shortly after his arrival at New Lanark Owen had to increase the length of the working day to 12 hours and, despite his desire to reduce this to 10 hours for children, difficulty with his partners in the concern kept hours to 12 until 1816 when they were reduced to $10\frac{3}{4}$.[19] In accord with his views on the age at which it was suitable for children to commence work and the length of time for which they should work, Owen proposed a bill to provide legal enforcement. Sir Robert Peel took this up and a parliamentary committee was set up in 1816, which continued over two sessions, hearing a variety of evidence for and against limitation of hours of work of children, including evidence from medical men who considered that no harm was done to children by working them for twelve and more hours per day. The evidence given before the committee showed that most mills worked $12\frac{1}{2}$ hours a day and $9\frac{1}{2}$ on Saturdays, a 72 hour week, but children were often kept back during the $1\frac{1}{2}$ hours additional time each day for meals and after work in order to clean machinery. There was, however, evidence of mills where considerably longer hours were worked—15 or 16 a day.[20] As a result of the report of the committee an Act was passed in 1819 to restrict the hours of work of children in cotton factories, although Owen had wanted to apply it to all textile factories. Despite evidence from Sir Richard Arkwright, a leading cotton manufacturer, that he employed no children under the age of 10, the Act instituted nine as the minimum age at which work might commence, in place of the age of 10 which Owen had proposed. Owen had wanted young people under 18 to work only $10\frac{1}{2}$ hours a day but the act settled for a 12 hour limitation on those aged nine to 16. Finally, while Owen wanted a paid inspectorate to enforce the Act, inspection was left in the hands of justices of the peace, some of whom were millowners or the friends of millowners and could not, therefore, be expected to be enthusiastic in the performance of their duty.

It is common practice in historical texts to regard this Act as of no importance. One historian has written, 'The Act was admittedly defective and it remained a dead letter—' and 'It set up no machinery —even the primitive regulations concerning inspection . . . in the original bill had disappeared.'[21] This is less than fair. Returns to the

Home Office[22] from justices of the peace show that inspection did take place and that as a result at least some of the provisions of the Act, such as regular whitewashing of the walls of the mills, were being enforced in particular areas. More important than the effect of the provisions of the Act was the fact that the legislature had seen fit to interfere with the hours of labour of free children (rather than the pauper apprentices of 1802) who had previously been considered capable of looking after themselves and moving to another job if they did not like conditions in their existing one. This legislation was only to affect children but it was the thin end of a wedge and similar arguments could be brought to bear on the ability of women and even adult male labourers to alter their conditions of work. Also the legislation only affected cotton textile factories, not because hours of work there were longer than in other fields of industry but because they were conspicuous concerns which could (in theory at least) be inspected with relative ease. Again this was the thin end of a wedge. It would in future be difficult to maintain the right of cotton operatives to protection when other children worked longer hours and eventually the difficulty of detection in some trades was to be overcome by the implementation of compulsory education for all children up to a minimum age.

In 1825 an amending act was passed, possibly as a result of the interest which the Home Office had shown in the previous year in the enforcement of the 1819 Act. It repeated the provisions of that Act, with the exception that the hours of work of children under 16 were limited to nine on Saturdays, to be taken in the period 5 a.m. to 4.30 p.m., thus creating the legal precedent from which the half-day Saturday movement was slowly to emerge. Again it seems unlikely that the Act had any general effect. Effective limitation of the hours of young persons under 16 would automatically have limited the hours of adult workers to 12 a day, since children made up a considerable proportion of the total employment in textile factories[23] and their labour, especially as piecers, was essential while the machinery was moving, without considering the work of maintenance which they were also expected to undertake. In passing legislation, Parliament did not consider this problem until after the report of the Royal Commission of 1833, hence previous Acts were in practice largely ineffective, since many manufacturers were not prepared to see their machinery idle for long periods. Of a further Act passed in 1831, relating only to cotton textile factories,[24] it is worth noting that it extended the 12 hour day to young persons under 18 and banned nightwork (between 8.30 p.m. and 5.30 a.m.) for all under the age of 21.[25] It, therefore, initiated two new ideas, although again it was not effectively enforced. Firstly it legislated for a normal day, between 5.30 a.m. and 8.30 p.m., and thus commenced the trend of limiting hours of work to set times during the day. Secondly, although this seems to have received little comment, at a time when life expectancy was considerably lower than it is today, the extension of legislation to cover all under the age of 21 was getting very close to a contemporary definition of an adult, and thus foreshadowed the agitation of the late 1840's for control of the hours of all textile factory workers.

Up to the end of the 1820's there had been little popular agitation for limitation of hours of work among factory workers, but in September 1830 Richard Oastler,[26] a land agent on a Yorkshire estate, having discovered the conditions of labour in some woollen mills, wrote a series of letters to the *Leeds Mercury*. Entitling them 'Yorkshire Slavery', Oastler compared the conditions in woollen mills unfavourably with the conditions of negro slaves working in the southern states of America. His letters raised an enormous storm of public opinion and controversy on the question of factory conditions and from them may be dated the major development of the shorter hours' campaign.[27] Readers of the letters were told that, in spite of the Factory Acts already passed, there were thousands of children in textile factories working at least 13 hours a day, often with only half an hour off for meals. Following this agitation came the Factory Act of 1831 but it was unacceptable to the factory workers, who, fired by the agitation which had arisen, began spontaneously to form themselves into independent short time committees. Among the earliest and most important of these were the ones formed in the West Riding woollen manufacturing towns of Huddersfield, Leeds, Bradford and Keighley, while following this the movement spread into the cotton districts of Lancashire where similar committees were formed under the co-ordinating organization of a Manchester group. The various committees organized meetings and petitions in order to keep up the agitation and Michael Sadler, member of Parliament for Newark, introduced a bill into the House of Commons aimed at limiting the hours of labour of persons under the age of 18 employed in textile factories to 10 a day.

In order to obtain information on conditions in factories, Parliament set up a select committee, headed by Sadler because of his interest in the subject, on the report of which the government would prepare a bill. It would seem likely that the report of the committee[28] attempted to show that the worst conditions in factories were commonplace, in order to support Sadler's demand for legislation.[29] Conditions which had been prevalent twenty or thirty years earlier were mentioned as if they were contemporary and much play was made with the deplorable conditions in the small old mills, while little notice was taken of the large modern mills, custom-built for their purpose, where conditions were often much better. Nevertheless, publication of the report caused much interest and inevitably controversy. General opinion was appalled by the conditions which it reported. Even among economists, traditionally expected to adopt an attitude of non-intervention by the state, there were some who were impressed by Sadler's report, J. R. McCulloch commenting,[30] 'I would not interfere between adults and masters; but it is absurd to contend that children have the power to judge for themselves as to such a matter' as conditions of employment. Not all were so affected. Nassau Senior stated that, 'the exceeding easiness of cotton factory labour renders long hours *practicable* ... The work, in fact, is ... mere confinement, attention and attendance'. Members of the short time committees, by contrast, were delighted with the report and were understandably furious when the government decided to set up a Royal Commission to undertake further investigation in order to confirm the findings of Sadler's committee. They believed that this was a time-wasting action which would lead to a 'whitewashing' of factory conditions and no legislation to reduce hours. There was consequently much opposition to the work of the Commission and the short time committees refused to give evidence before it. In its report the Commission, nevertheless, made what seems to be a very thorough study of conditions in textile factories at the time, with surveys on a regional basis by a number of assistant commissioners.[31] It confirmed that conditions in many of the smaller and older mills were deplorable and accepted the view put in much of the evidence that existing hours were too long for children to work. It, therefore, proposed that young persons should be limited to eight hours' work a day. Although humane, this was perhaps the major failure of the Commission's report. It seems likely, so determined were the commissioners to have an eight hour day for children, that they proposed a double shift system of children in order to keep the mills going, while ignoring evidence in the reports of the assistant commissioners which suggested that this was impracticable. This proposal did not please the short time committees, a fact which, on the surface, contrasts strangely with their earlier emotive language as to long hours being equivalent to child murder and their own demand for a ten hour day for children. The contrast is to be explained by the fact that the agitation outside Parliament was really aiming at the control of the hours of all workers in textile factories. Ten hours' legislation for children would mean that adults would benefit from similar hours, but two eight hour shifts for children would almost certainly mean an extension of hours for adults, up to 16 a day. Hence the opposition expressed by the short time committees to the proposals of the Royal Commission.

In 1833, the government brought in a bill, based on the report of the Commission, which was passed by Parliament. Children under nine were once more banned from textile factory work, except in the silk industry, but with no formal registration of births until 1837 it remained easy to avoid this provision. Children under 11 were to be limited to nine hours a day or 48 hours a week (and this was to be extended gradually to children under 13 in the three years following the passage of the Act). In silk mills children under 13 were limited to 10 hours a day. Between the ages of 13 and 18 young persons were limited to 12 hours a day or 69 hours a week with no night work except in lace manufacture. Two new clauses were added. Children were not to remain in any room with machinery after the appointed hours in order to prevent additional work in the form of maintenance and cleaning of machinery. Secondly, to meet the problem that some manufacturers, by working longer hours or reducing meal breaks, led others to follow suit,[32] a clause provided for the appointment of four paid factory inspectors to enforce the terms of the Act. Despite this clause enforcement continued to prove difficult for a number of reasons including the large areas the inspectors had to cover and the many factories they had to visit.[33] Nevertheless, the Act of 1833 may be described with some accuracy as the first effective Factory Act. It was not, however, acceptable to the factory workers. Oastler commented:

Finding himself very much annoyed by the innumerable petitions presented by the people to Parliament, he [Lord Althorp] told the Millowners, that the question could not be allowed to sleep, and that an Act of some sort must be passed, *in order to satisfy the demands of the people, and to put down the agitation, which was so annoying the Government.* After a good deal of 'backstairs intriguing', the *Millowners and the Government* concocted a Bill, and ... we are informed that it was supported by the Millowners, *because they knew it to be impracticable.*[34]

To some extent there can be little doubt that Oastler's opinion of the power of the agitation raised by the short time committees was correct. These committees were only the formal organization of a much more widespread feeling which had the power to unite some conservatives on the extreme right with some radicals on the extreme left.

Since the Act did not please the short time committees with their barely concealed desire for legislation which would indirectly limit the hours of adult workers, the extra-parliamentary agitation remained highly vocal. In 1836, Charles Hindley, member of Parliament for Ashton-under-Lyne, who had some sympathy with the short time committees in Lancashire, drew up a new 10 hours' bill but it was not introduced to Parliament. Its major point of interest was that Hindley had picked up the idea of legislation to restrict the hours during which the machinery of a factory could be worked. This topic had been much canvassed at meetings of short time committees since it had the advantage of establishing a normal day and preventing manufacturers working their adult employees for long hours by using shifts of children. Within Parliament in these middle years in the 1830's there was considerable support for a compromise bill to limit hours to 11 a day but this the short time committees would not accept. By contrast, Lord Ashley, who had accepted the parliamentary leadership of the movement at the request of the short time committees when Sadler had lost his seat in Parliament in 1832, would not introduce a 10 hours' bill in 1837 since he was opposed to the increase in the hours of children from eight to 10 to which this was expected to lead. That the operatives were prepared to accept this increase in the hours of work of children clearly shows that their professed concern for the condition of the children was at least to some extent a cover for their real desire for limitation of the hours of all factory workers. In the campaigns, led by Oastler, in the later 'thirties and 'forties, the need to limit the hours of adults was clearly stressed. Thus in the later 1830's the shorter hours' movement was to a considerable extent in a state of fragmentation with different sections supporting different means of carrying the movement forward. In this circumstance, the trade depression of the period 1838-42 made it difficult for the short time movement, as for any organization concerned with the alteration of working conditions, to retain its support. In addition there were, for many of the operatives, the counter-attractions of the anti-Poor Law and Chartist Movements to limit the availability of time and money to support the agitation for shorter hours. While the trade depression meant reduced hours of work, a shorter week and often unemployment for many factory operatives, Chartism appeared to offer a solution to all the problems which faced many working

men with the promise that the vote would enable them to choose a
House of Commons which would truly represent their interests and
not merely those of landowners and manufacturers. Indeed Chartism
took over much of the organization and the cause of the shorter hours'
movement as it did of the anti-Poor Law Movement. Of the leaders
of the ten hours' movement, Oastler and Joseph Rayner Stephens had
brief flirtations with Chartism, while others, including Lawrence
Pitkeithly, William Rider and Peter Bussey, became Chartist leaders.
Chartist orators were fond of encouraging their audiences with comments to the effect that 'the Charter means a good house, good food
and drink, prosperity and short working hours', O'Connor saying the
Charter was 'a means of ensuring a fair day's wage for a fair day's
work'.[35] A Wiltshire Chartist promised his listeners that when the
Charter was obtained they would get 'plenty of roast beef, plum
pudding and strong beer by working three hours a day',[36] and the
couplet 'Eight hours work, eight hours play, Eight hours sleep and
eight shillings a day' dates from the same period. Under these circumstances it is natural that the direct agitation for shorter hours,
both in and out of Parliament, should tend to quieten down and it
is worth making use of this brief chronological interlude to look at the
general hours of work about the year 1840 in some of the major
trades.

In textiles, publicity and the factory acts had probably had the
effect of reducing the longest hours of labour which had been 15 or
16 a day[37] to around 12 per day, or the 69 hour week which the 1833
Act prescribed for young persons from 13 to 18, who provided a
considerable proportion of the total labour force. Among craftsmen
hours were probably shorter than this. As early as the last decade or
so of the eighteenth century, some of the artisan trades, especially in
London, had succeeded in having their daily hours reduced to as low
as 10.[38] Although this was exceptional at that time, it became more
widespread during the early nineteenth century, especially among the
small and relatively powerful craft unions such as masons, bookbinders, tailors, etc. Among the engineers themselves, the millwrights'
societies had laid down hours of work in the early nineteenth century
of 6 a.m.-6 p.m. in summer and light to dark in winter, inclusive of
mealtimes, thus making a normal day of $10\frac{1}{2}$ hours' work.[39] In 1836
in London there was a strike, lasting eight months but ending in
success for the men, for a 10 hour day with overtime paid at higher
rates. There were similar strikes in Lancashire, the other main centre
of engineering, which also succeeded in obtaining a 10 hour day and
by the mid-'forties some engineering shops in both areas had obtained

a shorter Saturday, making their hours $57\frac{1}{2}$ or $58\frac{1}{2}$ a week, although for most engineers 60 was still common.[40] In 1834 the London tailors decided to demand a working day of 10 hours in the four summer months and eight hours for the remaining eight months, but they were defeated after a long strike.[41] A number of returns to the Chartist General Convention of 1839 by regional Chartist associations[42] would suggest that for craftsmen in the building trades, masons, carpenters, etc., and for groups such as smiths, the working week was generally standardized over the whole of the country at 10 or $10\frac{1}{2}$ hours a day. Not all workers were as fortunate in their hours as these. Agricultural labourers faced long hours during the summer months and, especially in the southern counties, unemployment during the winter. Workers on the newly developing railways often had exceptionally long hours, partly, in the case of railway enginemen, because of a shortage of capable men. On the Newcastle and Carlisle Railway, for instance, railway enginemen worked a 12 hour day, seven days a week,[43] and in other parts of the country hours of work for enginemen, signalmen and station staff were often longer, leading to slack performance of duties and, inevitably, to accidents. Finally, it may be noticed that there were trades where workers could often experience a shortage of work, quite apart from the exigencies of the developing trade depressions. These seem to belong to two particular types of workers. Firstly, domestic workers affected by competition from factory industry, such as many handloom weavers who could not get regular work and when they did had to work 16 or 18 hours in a day in order to finish their work on time. Secondly, workers who were hired for an annual or shorter period but were paid on piece rates. An example of the latter was the Staffordshire potters, who, after a major strike in 1836, gained an amendment to their annual contract by which the master potters had to give a minimum 16 days' work per month or the workmen could give a month's notice. The potters' union collapsed soon after the strike was over and the agreement was not held to.[44]

It will be seen that by the mid-nineteenth century the trade union was becoming a factor in the determination of the hours of labour. Among the old craft associations concern about maintaining traditions was beginning to die away and a more forceful policy was developing. Indeed with growing prosperity from the mid-1840's the relationship between the importance attached in strike action to wage increases and hours' reductions becomes obvious. Theoretically they have the same effect on the wage for any given period of labour offered, but the latter grows more attractive to workers as they become progressively better off. Nevertheless the mere existence of a united front to the employers through trade union pressure did not necessarily lead to reduction in hours of work. To a considerable extent this depended on the strength of the individual union. Many of the artisan trades, masons, carpenters, etc., were able to maintain considerable control over their working conditions while workers in poorly organized trades, such as farm labourers, could do little. In some trades the new time discipline was particularly severe, as in textiles, iron manufacture and engineering, because of their relatively high capital intensiveness, and there 'the contest over time became most intense'.[45] In other trades the need for strict time-keeping and/ or long hours was less and there was consequently less activity, while in some, opposition to time discipline led to an attempt by employers to introduce piece-rates but this again was strenuously opposed by working men, especially in the engineering and building trades. Here it is noticeable that it was the better-off artisans, the labour aristocrats, who had the greatest control over their hours of labour, and it is significant that it was the builders and the engineers who were to make the major break-through in obtaining the nine hours' day.

After 1840 the next major step in the agitation for reduction of hours came with the publication in 1842 of the first report of the Royal Commission on the Employment of Children in Mines.[46] With its startling illustrations and appalling evidence of the conditions in which very young children and women worked underground,[47] the report had perhaps an even greater effect on the public conscience than the publication earlier of Oastler's letters. It was shown that children, especially the youngest employed as trappers, had to remain underground for the whole time that a pit was being worked. This meant, on average, 11-13 hours a day with one hour for meals, almost invariably taken on the job, while in the colliery districts of Derbyshire and Scotland hours often extended to 15-18 and in the collieries of North-East England it was noted that it was not unusual to do an extra shift and therefore to stay underground for 36 hours consecutively.[48] The report helped to make the public aware that legislation with regard to hours and conditions of children in factories did not exhaust the need for protection and it helped to revive the agitation. In addition it led directly to the Mines Act of 1842, by which women and all children under the age of 10 were banned from working underground. It is noteworthy as being the first occasion on which Parliament had interfered with the work of women and no doubt was a major reason for the inclusion of the regulation of women's hours in the Factory Bills of 1843 and 1844.

Following the report on the conditions of children in mines there was a revival of the short time committees in the textile districts. Their agitation was directed towards the limitation of the hours of work for women with the hope that this 'petticoat argument' would in reality limit the hours of work of adult male workers which had not been affected as a result of the Factory Act of 1833. In 1843, under the pressure of considerable agitation led by Ashley within and the short time committees outside Parliament, Sir James Graham introduced a new factory bill on behalf of the Government. It proposed reducing to eight the age at which children might commence work but that children under 13 might work for only six and a half hours a day and would also undergo three hours' education daily. The bill had, however, to be withdrawn because of the enormous outcry by non-conformists against the proposition that religious teaching should follow the Anglican faith, even though non-conformists were to be allowed to opt out. Edward Baines described the Bill as 'a deep scheme for getting the education of the whole people into the hands of the Church, [and] a declaration of war against all the Dissenters in the Kingdom'.[49] As a result of this religious schism an incipient system of national education was held back until 1870, but control of hours in factories went ahead. In February 1844, Graham re-introduced his Bill. For the first time it included women with young persons to be limited to 12 hours' work a day and introduced the half-time system for children who were to work six and a half hours in either morning or afternoon and spend three hours at school in the alternate half-day. Women were also included in the restriction of night work for young persons and this meant virtually that no textile factory could work at night. When this last clause was before the House of Commons the short time committees came close to obtaining their much desired 10 hours' day. Ashley introduced, and succeeded in getting accepted, an amendment that night work should be taken as the period 6 p.m. to 6 a.m. and not 8 p.m. to 6 a.m. as was proposed in Graham's Bill, on the clear understanding that this would limit the hours of adult males as well. It meant that with only a 12-hour period allowed for work, of which $1\frac{1}{2}$ hours had to be taken in meals, the actual working day could be at most $10\frac{1}{2}$ hours. When Ashley went on and introduced his 10 hour amendment to Graham's 12 hour proposal for women and young persons, the House changed its mind and rejected the amendment. This left the proposals with regard to hours in chaos and Graham had to redraft his Bill, limiting the hours of young persons and women to 12 between 5.30 a.m. and 8.30 p.m. and this became law later in the session. Thus

adult males might still be obliged to work 13 hours a day, assisted by
two relays of children. Although not to the liking of the short time
committees, the Act was useful in tightening up the regulations of
the 1833 Act, largely as a result of the practical experience which the
factory inspectors had obtained.

Legislation on factories and mines emphasized by contrast the
unregulated state of other trades. In the debate on the 1844 Bill, Sir
Robert Peel had expressed this when he asked, 'Is it right to deal only
with one branch of industry and leave others altogether untouched, in
which it appears that female children work fourteen, fifteen, or sixteen or even as much as eighteen hours a day?'[50] In 1843 the report
of the Royal Commission on the Employment of Children,[51] had
obtained the evidence of long hours of work of children in other
trades from which Peel had quoted and it had stated the necessity
for legislation in several trades. All that was immediately done, however, was the passage of the Print Works Act of 1845, limiting the
working of children under eight, and of women and children under
13 at night (10 p.m. to 6 a.m.) in calico printing works.

Not all employers affected by the factory legislation worked their
employees to the maximum allowed by the law. Rising financial confidence among employers, who feared bankruptcy less the richer they
became, and also a growing realization that long hours might not be
good for productivity, led to some voluntary reductions in hours from
the mid-1840's. A number of cotton mills had reduced hours to 11
by 1845, including that of Robert Gardner at Preston, where it was
also planned to reduce them further to 10½ without fear of suffering
loss.[52] Similarly, among the skilled building workers and the engineers
in Lancashire, the 'English week', with early finishing on Saturday,[53]
began to spread in the 1840's without any legislative action. From
the 'fifties the same thing occurred in London, the other major centre
of agitation for reduction of working hours, with the bricklayers
involved in 1851 in a 16-week struggle for a five o'clock finish on
Saturdays.[54] The Early Closing Movement, of which Lord Ashley
had been founder-president in 1842, had also achieved quick results
and in 1850 the following could be written:

The early closing movement in Newcastle has had a beneficial
influence on the class connected with the retail trades. Before, they
had no time for reading and little taste for it. Many went straight
from the shop to the public house, because it was too late to go
anywhere else. What little time they had, they did not consider
worth improving; but those same parties who were known to do

so then, are known now to avoid the public house as well as every other scene of dissipation entirely, and to lay out their time in a rational and profitable manner.[55]

In the mid 'forties there occurred also the first major demand for the nine hour day. This was put forward by masons in Liverpool following a strike by local plumbers.[56] The employers concerned retaliated by locking-out all their building workers and by 'presenting the document' (a contemporary phrase meaning that the employers had demanded that their men sign a document renouncing trade union activity before they would be re-employed). The struggle was ended by mutual agreement with the withdrawal of the men's demand for nine hours and the employers' for the document.

The next development was a major one with regard to hours in textile factories. In 1846, John Fielden, M.P. for Oldham and himself a cotton manufacturer, had suffered a narrow defeat in the House of Commons on a 10 hours' Bill which he had proposed.[57] It was now only a question of the length of the working day to be stipulated and no longer one of whether or not there should be legislation, since there were many Whigs who were in favour of a limitation to 11 hours. Following the General Election of 1847, in which the Whigs regained office, Fielden re-introduced the 10 hours' Bill and although the Government preferred an 11 hour limitation, its amendment was defeated and Lord John Russell accepted 10 hours. Divisions on the bill were small and it seems likely that many Conservatives abstained from voting against the bill in order to gain revenge on the factory owners for repeal of the corn laws.[58] This was, however, not the main reason for the success of the bill. Within early Victorian England there were growing doubts as to whether individualism and deliberate abstention from state interference were suitable for an industrializing state. The Factory Act of 1847 looks forward to an era when welfare was coming to mean as much as wealth. The Act provided for an 11 hour day or 63 hour week for women and young persons as from 1 July 1847, and a 10 hour day or 58 hour week from 1 May 1848. There was great rejoicing among the short-time committees at this success after some thirty years' work but it proved to be rather premature. The Act had been passed with surprisingly little opposition from the textile manufacturers but this was largely due to the fact that at the time the Bill was before Parliament the economy was in the throes of the now regular decennial financial crisis. Trade was poor, few mills were working more than seven or eight hours a day and even to reach a regular 10 hour day seemed a visionary hope to most manufacturers. But in 1848 when revival from the slump began to occur there was some pressure from manufacturers for repeal of the Act and a number of operatives were either forced to work illegal hours or persuaded to do so for higher wages. It seems likely, however, that most operatives were happy to have their hours limited. One married woman weaver told Leonard Horner, a factory inspector, 'I get 10s. with ten hours, and would get 12s. with twelve hours. I prefer ten hours. I have my family and house to look after, and I can go to bed sooner than I used to. I have sometimes been up twenty hours out of the twenty-four.'

Much may be said, from various viewpoints, of the thought of a society which could pass such an Act as this after many years of debate. In the last decade the factory legislation of the second quarter of the nineteenth century has frequently been cited as evidence in the historical debate as to whether *laissez-faire* was a myth or a reality, as to whether individualism reigned supreme or whether the power of modern collectivist state policies was already beginning to be seen in the Victorian economy. Despite a recent attack[59] on those historians who support a theory of rising collectivism and intervention by the state in the economy, on the ground that they have adopted too literal an interpretation of *laissez-faire* and supported their case with various odd examples of intervention while the basic philosophy of individualism remained unimpaired, the evidence to support their case seems unimpeachable. Obviously if one looks at state intervention in early Victorian England from the stand-point of 1971 it will seem miniscule indeed, but the Victorians were unaware of our present standards and could only compare their present with the past. To them the developments in factory legislation seemed enormous steps towards controlling the individualistic nature of the economy. When, in 1844, the Government was defeated when it opposed Lord Ashley's amendment that nightwork should be taken as 6 p.m. to 6 a.m., an editorial in *The Times* commented, 'a few hours since ... one legislative House of the greatest Empire in this world resolved on the largest national interference in favour of poverty and industry to be found in the history of this or any other country'.[60] Between 1830 and 1850 there occurred a change in attitude, from one of concern for children because they were not free agents, through an extension of the age limit to 21 and then to cover all female workers in textile factories, to a final coverage of adult male workers in practice if not in formal legislation. This is surely evidence of growing pragmatism among legislators. Moreover there can be little doubt that this attitude of treating matters on their merits and interfering in those sections of the economy where interference seemed necessary was spreading among men of political significance and even among economists who were thought most strongly to support *laissez-faire*. In commenting on the deplorable state of the habitations of working men, the report of the Royal Commission on the Condition of the Handloom Weavers, largely written by Nassau Senior, stated that

> With all our reverence for the principle of non-interference we cannot doubt that in this matter it has been pushed too far. We believe that both the ground landlord and the speculating builder ought to be compelled by law, though it should cost them a per centage on their rent and profit, to take measures which shall prevent the towns which they create from being the centres of disease.[61]

In the period from 1850 to 1867 the pragmatical attitude led to the widening and extending of legislation as it was realized that there was a need for governmental interference beyond the conditions in textile factories. To contemporaries these extensions of the factory acts, together with control of merchant shipping, financial and public health legislation and many other instances of government action within the economy, must have seemed a rapid and considerable change in the rôle of the state and a far cry from the England of George III.

Nevertheless it would be facile to suggest that the various pieces of legislation had an immediate and total effect and not least was this true of the Factory Act of 1847. The factory inspectors reported considerable difficulty in limiting hours to those prescribed,[62] largely as a result of the fact that by using a system of relays some manufacturers were keeping their mills working for the full day of 15 hours, from 5.30 a.m. to 8.30 p.m., and although those persons whose hours of labour were restricted were perhaps working only 10 hours they were kept in or near the factory for 15. The short-time committees now cut short their rejoicings and began to agitate for a new Act and their demand was taken up by Ashley (now as Lord Shaftesbury with a seat in the House of Lords). The Government offered a compromise, giving a $10\frac{1}{2}$ hour day, and this was eventually accepted by Ashley, although the short-time committees were initially, and some of the extremists remained, much opposed to the change. J. R. Stephens renewed an old cry, advocating 'The Restriction on the Motive Power, without which no Bill, however framed, is worth the paper on which it is printed' and threatened 'let masters and government withdraw or tamper with the Ten Hours' Bill at their peril! Attempt to alter it, and the cry will be EIGHT, or for *no time at all*.'[63] The compromise Bill was passed in 1850, giving a 10½ hour day with 1½ hours for meals between the hours of 6 a.m. and 6 p.m. in summer and 7 a.m.-7 p.m. in winter, thus settling a normal day with fixed hours, and a 2 p.m. finish on Saturday. The 1850 Act still did not close all the loopholes to the working of long hours since children were not included with women and young persons in the limitation of 6 a.m.-6 p.m., an amendment by Ashley to include them having been defeated by Members of Parliament who realized that their inclusion would effectively control the hours of adult male workers. The short-time committees considered the Act as a repeal of their 10 hours' achievement and began a new agitation which ended in 1853 when J. M. Cobbett introduced a Bill to restrict the hours of women and young persons to 10 a day and stop factory machinery between 5.30 p.m. and 6 a.m. This was withdrawn and a compromise achieved when Palmerston, for the government, brought in and had passed a Bill which included children in the 6 a.m.-6 p.m. measure, their hours of work remaining six and a half a day or 10 on three alternate days as they had been set by the 1844 Act. Thus, after a long struggle, the male cotton operatives settled temporarily for a 10½ hour day, 60 hour week, which some of the more unscrupulous employers extended by manipulating the factory clock to their advantage at the beginning and close of the day and at meal-times.

There can be little doubt that the success of the factory movement in reducing hours in textile trades and the realization that conditions were worse elsewhere led to a widening of the demands to other trades. In 1850 the London Operative Bakers' Association began a campaign for shorter hours. In 1853 the London masons followed up the earlier demand of their Liverpool colleagues for the nine hour day but again unsuccessfully. The early closing movement, however, progressed and the Saturday half-holiday spread in many trades throughout the country. From the point of view of legislation we have seen that there had for some time been acceptance of the fact that conditions in many trades were deplorable, but the textile trades were the best known and the easiest to inspect. Now there came a change to doing something about other trades, particularly since some of the more liberal thinkers among the manufacturers had noted that the reports of the factory inspectors showed cases where more work was done in shorter hours and long hours led to losses. It was inevitable that those trades closely connected with textiles would be the first to experience legislation, partly as a result of the ill-feeling among employers already restricted, who could not see why closely related trades should remain unfettered. In addition, in 1853, the bleaching and dyeing workers formed short-time committees in Lancashire and Scotland, one of their memorials stating, 'we believe ... that short hours produce more work, and that of a better quality than under the old system.'[64] There was much agitation, discussion and drawing-up of bills until 1860 when bleach and dye works were placed under the factory acts and, with some exemptions, lace works were placed in the same category as other textile industries in the following year. As far as the basic textile trades were concerned, the 1853 Act remained the legislation affecting them for a long time, for although Cobbett re-introduced his 10 hours' bill in 1855, it was defeated and it was not until 1874 that the working week was reduced from 60 to $56\frac{1}{2}$ hours. Meanwhile, trade union action had been affecting hours in other trades. From its inception in 1851 the Amalgamated Society of Engineers had concentrated mainly on the reduction of systematic overtime and the abolition of piece rates (twin issues over which the 1852 strike and lock-out occurred), but by 1861 a survey showed that hours of engineers ranged from 58.2 a week in Lancashire and Cheshire to 60 in Ireland, with an average for the country as a whole of 58.8.[65] It seems probable that workers in some engineering work-shops were working only 56 or 57 hours a week. In 1861 the Amalga-mated Society of Engineers undertook a survey of the normal hours of work in engineering workshops throughout the country on which the above figures were based. In north-eastern towns the figures were: North and South Shields, Stockton and Middlesbrough, 61 hours; Darlington and Hartlepools, 60 hours; Newcastle and Gateshead, $59\frac{1}{2}$ hours; Jarrow $58\frac{3}{4}$ hours; and Sunderland, 61 hours in summer and 55 hours in winter. At Manchester, however, the normal week was $57\frac{1}{2}$ hours. By 1855 masons in London had achieved a four o'clock finish on Saturdays and from 1857 Lancashire builders had a one o'clock finish on Saturdays. Following the formation, in London in 1858, of a Joint Committee of Carpenters, Masons and Bricklayers, a demand was formulated for a nine hour day.[66] The committee petitioned four firms, including that of Messrs Trollope, who pro-ceeded to sack one of their masons who presented the petition. A strike commenced against Messrs Trollope and was followed by a lock-out by all the major London builders and the employers demanded the document before they would lift the lock-out. The Stonemasons' Society, which had considered the demand for a nine hour day to be premature, now took up the struggle against the hated document. There was much encouragement and financial support from many unions which viewed the demand for the document as an attack on trade unionism as a whole, and after a considerable struggle the affair ended with both sides dropping their demands. Although the building workers had been defeated in their attempt to achieve the nine hour day a considerable coalescence of forces within the trade union movement had been obtained and this progressed towards the trade union congresses of the late 'sixties.

Following the passage of the 1860 Factory Act, the example which it set made it easier for trade unions to negotiate or fight for a shorter day and during the 'sixties most organized trades managed to reduce their daily working hours and obtain the Saturday half-holiday. Not all trades were as fortunate, however. In 1863 the report of the Royal Commission on the Employment of Children and Young Persons[67] in hitherto unregulated trades showed that the deplorable conditions recounted in the report of 1843 still existed. It showed that in many trades children commenced work at the age of six or even younger, that hours were long, especially at the end of the week and when orders were pressing. Dressmakers worked 14 hours a day or more at the height of the London season, and the Commissioners came to the general conclusion that hours and conditions were often worst in the smallest establishments and that all should be brought under legislation. It is worth noting that among employers a new attitude to labour was developing. Many of the larger employers were normally quite willing for effective legislation, one telling the Commissioners that 'the only thing needed is that it [limitation of hours] should be quite general; but that cannot be ensured by any mere moral pressure or social influence. Government must do it if it is to be effectual.'[68] The immediate effects of the report of the Commission were minimal, only six small trades being brought under the Factory Acts Extension Act of 1864. As late as 1867 employees in hosiery workshops had a 14 hour day with children as young as five working and with especially long hours at the end of the week. Conditions were as bad in the small dressmaking and tailoring shops, although during the 'sixties various tailoring unions, such as the Amalgamated Society of Journeymen Tailors, formed in Manchester in 1866, adopted a demand for a 57 hour week with a two o'clock finish on Saturdays. Of one section of the very large retailing trade it has recently been written:

Working conditions were hard in the retail food trade and no better or worse at Sainsbury's than elsewhere. The staff were at work at 7.30 a.m. every day except Sunday. Some would get a half day from 2 p.m. on Monday when trade was slack. On Tues-

day, Wednesday and Thursday trading ended at 9.15 p.m., on
Friday 10.45 p.m. and on Saturday the shop was open till mid-
night, but staff seldom got out of it till 2 a.m. as the counters and
floors all had to be scrubbed down.[69]

It was not until 1911 that shop workers were to receive the protection of legislation but reduction of hours was much nearer for many
other overworked trades. Following the formation of the Railway
Guards, Signalmen and Firemen's United Society in 1866, pressure
was brought on railway companies to introduce a 10 hour day and
in March 1867 the North Eastern Railway did so under threat of a
strike by their men. This was not merely a matter of making working life easier but undoubtedly one of saving lives by reducing the
likelihood of accidents.

Of far greater importance than the achievements of individual
unions, however, was the passage of the 1867 Factory Acts Extension
Act. It showed the extent to which the parliamentary attitude towards
individualism had changed over a period of half a century and it was
a considerable portent of much greater state intervention to come.
The Act took the logical step, based on the long available knowledge
that conditions and hours in textile factories had not been worse than
those in many other industries, of bringing any premises, where 50
or more persons were employed together, under the Factory Acts.
Unfortunately there were numerous partial exemptions with regard
to particular trades, which limited the value of the Act but nevertheless it was a major addition to the trades in which there was some
control of the hours of work. It was of special use in trades where
the workers were poorly organized and undoubtedly proved a considerable encouragement to action for further reduction of hours in
other occupations. At the same time, in line with views, which had
been expressed by various commissioners on the employment of
children, that conditions and hours were often worse in the smaller
establishments, a Workshops Regulation Act was passed to cover
manufacturing establishments with less than 50 employees. No child
under the age of eight would be allowed to work and children between
the ages of eight and 13 were to work on the half-time basis as in
factories. As with the Factory Acts, young persons under 18 and
women were to work a 10½ hour day with 2 p.m. finish on Saturdays.
Legislative control of hours had thus spread to a considerable number
of workers throughout the country and not merely in the textile areas
as before. It should, however, be noticed that in trades other than
textiles the work of women and children was much less essential to

the continuation of work and, therefore, the hours of adult male workers often remained unaffected and this was of considerable significance for the total number of workers covered since, outside of textiles, adult males provided the largest part of the labour force. In reality the new Acts had probably only a marginal immediate effect because of the difficulty of inspection of the diverse places of employment covered. In addition, enforcement of the Workshops Act by local authorities was limited or non-existent and in 1871 administration passed to the already overburdened factory inspectors. By this time the initiative had returned to the organized trades for further reduction in their hours. In 1867 'J. R. Stephens ... presided at a conference representing the textile unions ... and it was decided to set in motion a general agitation for the eight hours' day'.[70] Among other groups of skilled building workers in the late 'sixties and especially during the great revival of trade from 1869, the masons in the north-east struck in 1867 for the nine hour day. It was achieved in a few cases by the more highly skilled workers but its general adoption had to await the early 'seventies, under the stimulus of the success of the north-east engineers.

There can be little doubt that many of the attempts, described above, genuinely aimed at reducing a work-load which was felt to be oppressive and increasing the opportunities for leisure and the increasingly available cultural activities. It must, however, be continually borne in mind that there were alternative reasons for wishing to reduce the hours of labour. As we have seen, the agitation to reduce hours in the textile trades used the 'petticoat argument', aimed at controlling the hours of work of men indirectly by limiting the hours which women and children might work. It would be totally unfair to suggest that the largely male short-time committees did not genuinely wish to see the hours of work of women and children reduced. It would be just as shortsighted not to suspect that the vehemence of the agitation owed much to the fact that the men hoped that their own hours would be reduced as a result of restrictions on the hours of women and children. A more complex aspect than this is the possibility that in agitating for a restriction of their working hours the workmen of any industry hoped that a demand for more employment would be created, that wages would rise and that they would obtain well-paid overtime work. It follows from this that there was a close connection in the minds of many workmen between an increase in wages and a reduction of the standard working week. In a period of prosperity the inevitable effect of a reduction of hours would have been an increase in wages. When they were negotiating for a reduction of their working hours, workmen expected to be paid the same as before and that in order to keep production at its previous level total wages paid would have to be increased. It is, therefore, sometimes difficult to decide whether a demand for reduced hours is a genuine demand for increased leisure or in fact a disguised demand for increased wages. It seems probable that both views could be held, the appeal of a reduction in hours being different to different workmen. A wage increase and a reduction of hours were often seen by contemporaries as having the same end and, as we shall see, in 1871 both the Sunderland and Tyneside engineering workers began by considering whether to demand higher wages or shorter hours, and settled for the latter.

NOTES TO CHAPTER 2

1. Thompson, E. P., 'Time, Work-discipline and Industrial Capitalism', *Past and Present*, 38, Dec. 1967, pp. 56-97.

2. See Pinchbeck, I., *Women Workers and the Industrial Revolution* (1930).

3. We are inclined to consider absenteeism as a twentieth-century phenomenon but the backward sloping supply curve of labour was as relevant in earlier centuries. St Monday was the name given to the holiday taken by many domestic workers, handloom weavers, nailmakers, etc., at the beginning of the week. It was not limited to these workers, however, being present in factory towns as well, and seems to have been endemic in the late eighteenth and early nineteenth centuries. It is interesting to note that many radical and Chartist meetings and demonstrations were held during the day on Mondays, showing that thousands of working men were free on that day. A study of St Monday is at present being undertaken by Raphael Samuel of Ruskin College, Oxford.

4. Mantoux, P., *The Industrial Revolution in the Eighteenth Century* (rev. edn. 1961), p. 332.

5. Flinn, M. W., (ed.) *The Law Book of the Crowley Iron Works*, Surtees Society, clxvii, 1957.

6. McKendrick, N., 'Josiah Wedgewood and Factory Discipline', *Historical Journal*, Vol. 4, 1961, p. 51. For additional evidence on attempts to discipline the industrial workforce see Pollard, S., *The Genesis of Modern Management* (1965), pp. 181-92, and Fitton, R. S. and Wadsworth, A. P., *The Strutts and the Arkwrights 1758-1830* (Manchester, 1958), pp. 232-40.

7. Power machinery was introduced slowly in engineering, at Hawthorn's, on Tyneside, not until 1823.

8. Henderson, W. O., *The Industrialization of Europe, 1780-1914* (1969), p. 131.

9. Quoted in Pollard, op. cit., p. 182.

10. See Barker, T. C. and Harris, J. R., *A Merseyside Town in the Industrial Revolution, St. Helens 1750-1900*, (Manchester, 1954), Chap. xix.

11. For a discussion of the increasing use of piece-rate payment in the nineteenth century, as against the traditional work load of groups such as the shipwrights whose employers had accepted their custom that a day's work was an agreed amount of work, see Hobsbawm, E. J., *Labouring Men* (1964), pp. 344-70. The men considered that the distinction between the two methods was that the agreed amount of work for a day ensured the continuation of a high standard of work and reflected the craftsman's pride in his work, while piece rates encouraged hurried and slipshod work.

12. For hours of work in coal-mining, see Ashton, T. S. and Sykes, J., *The Coal Industry of the Eighteenth Century* (Manchester, 1929), pp. 162-70.

13. Barker and Harris, op. cit., p. 123.

14. Ibid, p. 461.

15. Bundock, C. J., *The Story of the National Union of Printing, Bookbinding and Paper Workers* (Oxford, 1959), p. 2.

16. This view was formulated in Senior, N., *Letters on the Factory Act as it affects the Cotton Manufacture, addressed to the Right Honourable the President of the Board of Trade* (1837). See also Bowley, M., *Nassau Senior and Classical Economics* (1937), especially pp. 255-8.

17. Young, G. M., *Victorian England: Portrait of an Age* (1960 edn.), p. 50.

18. See the account in Hutchins, B. L. and Harrison, A., *A History of Factory Legislation* (2nd edn., 1911), pp. 7-9.

19. Podmore, F., *Robert Owen* (1906), pp. 72-92.

20. Hewitt, M., *Wives and Mothers in Victorian Industry* (1958), pp. 21-2.

21. Thomas, M. W., *The Early Factory Legislation* (Leigh-on-Sea, 1948), pp. 26-7.

22. Public Record Office (P.R.O.), Home Office papers (H.O.) 44/13 and 52/3.

23. Returns by the Factory Inspectors for 1835 show that there were 95,000 children under the age of 18 working in cotton factories out of a total of 219,000 workers of all ages. This figure was made up of 15,000 males and 14,000 females under 13 and 28,000 males and 38,000 females between 13 and 18. In woollen factories the figure was 37,000 out of 55,000; made up of 7,000 males and 7,000 females under 13 and 12,000 males and 11,000 females between 13 and 18. See Mitchell, B. R. and Deane, P., *Abstract of British Historical Statistics* (Cambridge, 1962), pp. 188 and 199. These authors comment that 'The Inspectors' returns were incomplete owing to the failure of some employers to send information, but it seems clear that the omissions were of little significance, even in the early years'.

24. Originally intended to apply to silk and wool, these sections of the Bill were withdrawn as a sop to the opposition of manufacturers.

25. Hutchins and Harrison, op. cit., p. 30.

26. See Driver, C., *Tory Radical: the Life of Richard Oastler* (1946).

27. For a detailed study of the movement and the part played by the short time committees formed by the workmen, see Ward, J. T., *The Factory Movement* (1962). I am grateful to Dr Ward and Messrs Macmillan and Co. for permission to make extensive use of material from that book in the ensuing section. For a concise study the interested reader might like to

consult Dr Ward's chapter, 'The Factory Movement', in Ward, J. T. (ed.), *Popular Movements c. 1830-1850* (1970).

28. Report of the Select Committee on the Labour of Children in Mills and Factories of the United Kingdom, *British Parliamentary Paper* 1831-2 (706) XV.

29. It should be emphasized that this view is my own and one that Dr Ward does not share. It is, however, a view that is cogently argued in Hutt, W. H., 'The Factory System of the Early Nineteenth Century', *Economica*, 1926, and which receives support in Pinchbeck, op. cit., pp. 194-6. For a recent, compelling refutation of some of the evidence on which the case for appalling conditions in early textile factories was built, see Chapman, S. D., *The Early Factory Masters* (Newton Abbot, 1967), pp. 156-209.

30. Quoted in Ward, op. cit., p. 91.

31. Reports of the Royal Commission on the Employment of Children in Factories, *B.P.P's.* 1833 (450) XX and (519) XXI, 1834 (167-1) XIX. The instructions given to the assistant commissioners, before they commenced collecting information, give some idea of the thoroughness with which the inquiry was conducted. There is some evidence before the Commission, that many, mainly female, workers opposed a reduction of hours because they feared a loss of wages. It is difficult to assess this evidence because it may have been influenced more by fear of employers than concern about wages. See Pinchbeck, op. cit., pp. 188-9.

32. It was often stated that the cotton industry was highly competitive and that 'without a legislative regulation of the hours of labour the kind and benevolent employer cannot stand against the competition of his less feeling rival' quoted in Hutchins and Harrison, op. cit., p. 50. The experience of employers such as Owen and Sadler would suggest that this was untrue. Although opposed to the ten hours' movement many manufacturers were anxious to ensure that any Act passed was made effective on all employers.

33. For the difficulties of enforcement see Thomas, op. cit., Chaps. 7 and 8.

34. Quoted in Cole, G. D. H. and Filson, A. W. (eds.), *British Working Class Movements: Select Documents 1789-1875* (1951), p. 326.

35. Quoted in Ward, op. cit., p. 194.

36. P.R.O., H.O. 40/48, December 1838.

37. Although even in the first two decades of the century this was becoming less common. In 1818, for instance, the Manchester mill of Moore and Wilson was working a 12½ hour day. Aspinall, A., *The Early English Trade Unions* (1949), p. 280.

38. Thompson, op. cit., p. 85.

39. For instance, at the Bedlington Iron Works, in Northumberland, in the early 1830's, hours were 12 a day including one and a half hours for meals.

40. Jefferys, J. B., *The Story of the Engineers* (1945), pp. 21-6.

41. Galton, F. W., (ed.) *The Tailoring Trade* (1896) p. xxxiv.

42. Rowe, D. J., 'The Chartist Convention and the Regions', *Econ. Hist. Rev.*, Vol. XXII, April 1969.

43. Tomlinson, W. W., *The North Eastern Railway* (1914), p. 428.

44. Owen, Harold, *The Staffordshire Potter* (1901), p. 42.

45. Thompson, op. cit., p. 85.

46. *B.P.P.* 1842 (280) XV.

47. There was considerable variation according to region. In the Northumberland and Durham coalfield, the most important in the country, women had not worked underground since the 1780's.

48. *Condition and Treatment of Children Employed in the Mines and Collieries of the United Kingdom* (1842), pp. 54-5.

49. Quoted in Ward, op. cit., p. 259.

50. Quoted in Hutchins, op. cit., p. 91.

51. *B.P.P.* 1843 (430) XIII.

52. Ward, op. cit., pp. 307-8.

53. In the north-east engineering shops the Saturday closing time was 4 p.m.

54. Postgate, R. W., *The Builders' History* (1923), p. 164.

55. *Inquiry into the Condition of the Poor of Newcastle-upon-Tyne, from the Newcastle Chronicle* (Newcastle, 1850), p. 51.

56. Postgate, op. cit., pp. 135-7.

57. The bill was actually introduced by Ashley, who subsequently resigned his seat because of his decision to support repeal of the Corn Laws and he was defeated at a by-election. John Fielden then took over the parliamentary leadership of the 10 hours' movement until Ashley was re-elected in 1847.

58. Throughout the 'forties as free trade in corn had become a more imminent possibility, under the pressure of the liberal manufacturers, enrolled in the Anti-Corn Law League and with the famine in Ireland in 1845, the question of factory reform within Parliament had become coloured with political overtones and vindictiveness. See for example McCord, N., *The Anti-Corn Law League* (2nd edn., 1968), pp. 69-70.

59. Crouch, R. L., 'Laissez-faire in nineteenth-century Britain, myth or reality', *Manchester School*, XXXV, 3 (1967).

60. *The Times*, 20 March 1844. Qd. in Hutchins, op. cit., p. 67.

61. Report of the Royal Commission on the condition of the Hand-loom Weavers, *B.P.P.* 1841 (296) x.

62. Hutchins, op. cit., pp. 71-7.

63. Quoted in Ward, op. cit., pp. 356 and 362.

64. Quoted in Hutchins, op. cit., p. 132.

65. Jefferys, J. B. and M., 'The Wages, Hours and Trade Customs of the Skilled Engineer in 1861', *Econ. Hist. Rev.*, XVII (1947), p. 32. It is interesting to compare these hours with those of draughtsmen at Robert Stephenson and Co., the locomotive builders. In 1846 their hours were 11 a day, of which one and a half hours were taken for meals, with a four o'clock finish on Saturdays, in other words a 55 hours' week. Warren, J. G. H., *A Century of Locomotive Building by Robert Stephenson & Co. 1823-1923* (Newcastle upon Tyne, 1923, reprinted Newton Abbot, 1970), p. 100.

66. Postgate, op. cit., pp. 168-77, and Webb, S. and B., *History of Trade Unionism* (1894), pp. 210-14.

67. *B.P.P.* (3170) XVIII.

68. Quoted in Hutchins, op. cit., pp. 163-4.

69. *J.S. 100, The Story of Sainsbury's* (1969), p. 33.

70. Cole, G. D. H., 'Some notes on British Trade Unionism in the third quarter of the Nineteenth Century', reprinted in Carus-Wilson, E. M. (Ed.), *Essays in Economic History* (1962), Vol. 3, pp. 207-8.

CHAPTER THREE

Trade Unions and Strike Action in the North-East before 1871

WE have seen that much of the initiative in the reduction of the hours of labour in the first three-quarters of the nineteenth century came through pressure for and the effect of legislation. It would, however, be unfair to neglect the part played by the growth of trade unions in fields where, before 1867 in particular, the state took no great interest. Of course trade unions were not formed merely for reduction of working hours, an aim which, as we have seen, was generally subordinated to the maintenance of existing craft restrictions, opposition to new conditions imposed by employers and, above all, higher wages.[1] Thus, before commencing a study of the dispute which led to the nine hour day for the north-east engineers, it may be illuminating to consider something of the development of industrial disputes in the north-east since the early nineteenth century.

Much of the economic background to the north-east in this period has already been discussed but it is worth reminding ourselves of some of the aspects which help to explain the way in which industrial disputes developed. In the first place Tyneside, in particular, and Wearside, to a lesser extent, had a long history of industrialization and of organization among working men on which nineteenth-century changes might build. The rapidity with which industrialization and the increase in population (particularly the blending of disparate groups as a result of migration) occurred, however, put considerable pressure on industrial relations, with the particular result of considerable turbulence in industries such as coal mining in the 1830's and 1840's. That there was fairly consistent industrial growth in the first half of the century, with few cyclical fluctuations, may have limited the extent of industrial disturbance. The level of unemployment in the region, as for instance during the general depression of 1837-42, appears to have been considerably smaller than in many of the other industrial districts of the country. This may account for the relatively successful integration of workers into the new industrial scene. Also of possible significance is the fact that in the early part of the century

58

there were in the region few large employing organizations where
size often meant remoteness between workers and employers, as
already there were in the textile industries. The relatively small scale
of units of employment often also meant difficulties of organization
among workmen in particular trades. Of similar significance may be
the fact that there was no industrial conurbation in the north-east and
even Newcastle was a small town, surrounded, within a matter of a
few minutes' walk for all its inhabitants, by fields. Industry was made
up of a number of disparate communities; iron-works at Bedlington,
Redesdale, Winlaton, Blaydon, etc.; coalmines and pitmen were
spread in communities from the Coquet to the south banks of the
Wear and from Shields to Wylam; and the lead miners had their even
more scattered communities on the northern-most slopes of the Pen-
nines. By 1850, of course, this was changing and even before that
date much of the industrial development, shipbuilding, chemicals
and glassworks, had been along the banks of the Tyne and Wear.
In a period in which the facilities for communication were still limited,
however, the diverse geographical locations of industry in the area
posed difficulties for organization among working men.

Since the economy of the area was based to a large extent on coal,
it is inevitable that it is in occupations connected with its mining
and transport that much of the story of industrial relations is to be
found. This sector holds one of the nationally important aspects of
trade unionism in the area, since the keelmen, who were responsible
for transporting coal in keels or barges from stocks at staithes on the
banks of the Tyne and Wear to the colliers waiting in the ports at
the mouths of the rivers, have some claim to be considered among
the first trades to be organized in a primitive form of trade union.[2]
By the early nineteenth century the keelmen's occupation was in
decline and in an attempt to maintain their economic position the
keelmen were involved in a series of strikes which throw some light
on industrial relations in the period. The keelmen may loosely be
described as a pre-industrial group of workers, similar to the wool-
combers and handloom weavers, who found themselves becoming
displaced by technological progress. Around the beginning
of the nineteenth century a new device, called a spout,[3] came into
use on north-eastern rivers, by which colliers could be loaded direct
without the intermediary use of keels. Thanks to the rapid growth
of coal exports and the fact that colliers were unable to get further
upstream than the low-arched bridge at Newcastle, the keelmen's
livelihood did not entirely disappear but it was much impaired and
this led to a series of strikes in attempting to maintain their position.

Throughout the eighteenth century the keelmen had had a reputation for being a well-organized and economically troublesome group of workers, who were involved in at least a dozen major strikes. Now there were strikes of considerable duration and importance in 1809, 1819 and 1822. In 1809, the strike followed the refusal of the employers to meet in full the keelmen's demand for an increase in their piece-rate wages. The demand was presented at the end of August, shortly before the keelmen were due to sign their annual bond. After some delay and discussion over the demands the strike began on 19 October and ended on 12 November when the employers made an offer which in some particulars exceeded the initial demands of the keelmen. During the three weeks of the strike the keelmen had forcibly prevented ships from being loaded with coal from the spouts and had turned back any strike-breaking keels which the coal owners had managed to man with blacklegs. Thus the whole coal trade of the Tyne, which was the major supplier of the London market, was paralysed for several weeks. The extent of the strike and the existence of some violence had led the mayor of Newcastle to request assistance from the Home Office and the Admiralty, and troops and a gun-brig were sent to his support. The magistrates made little use of these forces to break the strike, despite considerable pressure from the coal owners to that effect. Eventually, having rejected plans drawn up by the coal-owners for the use of the military forces to break the strike, the magistrates requested the coal trade to reconsider the keelmen's demands and this was done with the conclusion mentioned above.

For ten years the keelmen remained relatively quiescent, but in September 1819, in depressed trading conditions, with the spouts and drops making inroads into the amount of coal shipped by keel, they again came out on strike. On this occasion the strike was coincident with the fever of radical reform which followed the Peterloo affair of the previous August, and in Newcastle on 11 October there was a large reform meeting on the Town Moor. There is very little evidence that the strike was in any way connected with radical activity, a local magistrate commenting on 'the little interest which both the keelmen and pitmen took in the business'. The reformers made little attempt to draw the keelmen into their agitation, unlike the usual attempt to relate economic distress to lack of enfranchisement. Nevertheless, the coincidence of the strike and the reform agitation could not be overlooked in the eyes of the local magistrates and it must be remembered that their actions throughout the strike were tempered by the fear of a major commotion among the working classes. The

strike commenced on 27 September and was basically aimed at persuading the coal owners to limit the amount of coal that was shipped
by spout, although there were a number of other grievances. It concluded on 20 October with a settlement, negotiated by Thomas Clennell, chairman of the Northumberland magistrates, which was not
unfavourable to the keelmen, although it did nothing to solve their
major grievance about the spouts. The course of the strike had simi-
larities to its predecessor in 1809. The keelmen stopped any movement of coal on the Tyne and went so far as to prevent ballast being
unloaded from some ships at Shields which were to proceed up the
Tyne to load at the spouts; they also damaged some and threatened
to pull down others of the staithes along the river banks. Although
generally disclaiming any danger of serious disturbance the letters
from the mayor of Newcastle, Archibald Reed, to the Home Office
became more and more hysterical in their demands for military support. To some extent this was justified after 14 October, when there
had been an attack on the mayor and his party following the shoot-
ing of a member of a crowd at North Shields after a number of
strike-breaking keels had been escorted down-river. The mayor took
refuge in the Northumberland Arms and had to escape via a back
door when the mob broke into the inn. By this time there were a
sloop of war and two gun-brigs on the Tyne and several troops of
dragoons stationed in Newcastle: in addition, as a result of Reed's
demands following the incident, four troops of the 40th Foot were
despatched from Sunderland and two local units of Yeomanry were
called out, a dangerous expedient considering the feeling that existed
after Peterloo.The lack of repercussions and the fact that there were
no further incidents in the duration of the strike suggests that there
was little serious disaffection on Tyneside. Little use was made of
the troops called in, beyond one of guard duty, and no attempt was
made to break the strike by using the forces available. In the week
following the incident at Shields the strike was ended by the mediation of the magistracy and on 20 October Reed wrote to the Home
Office, 'The coal owners have acted most liberally and the corporation
of this town offered to employ every keelman who had not work'.
  Soon after the strike was over the coal owners were breaking the
1819 settlement and it was obvious that matters were likely to flare
up again and this happened in a strike, known as 'the long stop',
which began on 1 October 1822, and did not end until 7 December.
The extra length of the strike as compared with its predecessors
reflected the desperation of the keelmen to obtain a favourable conclusion and the determination of their employers to make no con-

cessions since they realized the declining economic importance of the keelmen. Again, the strike was basically an attempt to limit the use of the spouts. Considerable violence occurred on several occasions when strike-breaking keels were sent down-river from the above-bridge collieries. Military and naval forces were again drafted into the region and included five warships sent to the Tyne, although there was again no attempt to use them to break the strike. They were detailed to protect strike-breaking keels and by mid-November the above-bridge collieries were getting a lot of their coal down-river by this method. During this long period the keelmen had been supported from various friendly societies but when they realized that the coal owners had the matter in hand they endeavoured to re-open negotiations for a settlement but the coal owners were disinclined to make any concession and after a few more days the keelmen returned to work unconditionally. This was the last occasion on which they came out on a major strike. In the following year, however, they showed their considerable organizational ability by commencing an eventually unsuccessful legal action to have the spouts removed. There was less economic effect as a result of this strike than previously, since more coal was being shipped from the spouts below bridge, which were unaffected by the strike. Nevertheless the pitmen in the above-bridge collieries were laid off for some time with considerable loss of profits to the owners of those collieries. On this occasion the magistrates were not as sympathetic towards the keelmen as they had been during earlier strikes, although on two occasions they persuaded the coal owners to consider the keelmen's grievances.

One thing stands out from these strikes. There was no attempt at repression by the authorities and little by the coal owners, although in all the strikes examples were made of a few of the strike leaders by arresting them for breaking their bonds and committing them to a month's imprisonment, often in the House of Correction. This would seem to be a common element in strikes in the north-east in the first quarter of the nineteenth century, even if it is a surprising element to many who will have been brought up to believe that this was the archetypal period of repression of the working classes. The magistrates, especially in the first two strikes described, seem to have had considerable sympathy with the grievances of the keelmen and were unwilling to give the coal owners any assistance in their attempts at coercion—their aim being largely to maintain the peace. This attitude is true of areas other than the north-east in the same period and finds its reflection in the comments of the central authorities. Extracts from letters from the Home Office[4] to magistrates will emphasize this: 'The combination [of the Tyneside seamen] is, I trust, at last dissolved, and it is now my earnest wish that no prosecutions may be instituted except against the most prominent offenders, and that, as the law is no longer violated, that consideration and liberality may be manifested by the shipowners which is due to British seamen' and 'on the present occasion the master spinners appear to have acted with very little discretion towards their men.... Government and the magistracy must ever discountenance combination, but they have much to complain of those who give rise to the combination by relying on the support of the law instead of considering the justice of demands made on them.' Finally, on the occasion of the keelmen's strike in 1819, 'When the keelmen shall have ceased to transgress the law, their complaints shall be listened to with attention and indulgence, and if well-founded, the causes of them should, of course, be removed.' This comment is more revealing in that it was written in the disturbed period immediately before the Newcastle upon Tyne protest meeting on Peterloo. This may be of some surprise since the Home Office was, in general, more knowledgeable about the viewpoint of employers than of the workmen. To only a lesser extent it would also be true to say that employers themselves often acted not unfairly and sometimes quite generously towards their employees. At the close of the 1809 strike the employers made generous wage increases and in 1819 made a contribution of £300 to wipe out the debts of the keelmen's charity and levied a small charge on coal shipped from the port to ensure its future solvency. There is much truth in the remark of two historians that, 'The successful industrial capitalist, though a pushing fellow, was not always such a confirmed individualist as has been supposed. Nor was his workman in very many cases a lonely, isolated and helpless figure, entirely at the mercy of his master.'[5]

The second point of considerable interest lies in the fact that the moderate reaction of the authorities was towards strikes which occurred when the Combination Acts were in force and in the case of the first two strikes, when the country was respectively at war and under the cloud of the reform agitation after Peterloo. Although there is no evidence that the keelmen had a formal trade union organization, their strikes were in restraint of trade, but at no stage during any of them was there an attempt to prosecute them under either the 1800 Combination Act or the Common Law, nor even any mention of the possibility of such prosecution in the papers of the local magistrates or those of the Home Office. The only action was the prosecution of a few leading strikers for breaking their bond of employment. It has become, perhaps, too much of a tradition that the Combination Acts of 1799-1800 were particularly repressive pieces of legislation and that they prevented the development of trade unionism and the use of strike action. The view has no doubt been fostered by the anti-Jacobin scare in which the Acts were passed and the importance which has been attached to their repeal in 1824 under the aegis of Francis Place and Joseph Hume. That repeal was followed by a wave of strikes has also been used to adduce the repressive effects of the Act, whereas this was largely due to a period of rising trade after a long depression after the end of the Napoleonic Wars. It seems probable that strikes and combinations, similar to those of the keelmen, occurred in considerable numbers in other areas of the country and were not proceeded against, and that the Acts were important for their psychological effect rather than practical enforcement.

The third point of significance is that the keelmen would appear to have received no support or encouragement from other groups of working men in their struggles against their employers. There are, of course, a number of reasons which might be adduced to explain this phenomenon. The keelmen were a relatively well-organized economic group but they were an insular community, living, as well as working, in close proximity with each other, and this may suggest that they were to some extent divorced from other working groups. It may also be said that they were fighting a losing battle against inevitable redundancy[6] and that they had, therefore, special problems which did not attract the support of other working men. Nevertheless the northeast would appear to be an area in which the much vaunted growth of a self-conscious working class[7] during this period was conspicuous by its absence. As a result of their strikes the keelmen put both pitmen and seamen temporarily out of work, yet there is nothing to show that either of these groups took this opportunity to further their own grievances against their employers or to assist the keelmen. The only exception to this came during the 1822 strike when a body of sailors, from the large colliers immobilized at Shields by the strike, moved up the Tyne preventing the small ships from loading at the spouts. They were, however, quickly apprehended by the magistrates with the support of the military. The mayor of Newcastle informed the Home Office that the seamen were 'in concert *probably* with the keelmen'[8] but it would seem more likely, no other evidence supporting his comment, that the seamen were envious of the fact that their fellows in the smaller ships were obtaining work and pay when they were not. Since both seamen and pitmen were on piece rates and would receive no wages while off work because of the keelmen's strikes (the first of which paralysed the trade for three weeks, the second was largely effective for three weeks, and the third cut off up to one-half of the trade for approximately two months) it is surprising that they showed no overt signs of sympathy for their fellow workers. It is not even possible to suggest that pitmen and seamen were satisfied with their conditions of employment and, therefore, that they considered the keelmen to be misguided and an inconvenience to their own earning prospects. On the contrary both of these groups of workers had a turbulent industrial history and were frequently in dispute with their employers, yet their respective strike actions never coincided with each other or with the strikes of the keelmen. Indeed it would almost seem as if there was a deliberate attempt by each of the groups to avoid coinciding their demands, despite the fact that strike action by one group inevitably affected the employment of the others. This was partially overcome in the case of the pitmen by the fact that it was possible for coal to be stockpiled for a short period and inevitably a considerable number of seamen were always away from the port, although a stoppage of a month would lead to very large numbers of colliers confined in Shields harbour. We may now turn to the second of these groups, the seamen.

The end of the Napoleonic War saw a considerable reduction in naval employment offered by the government, with unemployment among seamen and consequent troubles in ports from London to the Clyde, although the major disturbances were centred on the ports on the Tyne and Wear.[9] In mid-August 1815 the seamen put forward a demand to the mayor of Newcastle that no foreign seamen should be employed while local men were unemployed. While informing the seamen that he had no power to enforce their demand, the mayor passed their request to the Admiralty, confirming that there was considerable distress among the seamen but requesting the presence of a warship on the Tyne to prevent disturbances. The Admiralty was unfavourable to these requests, although it made some concessions to the seamen, including the expansion of recruitment for the Royal Navy. By early September the level of unemployment had increased and the men presented a series of demands to local shipowners. More important than the question of foreign seamen were grievances over wages and the number of crew to a ship. Wages had been reduced from the high war-time level of £8 or £9 a voyage to London, and the men now demanded £5 which was soon conceded. The manning demands caused more serious trouble. During the war-time shortages, ships had sailed with reduced crews and when the war was over ship-owners had endeavoured to keep to reduced manning, in order to save wages, even though there was chronic unemployment among seamen. The men wanted a fixed scale of five men and one boy per 100 tons. By the end of the first week in September, in order to give point to their demands, the seamen had paralysed the trade of both Tyne and Wear, as well as ports on the smaller rivers, with the exception of a few ships which met the manning requirements: these were given a licence to sail after contributing to the strike fund. Other ships were prevented from leaving by means of forcing their crews ashore. It was obvious that the seamen were very well organized. Quite expecting rejection of some, at least, of their demands by the shipowners, the seamen petitioned the Admiralty, through Captain Caulfield, the Regulating Officer in the north-east, to support their demands. On 15 September the seamen received the Admiralty's disappointing reply that it would facilitate entry into the Navy, but could interfere no further. Meanwhile the shipowners had been endeavouring to persuade the mayor of Newcastle to intervene to open the port and crush the strike, but the magistrates had considerable sympathy with the seamen and finally told the shipowners that they were far too busy on the town's affairs to interfere in the strike unless violence occurred. Nevertheless the mayor requested military assistance and although three troops of the 5th Dragoon Guards were sent to Newcastle, he was firmly told by the Admiralty that a ship of war could not be sent and that he must rely on the civil power. Contrary to its readiness to provide assistance during the strikes of the keelmen, the Admiralty was obviously opposed to the use of naval forces in the event of possible action against the seamen. The attitude adopted by the Sunderland magistrates was very similar to that in Newcastle.

Although continuing to refuse to act against the seamen, towards the end of September the magistrates were very concerned about the continuation of the strike and the mayor wrote to Lord Sidmouth at the Home Office, emphasizing the vulnerability of his forces, the danger that the pitmen and keelmen might become involved and requesting him to use his influence to obtain a warship from the Admiralty. This was done on 27 September, although the captain of the 20-gun ship ordered to the Tyne had instructions that his crew was not to be used in action against the strikers. With the strike still in full effect the shipowners tried to force the hands of the Newcastle magistrates when, on 2 October, they sent a memorial requesting that they would assist in releasing the ships which were illegally (under an Act of 1793) detained in the river. Still reluctant to act to bring the strike to an end, despite pressure from the Home Office to do so, the local authorities on Tyneside merely decided to act as mediators to try to obtain an agreement between seamen and ship-owners. These negotiations took place on 4 October and ended with the magistrates agreeing with the seamen that a scale of manning should be agreed, although this was turned down by the ship-owners. On 7 October another attempt at mediation, including the Northumberland and Durham magistrates also failed, and the magistrates began reluctantly to accept the need to break the strike, calling on the Home Office for further reinforcements. On 11 October the whole of the Middlesex militia was ordered to Wearside. By 14 October there were seven naval vessels on the Tyne, carrying large numbers of marines, and on 18 October the Royal Westminster Regiment moved into barracks at Tynemouth Castle. The Home Office was no longer prepared to tolerate inaction and the local authorities were told that the forces available to them were now sufficient and they must act to break the strike. When a request to the seamen to return to work was ignored the magistrates, using the forces sent to them, took control of the harbour and the boats on which the seamen depended early on the morning of 21 October, meeting very little resistance. The seamen met and decided to return to work on the terms which the ship-owners had already offered, and although the latter tried to get out of some of these concessions, this settlement was agreed. On the same day a settlement on the Wear was obtained as a result of the mediation of a magistrate. Sympathy for the seamen continued to exist among local magistrates and both they and the Home Office were completely opposed to any extensive reprisals against the seamen. Dr McCord found only seven instances of prosecution following the strike, with sentences ranging from two to twelve months, the latter on two ringleaders in the forcible boarding and prevention from sailing of a ship in Shields harbour.

Most of the comments made on the strikes of the keelmen are again relevant. The authorities were surprisingly moderate, since one would expect from their social and economic position that they would side with the ship-owners. Even more than the keelmen, the seamen had extremely effective organization and controlled the ports for over six weeks. In doing so they affected other working groups, but again there was no coalescence of forces. During their period of control the seamen's leadership maintained an effective organization over its rank and file and violence and disturbance were kept to a minimum. Again it would seem that the strike was purely an industrial dispute with no political overtones. During the strike the veteran reformer,

Major John Cartwright, spoke in Newcastle but the strike was not mentioned, nor did the seamen take any interest in his meeting, and, as in the case of the strikes of the keelmen, the local radical newspaper, the *Tyne Mercury*, expressed strong opposition to the strike.

Subsequent strikes among the seamen continued to show their sound organization. In 1818 they gained an advance of wages by threat of industrial action and it is possible to see a change in the attitude of the authorities, especially of the Home Office, probably affected by fears of growing radical unrest. On being informed of the seamen's action Lord Sidmouth told the mayor of Newcastle that '—it is to be regretted that if an advance in the seamen's wages was proper, it should appear to have been obtained by combination and menace; and if improper, that it should have been obtained at all. My hopes of the continuance of quiet are never sanguine, if it is the result of concession under such circumstances.'[10] Nevertheless the lack of material in the Home Office disturbances files for the northeast in the period 1816-20 is a significant indication that it was an area which was to a considerable extent by-passed by economic and political troubles. In 1825 there were further troubles between seamen and ship-owners in the north-east coast ports.[11] In 1824 a seamen's benefit society, called the Seamen's Loyal Standard Association had been formed. By its articles of agreement it was formed to make provision for seamen and their families 'in case of shipwreck, sickness, superannuation and death'.[12] Article 18 made it clear that the Association would not countenance industrial disturbances.

> Should any Member or Members of this Association muster on the River Tyne, in a tumultuous or riotous manner, to stop or detain any ship or vessel, on any pretence whatever, or to take the crew of such ship or vessel out of her against their own consent, such Member or Members shall be fined ten shillings each. And should any Member or Members be committed to prison for such disorderly conduct, they shall not be supported or relieved by this Association. Likewise, we further agree, that should any Member or Members speak contemptuously of the present king and constitution, he shall be fined five shillings.

Similarly, in their evidence before the 1825 committee on the repeal of the Combination Acts, Henry Woodroffe and Thomas Hodgson, secretaries of the Association at Newcastle and Sunderland respectively, tried to make it clear that their Association took no part in industrial action. It is, nevertheless, clear that the Association was adopting the functions of a union, with several of its members, including John Harrison, a committee member, being convicted for their parts in the 1825 disturbances against non-union seamen.

During the strike of July/August 1825, the leaders of the seamen's organization[13] issued *'A Dialogue between Tom and Harry on the Duties of Seamen and the just and equitable rewards for their services. Addressed to the seamen of the Tyne.'* In it they complained of the low level of wages, the extra duties they were required to undertake, such as casting ballast, and encroachments on their employment such as ships' carpenters being appointed as mates. The dispute affected all the ports of the north-east coast. The magistrates of Scarborough informed the Home Office that the union seamen there had been using bribes and threats in order to prevent blackleg seamen, brought in by the owners, from manning ships. Soon after this the owners agreed to an increase in wages but the Scarborough shipwrights had also come out to demand higher wages. On the Wear the Sunderland magistrates told the Home Office that, 'the Civil Power being incompetent to secure the tranquillity and good order of this and the adjoining towns',[14] they needed a permanent military force. A force of dragoons had already been obtained from Newcastle by the Sunderland magistrates and with these they had to be satisfied. In order to prevent the union seamen from forcing crews to leave the ships on the Wear, the magistrates had placed guards of constables and specials on board, but these proved little match for the union seamen, who, on 3 August, used a number of small boats to get out to the ships and overpower the constables. Assistance having been sent for, a detachment of dragoons with a magistrate arrived on the scene and the Riot Act was read. When the dragoons had re-captured the ships from the seamen, they were pelted with stones by a crowd on the bank of the river and 'Mr Davison, for the preservation of the lives of himself, and the Constables and Soldiers, directed the latter to fire, and four men were unfortunately killed in consequence'.[15] The control of the soldiers was obviously incompetent. The reports of the affair at the inquest do not make it clear that there was any necessity to fire at the mob. Nevertheless, verdicts of accidental death were passed on one of the seamen and of death from gun-shot while in a riotous mob on the others. After the incident a few ships managed to get away from the Wear but a few days later, on 11 August, the shipowners sent a memorial to the Sunderland magistrates in which they stated that 'The trade of the port, [is] if possible, in a worse state than before the late unhappy events, in consequence of the lawless conduct of the Union Seamen'.[16] The seamen were still managing to prevent ships from sailing by intimidation of their crews but, although the magistrates requested more military assistance, the strike was moving towards a negotiated settlement. This was achieved on 17 August with a wage increase and the ship-owners agreed to taking an extra man per ship in order to avoid distress until strike-breaking seamen whom they had brought in had returned to their own ports. Ten days later, however, there was a further incident at Sunderland. The seamen demanded the dismissal of two stranger seamen on one ship and claimed that the extra man taken on the ship was also a stranger, although this was denied by the shipowners. During the night the crew were beaten up and forced off the ship by union seamen. After this incident all remained quiet at Sunderland, although the shipowners were much disturbed at the continuing existence of the seamen's union. Nevertheless, they remained relatively apathetic towards action to put the union down, hoping that the authorities would do the job for them, but they were told firmly by Robert Peel that, '—all that the Government can do is to *assist*. It depends on the shipowners themselves who are immediately affected by the combination, to put it down, if they are true to themselves and to each other, they will succeed. But every con-cession on their part adds to the strength of the combination and renders it more formidable.'[17] It is obvious that a considerable change had taken place in the official attitude since the 1815 strike, partly as a result of the radical disturbances of 1816-20 and partly the rapid growth of serious industrial disputes, both of which had caused local magistrates and the Home Office a considerable amount of work.

The third group among the north-east's more troublesome workers was the pitmen. They had caused little serious concern in the years immediately after the end of the Napoleonic War but in 1825, follow-ing the repeal of the Combination Acts and in a period of prosperity, they had formed the United Association of Northumberland and Durham Miners, a short-lived trade union. At the beginning of the following year the union commenced an agitation to abolish the bond, which it claimed meant that the employers could give the pitmen as little work as they liked in times of depression or when they wished to keep coal prices high, and prevent the men from obtaining work elsewhere. A temporary settlement, with amendments to the bond, kept the miners quiet for a brief period but there was a more serious dispute in 1831. This was part of a widespread movement among miners, since, in the period from the autumn of 1831 to the spring of 1832, there were strikes among the colliers of various places, including Lancashire, Shropshire and North Wales, which had concluded with wage increases.[18] The Northumberland and Durham pit-men had again formed a union in preparation for a long struggle against the owners. In March a meeting on the Town Moor, New-castle, emphasized the need for a new bond acceptable to the men, shorter hours for boys, who at this time might work from 4.30 a.m. to 5.30 p.m. and often for even longer hours, and educational facilities. The mayor of Newcastle was requested to act as mediator. Since the coalowners were not prepared to agree to their demands, the pit-men eventually struck work at the beginning of April, the time for renewing their bonds. There was a certain amount of damage and violence caused by the union men in order to make the strike effec-tive and this led to military forces being sent to the area at the request of Archibald Reed, again mayor of Newcastle. This elicited one interesting piece of information with regard to the strike, since Colonel Sir Hew Ross, in charge of the forces, wrote to inform his commanding officer, 'that so far from the coal owners being anxious to come to an immediate accommodation with their workmen the very reverse is the case, they consider it for their interest to enhance the price of coals by a temporary stand'. He continued, 'it appears to me more than ever necessary to throw those Gentlemen upon their own resources, and that they may protect their property with a civil instead of a military force'[19] : consequently he refused to provide a guard for individual collieries. Within a couple of weeks, however, as the pitmen realized that they were getting nowhere, they decided to make the strike more effective by forcing those collieries which were still working to close down.[20] On 18 April, Michael Longridge, of the Bedlington iron-works, informed Lord Melbourne that 1,000 pitmen had attacked Netherton colliery, destroyed the steam engine and forced the pitmen to join the strike.[21] He was concerned that his iron-works would be forced to cease production and, no doubt, other Tyneside and Wearside manufactories, dependent on land-sale coal, were beginning to be affected by the strike. On 19 April, Reed similarly informed Melbourne that Jesmond Colliery had been attacked and stopped and corves and ropes thrown down the shaft;[22] a number of similar incidents occurred at other collieries. By 24 April, Reed could write, 'at present there is not a colliery between the Tees and Tweed at work, the keelmen are destitute of employment, the sailors are in a similar situation as the collier ships are laid up as soon as they enter port, all the extensive manufactures [sic] upon the Tyne are at a standstill for want of coals, nay even in the Town and adjacent counties they have not a coal fire in many houses, and numbers of the lower classes are without'.[23] As a result of these developments military guards had been placed on individual collieries and reinforcements had been sent to the area. Informing the Duke of Northumberland that the *Saramang* [*sic*] with 80 marines had been despatched, Melbourne added the heavy hint that he hoped the Newcastle authorities would act 'to preserve the tranquillity of the Town and Neighbourhood'.[24] Melbourne doubtless remembered the reluctance of the authorities to use force during earlier strikes. His suggestion was not adopted, although by placing guards at the collieries the magistrates did succeed in curbing the earlier violence. After seven weeks of the strike, with the pitmen's union seemingly still able to maintain its members and with a tremendous shortage of coal, Lord Londonderry capitulated and agreed to the men's demands. It was expected that the other coal owners would speedily follow his powerful example but the strike dragged on for a further couple of weeks, Londonderry's pitmen coming out again because they were dissatisfied with some of the terms agreed. By the end of May most of the collieries had returned and Northumberland wrote to Melbourne, 'In many cases new covenants have been made upon fair and tenable principles, abrogating some hard and indefensible customs and giving an advance of wages upon an average of £10 per cent. In some cases a precipitate and absolute concession has been made to the demands of the pitmen,—more I apprehend in the eagerness of mercantile zeal, than from any positive and impending intimidation.'[25] Apart from the increase in wages mentioned, the pitmen also obtained an agreement that boys working underground should have a maximum 12 hour day, a demand which was obviously influenced by the factory agitation of the time.

In his letter, already quoted, Northumberland went on to say, 'that so long as the great and prominent evil—"The Organization" shall continue, so long the regularity of the trade and the peace of this populous district will be liable to interruption,—for it is admitted on all hands that "the Organization" is complete and that the mandates of its directors,—however inconvenient to the objects of them, are received with prompt and unquestioning obedience'. There was a further short strike at Lambton colliery in the autumn of 1831 but it was crushed when the leaders were gaoled and not re-employed. The union organization remained, however, as did some unrest among the pitmen, and this built up towards a climax at the binding time in 1832. As early as December of the previous year some of the pitmen at Waldridge colliery were on strike because of the employment of non-union men, and on 24 December a crowd estimated at 1,000 gathered and stopped the pumping engine and threw colliery equipment down the shaft. The colliery offered a reward of £250 to which the government added £250 and a Crown pardon[26] to anyone giving information leading to conviction of the leaders, an unusual proceeding which suggested the determination of the Home Office to dissuade the union from further action. Unrest and disturbance such as this built up to a serious strike which began on 3 March and when the bonds of the pitmen ran out at the end of the month the strike became virtually complete. Initially the pitmen were moderate in their action but this changed as they realized that the coal owners were well prepared for them on this occasion. Many owners had private patrols to protect their collieries and they were well advanced in plans to bring in blackleg workers, who were able to earn more money in northern collieries than in areas such as the Midlands, from which many of them came. This policy did not always work. For instance in July, 48 Welsh miners who had just arrived at Ouston left their employment and joined the strikers. Nevertheless the tactics of the owners began to prevail, especially since they began, under the leadership of Lord Londonderry, to evict pitmen on strike from their tied houses, which helped to break the men's resistance. Legally the coalowners had the right to do this, since the men had either broken or not re-signed their bonds. In an attempt to combat the effect of such moves the union increased the weekly allowance to striking pitmen from four to six shillings, but as desperation increased, so did violence, and with it the earlier neutrality of the magistrates disappeared. As early as 4 May the magistrates and military took prisoner 41 pitmen who had overcome the special constables at Tyne Main Colliery and used their weapons to fire on the military party.[27] Other collieries, including Friars Goose, were similarly attacked and specials overpowered. In June the violence reached its most unpleasant level when Nicholas Fairles, a rather autocratic Durham magistrate, was attacked by two pitmen and died from his wounds. A fortnight later a watchman at Jarrow Colliery was murdered by a union pitman among a crowd of 100, none of whom would come forward to give evidence,[28] perhaps because it was obvious that the authorities were incapable of offering protection to an informer. Beside these incidents the usual run of attacks on blackleg miners almost pales into insignificance. One, however, deserves the telling. At Pittington, on 1 July, five lead miners were attacked and beaten by union pitmen, as were two special constables who went to their assistance. The deposition of one of the specials shows something of the quality of that group and suggests the reason for the ability of the pitmen to overpower guarded collieries. Edward Forster, who signed with a mark, stated that seeing

the crowd attacking the lead miners 'I went right into the body of
the men and I cut right away among them [with a sword]—I cut
several of them—many a one.'[29] The magistrates had to rely on
special constables because of the unwillingness of the central
authorities to provide troops for guard work. This acted as a two-
edged sword. It meant that the magistrates were powerless to take
effective action against the pitmen and then had to face salvoes from
the Home Office for not getting the situation under control. Growing violence was really an intimation of impending defeat of the
union and from the end of July pitmen began to drift back to work,
their spirit broken. The union collapsed, holding its last meeting in
August. Thomas Hepburn, its main leader, had to renounce unionism
in order to obtain work and by mid-September after six months the
strike had been defeated.

Meanwhile, sandwiched between the pitmen's strikes, there occurred
a strike of the Tyneside seamen early in July 1831. So little was there
a self-conscious working class as against employer feeling, that it
seems that the seamen had waited for the end of the pitmen's strike
rather than combine with them. This was in fact the case. During
the 1831 strike of the pitmen the local authorities, who were concerned that the seamen put out of work by the strike might support
the pitmen's cause, came to an understanding with Henry Woodroffe,
the secretary of the South Shields Seamen's Loyal Standard Association. In return for an agreement that Woodroffe and his associates
would keep the seamen quiet for the duration of the pitmen's strike,
Archibald Reed sponsored a semi-official collection to relieve the dis-
tressed seamen.[30] When the pitmen's strike was over and his agreement had lapsed, Woodroffe then brought the seamen out on strike.
The seamen were aggrieved at having been out of work as a result
of the pitmen's strike and requested £4 against the existing £3 a
voyage. To this some of the owners agreed and the bows of their
ships were marked with a large 4 in chalk. The remaining owners
refused to negotiate with the seamen and a group of 14 men
endeavoured to enforce the strike by boarding the *Atlas* brig, which
was under way, in order to prevent it leaving Shields. The seamen
were quickly detected in this action by the crew of the sloop *Orestes*,
which was stationed in Shields' harbour, and were taken prisoner
without offering resistance. Like many other serving officers drafted
to the area during strikes, Commander Glascock of the *Orestes* was
impressed by the strikers and informed the Admiralty, 'That the
seamen have some reasonable grounds for complaint there can be no
question, and this is admitted by some of the most respectable and

influential shipowners of North Shields.'[31] Glascock was also influential in persuading the Admiralty to receive a petition from the seamen, which requested the Admiralty to use its influence to support the men's case. The strike gradually petered out as some owners gave in and some seamen returned to work but as late as February of the following year there was still trouble with crews refusing to sail.

The period of the middle and later 'thirties was a relatively quiescent one from the point of view of industrial disturbances in Northumberland and Durham, there being no major strikes to attract attention. To some extent radical agitation and especially Chartism from 1838 made up for this but radicalism is only of significance here in that it may have detracted energies from trade union activity. Although the north-east was little affected by the growth of general unionism in the mid 'thirties, its unions taking no part in the Grand National Consolidated Trades Union for instance, there were still a number of industrial disturbances although they made little of a stir. During July 1833 there had been disturbances among a fourth local group of workers, the shipwrights, particularly on Tyneside. As the power of the Shipwrights' Company had failed in the eighteenth century, there had sprung up friendly societies, and by the early nineteenth century, the shipwrights were well organized in trade unions. In the spring of 1824 the Tyne and Wear shipwrights were pressing for an advance in wages and endeavouring to defend their traditional apprenticeship rules against changes which the employers wished to introduce. Through the shipping insurance associations the shipowners brought pressure against the employment of union shipwrights and presented the document. The shipwrights tried to obtain a meeting with their employers but the only response was a handbill stating that, 'the Committee of Ship and Dock Owners is of opinion, such a Meeting is not necessary, as the Carpenters have *only* to relinquish their adherence to a "Union" which has been the means of their setting up most unwarrantable pretensions, to be *immediately employed* by the Ship and Dock Owners.'[32] The shipwrights seem to have returned to work without achieving their demands but without any concession on the seven-year apprenticeship rule and the power of their union was unbroken. In 1833 the Tyneside shipwrights were again involved in disturbances. On 25 July some union men attacked the yards of Robson and Holt and broke the tools of non-union shipwrights who were being employed at wages below the level stipulated by the union. The following year there was trouble at Hartlepool during the building of the dock but this seems largely to have resulted from racial and religious differences between the English and Irish labourers employed there. In addition there were periodic strikes among many bodies of craftsmen in the north-east, but these did not have the major effect on the economy of the area which those of the workers connected with the mining and transport of coal had. The dissatisfied pitmen also struck in this period, commencing an unsuccessful attempt to obtain the abolition of the bond in December 1836. With the following years devoted to a considerable extent to Chartism little of interest with regard to trade unionism occurred until the formation of the Miners' Association of Great Britain and Ireland in 1842. The initial moves to form the union came from West Riding miners but from 1843 Newcastle became its headquarters. The idea of forming a national union was in some ways an eminently sensible one since it could possibly make available greatly increased bargaining power. The foremost aim of the union was 'to *equalize* and diminish the hours of labour and to obtain the highest possible amount of wages'. These ends were to be achieved by the use of peaceful methods. A fund was raised to contest the trials of pitmen who had broken their bonds and after some earlier failures, W. P. Roberts, the Chartist solicitor of Bath, was retained on a large salary.[33] During the next two decades he gained an enormous reputation as the 'miners' attorney-general'. Roberts was one of the main driving forces behind the miners and in the legal actions which he argued, a public airing was given to the miners' grievances of wage reductions, long hours, increasing fines, deterioration of working conditions, annual hiring under conditions which they could not understand or were not given time to read, and many others. It was also brought out that the miners had no method of improving their conditions, except by strike action, since the coalowners refused to listen to these grievances. Roberts also made clear the disadvantage under which the men laboured;

> But the men and the masters did not stand on a par. The utmost the men could do was to summon their masters for wages, where, perhaps no jurisdiction could be found; but the masters could send the men to prison, however gross the fraud committed against them. It was reserved for this country to have a law to give the rich man the power of inflicting imprisonment whilst it did not give the same power to the poor man.

In January 1844, with the spirit of union high among the nation's miners, the union formally addressed the coalowners, stating their grievances and requesting a meeting to consider ways to overcome them, but there was no response to this or to the specimen bond which was drawn up by Roberts to cover the men's demands. The owners refused to negotiate because they had no intention of recognizing the union. Following this failure the union authorized a strike of the miners in Lancashire, who refused to postpone their action until April, when they would be joined by the north-east miners as their bonds ran out.[34] Rightly, the national miners' union had been opposed to this partial action and after a month the Lancashire men returned to work defeated and there was some loss of union membership in the area. At a national meeting of the Union, held in March at Glasgow, the north-east delegates, with Martin Jude prominent, obtained permission, and promise of support, for a strike beginning on the next binding day. Since the owners had refused to consider Roberts' revised bond, which had included a six month contract in place of a year, a 10 hour day, a guaranteed four days' work a week and the abolition of fines, the pitmen refused to sign on the old terms and the strike began on 5 April.[35] The story is much the same as that of 1832. The owners were prepared and drafted in blacklegs. They evicted pitmen from their tied cottages, thus with one stroke solving the problem of accommodation for the blacklegs and making it more difficult for the pitmen to maintain the strike. At least at first, evictions were aimed at the union leaders, Sir James Graham writing to Londonderry on 29 May, 'It appears to me that the determination of the coal-owners, not to turn the men generally out of their houses, but to select a few of the prominent leaders of the movement, is on the whole judicious.'[36] The local magistrates again called for military assistance for the civil power and to some extent their demands were met. On 15 April, however, the Durham magistrates were told that they must do their utmost to prevent disturbances by using the civil power and when a large meeting of pitmen was held in mid-June instructions were given that the military force should not be brought within sight of the crowd, 'which might have the effect of exciting and irritating the people assembled, as if done for the purpose of overawing'.[37] Thus, intelligent use was made of military assistance and there were none of the unfortunate clashes of earlier years. The pitmen for their part adopted the standard policy of endeavouring to persuade non-union men to join the strike and then of forcing collieries to stop work, but in general the plans of the owners were too well laid. Despite considerable criticism of the strike in the local press, the pitmen made a great attempt to obtain public support, by explaining the conditions in the mines and the grievances against which they were striking. Time, however, was against the strikers. Gradually the owners got more pits working with the assistance of blackleg labour, the attraction of high wages overcoming appeals from the miners' union and the *Northern Star* to workmen in other parts of the country not to go to the north-east. Further evictions, involving some cruelty and smashing of property raised the temperature in the strike and brought some public sympathy for the miners but this could do little to counter-act the positive measures taken by the owners. On 20 July, this pressure was increased by the notorious direction from Londonderry to shopkeepers in 'his' town of Seaham Harbour to refuse credit to striking pitmen and this development, adopted by other coalowners, proved a severe blow to the morale of the strikers as well as to their comfort and welfare. By the end of July the union in the area was virtually broken and men began to trickle back to work, the Durham men first, having experienced the worst of the evictions and lack of credit and the Northumberland men early in August. The strike was broken as it inevitably had to be if the owners stuck to their determination not to recognize the union. The sympathy which the pitmen received from the general public and also from some magis-trates and senior military officers[38] was of little tangible assistance. The men returned on the owners' terms with no concessions. They were forced to accept a monthly contract, which the owners had offered before the strike. The pitmen had earlier rejected this because of the insecurity it involved but were soon to be found extolling its virtues in comparison with the slavery of the annual bond.[39] Fostered by Jude and Roberts the local union carried on a semi-secret exist-ence for a number of years but was never again a powerful force and the industry settled into a peaceful existence.[40] It is, however, worth noting that Jude continued to be of importance in industrial relations in coal mining in the area, which implies the continuation of some local organization. In 1850 he passed on to the Home Office a memorial from the pitmen of Jarrow Colliery, which complained that blasting was still going on in that dangerous mine. This led to a letter from the Home Secretary to Matthias Dunn, a newly appointed mines' inspector, drawing his especial attention to the memorial.[41]

During the middle years of the century the north-east began to experience rapid population growth, which, together with the growth of the engineering trades, meant a change in the traditional character of industrial relations, which became less exclusively concerned with occupations connected with coal and more with the new technological industries in which the time discipline discussed earlier was of

importance. In the decade 1851-61 population in England and Wales
grew by 11.9% but in the north-east by 24.2% and in Gateshead by
32.6%. In the following decade the figures were England and Wales
13.2%, north-east 26.5%, Gateshead 44.8%, Stockton 107.8%.[42]
Growth in population such as this placed a considerable strain on
traditional relationships and increased the likelihood of industrial turbulence, especially since the population growth resulted largely from
migration, with the inevitable possibility of racial and regional disharmony. It was among the engineering trades, which were developing rapidly during this period, that the agitation leading to the nine
hours' day commenced. Already, by 1851, although there were many
small engineering shops in the area the trend towards domination by
large scale firms was evident with both Hawthorns and Stephensons
having more than 800 workers. By 1863 Armstrongs employed 3,800
and four other firms each had more than 1,000 workers. The 'fifties
was a period in which the skilled engineer was in a seller's labour
market and even when there was a shortage of work it was common
for employers to keep their men on in order to avoid losing skilled
labour. It is, therefore, not surprising to learn that there was a tradition of staying with one firm and that industrial relations were good,
with no recorded dispute in engineering during the 'fifties. An inevitable corollary to this was that trade unionism was weak among the
engineering workers compared with the organizational strength we
have seen in occupations connected with coal (see Table 2 below).
Among the engineering workers there had been little desire to fight
the employers and this lack of organization was a considerable disadvantage during the disputes which occurred in the 'sixties.

It was in shipbuilding that the standard of industrial dispute was
raised during the 'fifties.[43] Unlike the engineers the shipwrights were
skilled unionists and the transition to iron-shipbuilding, controlled
by the boilermakers with their opposition to piece-rate methods of payment, and disagreements between skilled and unskilled men, provided plenty of ammunition for disputes. In 1850 the Tyne shipwrights
revised their rules but the employers refused to accept the changes in
the working rules and this led to a strike of more than 1,000 shipwrights. The employers' main objection was to the seven-year apprenticeship rule, which had been in dispute in 1824. The shipwrights
insisted on this rule in order to maintain their craft standards and
also a relative labour shortage. By 7 March a settlement had been
agreed without any change in the apprenticeship rules. The control
exercised by the shipwrights' unions may clearly be seen from the
fact that the rules adopted by the shipwrights were widely accepted

Table 2 shows the growth of membership of the Amalgamated Society of Engineers between 1851 and 1868. In addition a small number of iron shipbuilders, for whom we have no figures, belonged to the Boilermakers' Society.

Table 2

Membership of north-eastern branches of the Amalgamated Society of Engineers 1851-68

	1851	1852	1853	1854	1855	1856	1857	1858	1859
Newcastle upon Tyne	80	57	52	62	75	76	115	96	111
North and South Shields	42	20	31	55	64	50	44	41	51
Stockton	16	21	19	21	45	49	53	65	62
Sunderland	7	6	7	12	15	25	22	24	32
Middlesbrough	—	24	30	40	54	44	50	70	67
Hartlepool	—	—	—	12	23	36	42	39	45
Jarrow	—	—	—	—	15	13	14	17	26
Darlington	—	—	—	—	—	—	—	—	21
Total	145	128	139	202	291	293	340	352	415

	1860	1861	1862	1863	1864	1865	1866	1867	1868
Newcastle upon Tyne No. 1	172	264	210	176	160	226	225	220	227
Newcastle upon Tyne No. 2	—	—	94	106	135	152	161	162	168
North Shields	73	80	100	119	118	130	30	40	32
South Shields							135	133	114
Stockton	56	56	70	72	74	93	87	93	96
Sunderland	38	60	78	96	122	140	140	169	247
Middlesbrough	62	98	110	126	120	154	138	141	164
Hartlepool	56	82	95	85	128	104	73	70	72
Jarrow	26	40	45	57	57	85	84	77	91
Darlington	28	31	40	66	44	52	60	50	58
Gateshead	—	—	—	—	53	65	70	73	82
Howdon on Tyne	—	—	—	—	15	16	14	13	15
Total	511	711	842	903	1,026	1,217	1,217	1,241	1,356

Source: Royal Commission on Trade Unions, 1867-9, Appendix J.

by the employers. In October 1851 a strike occurred at Hylton on the Wear when the employers attempted to adopt the Sunderland working conditions which involved an extra hour a day and the abolition of the men's beer allowance. Shortly before Christmas the mayor of Sunderland, himself a major employer, arranged a conference between employers and shipwrights at which he presided. The conference came to some agreement on a number of points but the shipwrights insisted that 'boring' should be kept for old and lame shipwrights although some yards were employing labourers on this work since their wages were lower. There was obviously considerable pride among the shipwrights in their craft history and their traditional rules. After the meeting they issued a statement claiming that the dispute originated 'with the masters ... it was their intention to deprive us of certain privileges or regulations which we have been in quiet possession of for a number of years'. Economic pressure on the striking shipwrights was reduced since many of them found jobs on other rivers and some went to sea as ships' carpenters, while the Sunderland shipwrights contributed £100 to support the men who remained unemployed. The Sunderland shipwrights attempted a negotiation in mid-March, but could obtain no concession from the employers and after 21 weeks the Hylton shipwrights had to give in with no limitation on the number of labourers employed but preference was to be given to old hands for 'boring' work. Within a few weeks the Hylton men were again on strike following the engagement of two non-union men in one yard and the dispute was finally settled in mid-June, against the men, with the general adoption of the Sunderland rules.

During times of rising trade there was often accord between shipwrights and employers, as in February 1853 when on the Wear they amicably agreed an increase from 4/- to 4/6d. a day. Even so there were successful strikes for higher wages at Middlesbrough and on the Tyne. The Tyneside shipwrights showed the growing prosperity of the period and the increasing interest in leisure by offering to accept a half-hour tea break in lieu of sixpence of their demand. As a result of these wage increases the standard wage for the shipwright on the north-east coast became thirty shillings a week. It was also typical that in a period of prosperity the shipbuilders and shipwrights of the Wear should meet in January 1853 'to consider whether a better understanding between the masters and men could not be established'. From the meeting resulted one of the country's earliest joint industrial conciliation boards to which 'any question of dispute, either between an individual master and his men or the whole body

of builders and shipwrights' was to be presented to obtain an amicable
settlement. The Board did some useful work in settling uniform
working conditions for the Wear and the hours of work. In October
1854, however, the employers posted a notice to reduce wages from
the six shillings to which they had risen because of activity connected with the Crimean War to five. The men wanted to put the
matter to the Board but the employers refused and the Board went
into abeyance. A strike took place but it was only partial since some
employers continued to pay six shillings, there still being a surfeit of
work. The employers managed to extend the reduction to some
yards on Tyne and Tees but by mid-December the yards were so
much in need of men that the reduction notices were withdrawn and
the strike was over. Prosperity in iron shipbuilding at least, led, in
March 1856, to the unforced introduction by the employers of a 1
p.m. closure on Saturdays, reducing the working week to about 57
hours. At the same time came the end of the war and a falling-off in
shipbuilding output, and in November the employers on the Wear
posted a notice of a shilling a day wage reduction. The shipwrights
decided to oppose the reduction since other ports in the area continued to work at six shillings a day as did some Wear yards, and
more than 1,000 shipwrights were soon on strike. Again pressure of
work led the employers to withdraw the notices early in January
1857 but, with the immediate pressure of work over and a general
trade depression apparent, the reduction had to come. The Wearside
employers wanted a reduction to 4/6d but the men offered to accept
5/- with which the employers agreed and a strike was averted, although
3,000 men on the Tyne and at Blyth came out on strike but had
eventually to accept the same reduction. Later in the year a serious
financial crisis set in, the Northumberland and District Bank collapsed
in November, and there was heavy unemployment in shipbuilding as
in other trades and the powerful unions were unable to prevent wages
falling to around two shillings and six pence a day with work shared
out among the shipwrights. During the early months of 1859 many
Wear shipwrights left the area for work in government dockyards, the
union giving married men 20 and single men 15 shillings to assist
them on their journey. By May a shortage of hands was apparent
and on the Tyne and Wear a strike for an extra shilling a day was
commenced but the men had to return without an increase since the
expansion of work proved ephemeral. Thus the 'fifties ended on an
unpromising note for the shipwrights. The decade was, however,
memorable for the positive attempt to avoid strikes through the joint
conciliation board, however short-lived it was, and also for the several

occasions on which wage reductions and increases were negotiated without industrial action.

The 'sixties were to see a revival in mining trade unionism, following the long period of quiescence after the 1844 defeat. A new union was formed in Northumberland at the end of December 1862, after a strike at Seghill colliery, provoked largely by a threat from the Northumberland employers to reintroduce the bond and reduce wages.[44] To this a number of Durham collieries affiliated in the following months but the resources of the union were extremely limited and it received a number of defeats over strikes which it had been forced to authorise in the autumn of 1863. Despite considerable local public sympathy and the support of Joseph Cowen's *Newcastle Chronicle*, the union was too weak to stand the ill-prepared Durham strikes. Early in 1864, when the Durham pitmen accepted the re-introduction of binding, Thomas Burt and others called on the Northumberland men to secede and formed them into a separate organization, the Northumberland Miners' Mutual Confident Association. Under Burt's direction this union became based on the principles of high subscriptions, dependable members, no strikes and recognition by the owners. When he became secretary in July 1865, however, the union had only 20 colliery lodges with 4,000 members, which did not include most of the large collieries near Newcastle. There were no funds and there was an eight-week old strike on hand at Cramlington with six or seven hundred pitmen out.[45] The strike had begun with a demand for higher wages and several attempts at negotiation almost led to an agreed increase but these were always prevented by unacceptable conditions. After 15 weeks, with a settlement unlikely, the owners called on the pitmen to vacate their houses and followed this up with evictions a couple of days later. Houses were barricaded and the 'candymen' (bailiffs) used considerable force in their evictions. The pitmen were re-inforced by others from Seghill and other nearby collieries and the bailiffs and their police escort were attacked with stones but no serious damage was done. Half a dozen of the leaders were later tried and imprisoned for six months. The union supported the evicted miners and endeavoured to prevent the employ-ment of blackleg labour but after nearly a year 400 Cornish miners and their families were brought in and the strike petered out, the men finding work in other counties. Cramlington was the last strike in the mould of 1832 and 1844. In the following years Burt built up the union's membership and funds and managed to get the employers to accept that negotiation was better than the old anarchic conditions. In Durham, following a strike at Monkwearmouth over the legality of

the bond, the spirit of unionism revived and the Durham Miners'
Association was formed in 1869, adopting the ideas of its Northumberland counterpart. One of the aims of both unions was the reduction
of hours of labour of boys. In 1863 the Northumberland and Durham
delegates had opposed the national miners' association's call for a
legal eight hour day. In the two counties a two-shift system was
worked, by which each pitman did only about seven hours work a
day. But the boys who transported the coal were underground for
both shifts and worked 12 or 13 hours, although from 1871 at the
instance of the unions these hours were generally reduced to 11 a
day.

The decade of the 1860's was also to be a disturbed one for engineering and shipbuilding and was to see the developments which led to
the demand for the nine hours' day in 1871. It was a prosperous
decade for both industries with output rising to the middle of the
decade, two years of depression in 1867 and 1868 following the
financial crisis in 1866 and then the beginning of a boom which was
to grow in the early 'seventies. The first industrial dispute of importance occurred at Armstrong's in May 1862, when new methods of
payment for night workers in the armaments section would have
meant a 20% reduction in weekly wages. Some fifty men demonstrated their disapproval by leaving work early on 30 May and were
promptly dismissed. No explanation of the reason for the reduction
had been given and there being no union organization, the men had
no immediate means of negotiation with the employers. On Monday,
2 June, approximately 1,000 men from Armstrong's held a meeting in
Newcastle to consider the situation. Agreement among the men on
a common approach to the employers was made difficult by a division
between skilled men and labourers. Piece-rates were the ruling
method of payment at Armstrong's. A team-leader or piece-maker
received a contract from a foreman and was paid by him and in his
turn he employed semi-skilled men and labourers from Armstrong's
work-force to assist him and paid them himself. It seems probable
that in some instances piece-masters paid only time rates to their
assistants and pocketed the whole of the surplus for their own
trouble.[46] For the employers the system had the advantage of reducing the number of foremen needed, although it did not make for
harmony between skilled and unskilled workers. Disharmony was
increased at the meeting, by the fact that the skilled men had been
informed during the day that the reduction was not intended to apply
to them—something which had been far from clear a week earlier,
and the skilled men therefore opposed a strike. A vote was taken, the

unskilled men, who made up the vast majority of the meeting, not being allowed to vote, and strike action was rejected. The skilled men then decided that they would negotiate on behalf of the labourers, in an endeavour to prevent the labourers' wages from being reduced. They presented a petition, which is worth quoting for the humility of its wording.

> We, your petitioners, fully believing that the present disputes are alike detrimental to the interests of the employer and employed, would beg humbly to approach you as mediators; ... We would humbly submit a few considerations which have influenced us in our present proceedings. We believe the men committed an error in making a hasty determination to leave their work, and this may have caused some unnecessary irritation to their employers. We would, however, plead on their behalf the short period allowed them to consider the new rule ... Trusting you will reconsider the case of those who have recently been discharged from your employ, and receive them on such terms as they enjoyed heretofore, or such as will tend to conciliate and inspire confidence in your good intentions towards them.

No doubt it was easy for the skilled men to be humble on behalf of the labourers but they must also have been aware of the intransigent attitude adopted by the management of Armstrong's in matters of industrial dispute. The humility had no obvious effect, the petition being rejected by the management and the new rule with its consequent wage reduction took effect. The division between skilled men and labourers and the lack of union organization made it very simple for the employers to wield enormous power with regard to changes in conditions.

In shipbuilding the 'sixties was a decade of major change from wood to iron building as well as seeing a speed-up of the transition in motive power from sail to steam. The former change inevitably led to much bitterness between shipwrights, the wooden builders, and boilermakers, who claimed the sole right to build iron vessels. A further difficulty was that the boilermakers were paid exclusively on piece-rates while the craft-conscious shipwrights clung to time-rates. Perhaps because the change came relatively slowly, especially on the River Wear, there were surprisingly few industrial disputes in shipbuilding. The fact that some shipyards, for example Pile's on the Wear and Smith's on the Tyne, employed shipwrights to build iron vessels, although it increased bitterness between shipwrights and boilermakers, did continue to provide employment for shipwrights and thus prevented too sudden a decline in employment opportunities for them. There were, however, some disputes. In March 1863 many of the ancillary workers in the shipbuilding yards, including sawyers, struck work for a wage increase but were defeated when the shipwrights, who had negotiated an increase with their employers, undertook such tasks as sawing timber themselves. It is evident that the lack of community of interest between the various working-class groups, mentioned earlier, was still extant and was increased by the fact that shipbuilding was organized on a craft rather than an industrial basis. In 1864 a strike against a wage reduction at Palmer's at Jarrow offers an illustration of the contemporary use of the courts as a method of intimidating workmen. Eight men were prosecuted and sentenced to periods of one or three months' imprisonment and, no doubt, this kind of action had some effect in making workmen reluctant to strike, if by doing so they were breaking a contract of employment. There were strikes at the works of the Tyne Iron Shipbuilding Company and at Bolckow and Vaughan's ironworks at Middlesbrough against unpopular foremen. In both instances the resignation of the foreman resulted, which demonstrates the growing industrial power of the workmen concerned. There were further disturbances of greater importance at Jarrow. Charles Mark Palmer was strongly opposed to trade unionism, which was therefore unwelcome in his yards and this did not augur well for conciliation in industrial relations at Jarrow. In 1865 the ironmasters of the north-east acted together, Palmer among them, to secure a reduction in wages. The iron-workers at Jarrow reacted by striking but were unable to obtain any concession from Palmer and, therefore, ended their strike and desired to return to work. They were accepted back but Palmer demanded a pledge that they would send no contribution to their fellows in other parts of the country who were still on strike against the reduction. It would seem likely that this first industrial dispute at Jarrow gave Palmer a deeper insight into industrial relations for his handling of labour questions was more skilful in the years which lay immediately ahead.

    In the year after this strike at Jarrow came the first major demands for the nine hours' day in the north-east, prompted by the prosperous conditions of the time. Following the demands of the London building workers in 1859, George Potter, one of their leaders, spoke on the subject in Newcastle in April 1861. Shortly after this, local committees of the building trade workers were organized to work for reduction of hours. During 1864 the iron shipbuilders and some factories obtained reductions in working hours and on Tees-side many carpenters gained the nine hours' day which was also adopted by Pile's shipyard at Hartlepool in 1865. By this time it was becoming obvious that these were only the more far-sighted employers forestalling a general movement and in 1866 there was evidence of considerable organization in preparation for the nine hours' movement. There was also evidence, at least among some of the leaders of the movement and their middle-class supporters, that this was not just another industrial dispute but was connected with a contemporary concern for social and educational improvement.[47] Long working hours left little time for anything but eating and sleeping and there was much contemporary discussion as to the fact that what time was available was usually spent in a public-house. The argument then ran that if the working day was shortened the longer time available in the evening could be used profitably—it was the great period of the Smilesian philosophy of self-help—that the scope for the working man was endless if he would only work hard and improve himself. The chairman of a meeting of Tyneside engineering workers in February 1866, Mr Rea, of the North-Eastern Railway Works, said that the issue of the nine hours' day 'was one of more importance than that relating to a mere advance of wages, as it affected their social and intellectual condition'. Much enthusiasm was shown at this meeting and comparisons were made with the eight hours' day in the United States of America. The meeting was strongly opposed to strike action and resolved: 'That in the opinion of this meeting the time has arrived when the employers ought, as a tribute to the intelligence of their workmen, to concede, without struggle, the reduction of the hours of labour from ten to nine per day.' Even though the workmen had seen the necessity of meeting to consider the subject they were still far from obtaining their aim since they had no means of negotiating with their employers and could hardly expect them all to follow the example of the few employers who had volunteered a reduction in hours. At the meeting, mentioned above, a Mr Green urged that only through trade unionism could the reduction be obtained but the chairman intervened to prevent Green from expanding his argument. It was obvious that workmen in the engineering trades on Tyneside did not view the trade union as an obvious vehicle for obtaining higher wages or reductions in hours of work. No doubt this stemmed from the cautious and moderate policy adopted by the Amalgamated Society of Engineers, of which very few were members.

After the meeting the Jarrow workmen wrote to inform Palmer of their views. Some extracts from the letter are worth quoting, not only as showing the arguments used but to show the change from the humble approach of the petition to Armstrong in 1862 to one still respectful but also forceful.

> We ... beg to acquaint you that an association has been formed on Tyneside for the reduction of the hours of labour from ten to nine per day; and also to inform you that we have identified ourselves with this movement, believing that the period has arrived when such reductions may reasonably be expected.
> We submit the following reasons as the ground for our request:
> By the introduction of improved machinery into the various departments of labour the profits of the employers have been considerably increased, while no corresponding benefits have accrued to the working classes, though in most instances such improvements in machinery are mainly attributable to the increased intelligence and application of the artizans themselves.
> No suggestion is required to prove that machinery, however complicated or simple, is safer in the charge of intelligent and moral workmen, than men without education and moral rectitude; and as the shortening of the hours of labour will afford opportunities for mental and moral training, thereby a mutual advantage could not but be realized by both employer and employed....
> We submit this memorial for your careful consideration and respectfully request your answer on or before March 1st, 1866.

On 22 February Palmer called a meeting, which was attended by 2,000 workmen. That afternoon a meeting of employers from all over the north-east had decided to resist the demand for nine hours and Palmer informed his men of this, telling them that, although he would like to see shorter hours, his labour costs were higher than those in other parts of the country and there was the fear of foreign competition. He went on to make it clear that if the men did not continue to work on the basis of a 59 hour week, or if some of them went on strike, there would be a full lock-out. The meeting ended with a resolution that each section of the works should appoint delegates to meet the employers but although discussions went on for some time it was clear that Palmer's address, backed by the knowledge of the united front by other employers, had nipped the incipient movement in the bud. As a result there was no strike, except among the joiners in a number of yards, who had the alternative of employment in the building trades.

On the Wear, with its large number of yards still building in wood, everything remained quiet, but towards the end of January, the iron shipbuilders on Tees-side gave a fortnight's notice to their employers of their intention to strike if the nine hours' day was not conceded. Before the notice expired the employers offered to reduce hours from 61 to 59 but this was not acceptable since, as we have seen, Pile's yard was already working only 54 hours, and the strike commenced on 7 February. Lacking the trade union which might have been able to negotiate with the employers, the men at both Stockton and Middlesbrough had formed committees to conduct the strike. While most employers locked out all their workers, Piles continued to work a nine hour day, 54 hour week, and this was also conceded by a small Middlesbrough yard and by the Tyne steam tugboat makers. There were several meetings between groups of men and their employers on the Tees but these negotiations were unsuccessful. On 26 February the employers met and decided to open their yards to men who would return on a 59 hour basis and that they would support those employers whose workmen remained on strike. On 28 February the employers informed a small meeting of workers of this decision but the men decided to remain out. Solidarity was, however, weakening, since only the few trade unionists belonging to the Boilermakers' Society received strike pay and the unskilled men almost certainly had no savings on which to fall back, and some expressed their willingness to return for nine and a half hours a day.

The employers' next step was to make use of the courts. Pearce and Lockwood obtained 26 summonses for breach of contract, all but one of which were heard at Stockton on 3 March with W. P. Roberts to defend the men. The employers claimed that the men had made a verbal contract to work until a certain ship was completed and this was upheld by the court, Roberts' claim that the employers' lock-out notice had ended the contract being rejected. The first two men were sentenced to one month's imprisonment but these were suspended when the men, after consultation with Roberts and seeing that all the cases would go the same way, offered to return to work. It was now generally imagined that the strike was over and Pile's yard issued a notice to increase hours to 59. The possibility of prison sentences, however, caused the Manchester headquarters of the Boilermakers' Society to act. A telegram, which appeared to offer strike pay of ten shillings a week, was sent to the Tees-side men. On the following day a Mr Swan, of the Boilermakers' executive, was reported to have confirmed this. This altered the situation and the next day Swan addressed a large meeting at which he was careful to repudiate the idea that strike pay would be available to all boiler-

makers whether they were members of the union or not. Meanwhile
at Middlesbrough the morale of the strikers was boosted by the
decision of the local branch of the Amalgamated Society of Engineers
to give financial assistance to keep the strike going.[48] Swan now
succeeded in persuading the employers to arrange a conference to
which the men should send delegates with power to come to a negotiated settlement. Middlesbrough stuck to nine hours and refused to
send delegates but Hartlepool elected its delegates and the Stockton
men voted narrowly in favour of a compromise and elected delegates.
The conference met but the employers were unprepared to make
further concessions beyond 59 hours and after consulting with the
delegates Swan had to stand on 56 hours, which was the compromise
agreed by the men, and so the strike continued and the employers
reverted to taking out summonses. The men at several more yards
came down in favour of the compromise and those at Pile's tried to
gain 56 hours but they were locked out on 15th March when they
refused to work the 59 hours of which notice had been given. At
Hartlepool the difficulties of the strikers and the men locked out
from Pile's were increased when the town's grocers made a public
announcement that they would refuse credit to the men. One of the
major difficulties which the men faced was their lack of organization
which made it difficult to obtain money, although appeals were made
and meetings in various parts of the country addressed by travelling
delegates. On the Tyne the men had decided to await the outcome
of the Tees-side dispute before they acted. Again the lack of union
organization told against the men. Had the men on all the north-east
rivers been called out at the same time there would have been much
greater pressure on the employers, but only the joiners came out on
the Tyne and most of them found jobs in building works. Meanwhile
meetings of the Tees-side men continued and, following a notice
announcing a meeting of employers, which would negotiate with the
men, delegates from most of the Tees and Tyne yards were elected.
The meeting took place on 24 March but, like its predecessor, was
patently a waste of time, since neither side to the negotiations was
prepared to move from its entrenched position. Both reiterated their
views and the meeting broke up.

Possibly the fact that Palmer had led the employers at this meeting, with its uncompromising attitude, and the close contact between
the Tyne men and the Tees-side strikers, led the Jarrow workers to
hold a meeting on 30 March. At that meeting Andrew Gourley moved
that a month's notice be given to Palmer of the men's demand for
nine hours and that if this were not conceded they would come out

on strike when the notice period had been worked. After some discussion an amended notice period of only seven days was approved
amid much cheering. Second thoughts were then had, since it was
realized that this resolution might lead to a lock-out throughout Tyneside and it was eventually decided that workshop meetings should be
held at Jarrow to consider the matter and report to a general meeting a week later. With these meetings under way the *Newcastle
Chronicle*, a very influential, progressive paper, which, under the
ownership of Joseph Cowen, had been particularly sympathetic to
the aims of working men, published an important editorial on the
dispute. It commented on the futile negotiations of the previous weeks
and pointed out that in the present state of trade the employers were
not in a position to concede the men's demand but were well organized to contest the dispute, while the men were poorly organized
and unlikely to succeed. It is always difficult to assess the importance
of communications media in influencing events but it is perhaps
sufficient to comment that the *Chronicle* was much esteemed for its
support of working men and that the general meeting held on 10
April voted heavily against strike action. It was resolved to send a
deputation to Palmer to ask for 57 hours, an amendment to accept
59 hours being defeated. The proposal of one delegate to request
payment of wages weekly, which he said would be the equivalent of
a rise of two shillings a week, since the men would be able to dis-
pense with obtaining expensive credit, was also accepted. It is significant that two of the deputation were Andrew Gourley and John
Burnett. The leaders in the major dispute in 1871 were already in
the van five years earlier. Palmer rejected the 57 hours compromise
and the men had to be content with the 59 hours which had been
offered by the employers several weeks before. At the same time those
of the Tyneside joiners who had not moved away or found employment in the building trades returned to work and the river was again
peaceful. Meanwhile on Tees-side the joiners were still out at the
beginning of April, as were the boilermakers supported by their
labourers. The latter made up by far the largest portion of the strikers
—at Pile's only 300 of the 2,000 men were boilermakers, and the
determination of the labourers to see the strike through was all the
more meritorious in that they had no union organization and received
no regular strike pay, unlike those of the boilermakers who belonged
to the Boilermakers' Society. At the end of March support was
received from some Manchester unionists and a distribution of 12s.
to union members and 10s. to non-union men and labourers was
made. The effects of the long strike, lack of organization, and the

sight of strike-breaking labour began to tell on the men's determination, however, and some began to trickle back to work. By mid-April
a number of yards, including Pile's, had all their men back at work
or were able to replace those missing. Only at Middlesbrough did
the majority of the boilermakers remain out and, faced with the knowledge that the labourers were learning plating, they began to return
at the beginning of May. As at Jarrow the Tees-side strikers returned
on the basis of the employers' offer of a 59 hour week but they also
obtained weekly payment of wages.

To a considerable extent the men were defeated by the decline in
economic conditions with the down-swing in the trade cycle which
led Pile's yard to bankruptcy in September 1866. Even with the sound
organization which they possessed the employers would have been
unlikely to have accepted a long strike (twelve weeks at Middlesbrough) had trade been buoyant and would almost certainly have
compromised with the men on 56 hours. As it was, however, Pile's
had only one ship under contract in March 1866 and during one of
the meetings at Stockton an employer had said that it was advantageous to them to have the men on strike at the time. Nevertheless
the strike had a value to the men beyond the achieving of a 59 hour
week and weekly pay. Most important of all it taught them the need
for organization. This they might have learned from the earlier history
of industrial relations in the region, from the examples of successful,
well organized, strike action by such groups as the keelmen and
seamen. They did not, and had to learn from their own experience
by coming against a strong *ad hoc* employers' organization, deter-
minedly led by Palmer. Beyond a small number of boilermakers and
engineers there were no unionists among the men. This made the
financing of a strike difficult and there was little co-ordination between
the workmen of the three main rivers. Given the boom conditions of
1871 and an increase in union organization in the north-east, it is not
difficult, with the advantage of hindsight, to predict that the outcome of a renewed agitation for the nine hours' day would be different.

There are a number of consistent features of the strikes outlined
above to which attention may be drawn and which were often of
significance for the events of 1871. There is a regular tendency for
the workmen's side in industrial disputes in the north-east during
this period to throw up its own leadership, whether among engineers
or pitmen. In most instances this leadership was not apparent to
outsiders beforehand but appeared as a result of the strike. What is
more, there seems to have been only limited continuity of leadership
from one industrial dispute to another. Strike action was almost in-

variably on a regional and often on a sub-regional basis, with no imposition of leadership from outside, even within such industries as shipbuilding and coal mining which had links with unions throughout the country. The creation of sub-regional leadership, i.e., on the Tyne or the Wear, seems often to have led to a failure of the men within a particular occupation to co-ordinate regional action. One of the difficulties experienced by the workmen in shipbuilding and engineering in presenting a united front to their employers was the division which frequently existed between skilled men and labourers. This division was both social and economic. The two groups often lived apart and would frequent different public-houses, while the skilled men played a part in the social life of the community, as in the cholera inquiry, which was denied to the labourers. The division was economic, as in the case of iron shipbuilding where the boiler-makers were paid piece rates and their labourers time rates, which caused many disputes and much ill-feeling. Compared with their internecine warfare over wages, it could be seen that it was possible for skilled and unskilled workers to combine for a reduction of the normal working week, as at Tees-side in 1866 and this was to occur again in 1871.

The fact that there was only a partial response from the working men of the region towards trade unionism meant that at times of dispute the men elected delegates to represent them. In itself this dependence on delegates was doubtless one factor in limiting the growth of trade unionism among workmen in such industries as engineering. It also limited their power to remain on strike since they lacked the strike pay which union backing provided, although friendly societies and benefit clubs, as well as subscriptions from well-wishers, were useful sources of finance. There are numerous instances above, and further examples in the 1871 strike itself, of committees being deputed to conduct the strikers' case. Although we know nothing of the procedures by which such committees or delegates were selected it seems inherently likely that they were chosen for their prominence and prestige among their fellow workmen. It may well be that such a mode of selection was more likely to turn up men of intelligence and ability than would formal trade union organization. This was particularly true of Andrew Gourley and John Burnett, who were among the delegates appointed by the Jarrow engineering workers in the unsuccessful attempt to obtain the nine hours' day there in 1866. Five years later, although members of the Amalgamated Society of Engineers, they were selected because of their organizational ability and not because of their union links to be the major leaders in the

Sunderland and Newcastle agitations which achieved the nine hours'
day for the engineering workers. The reasons for the satisfaction with
representation by delegates rather than trade unions in many occupations seem to stem from the facts that there was no readiness to see
industrial disputes in terms of the class struggle and that employers
were often willing to negotiate with deputations from their employees.
Indeed the fact that employees often showed a willingness to negotiate rather than precipitate a conflict seems to follow from these points
as does the general willingness of strike leaders to maintain order
among their followers.

Even where direct negotiation between workmen and employers
did not take place or broke down, one of the abiding aspects of industrial disputes in the region was the appearance of local magnates as
intermediaries. From Thomas Clennell in 1819 to R. P. Philipson,
whose intervention brought the 1871 dispute to a close on Tyneside,
these men had similar backgrounds. Usually magistrates, or high-
ranking members of a local authority, they were felt by the men to
be at least impartial, and also, as they were frequently local industrialists, they had influence with the employers' side in the dispute.
Despite their social and economic assimilation with the employers
they were often sympathetic towards the men's demands and ensured
that they were fairly considered. To the intervention of such negotiators may be attributed the peaceful settlement of many disputes. That
impartial negotiators were frequently needed may be attributed to
the not uncommon intransigence shown by employers. This was an
attitude which is not surprising from men who felt that their
employees had no right to challenge decisions which they had made.
Nevertheless, they were often outwitted by the strike leadership,
which frequently managed to obtain public support and the sympathy
of impartial observers, such as local magistrates and serving officers,
for the men's cause. It follows from this that there was usually no
coalescence of the forces of authority with the employers against the
strikers. This extended to the attitude adopted by the central authorities at the Home Office. At the conclusion of the seamen's strike in
1815, when the Combination Acts were in force, Lord Sidmouth
wrote to a Tyneside magistrate:

It is now my earnest wish that no prosecution may be instituted
except against prominent and flagrant offenders, and that the seamen who have been engaged in the late unhappy disturbances,
having experienced the power of the laws which they had violated,
may find that all resentment has ceased with their misconduct,

and that they have not permanently forfeited the confidence and goodwill of their former employers.[49]

It seems hardly necessary to point out that comments such as this are incompatible with the thesis that this was a period of repression and one cannot help but be left with the feeling that working men in the north-east had a surprising ability to influence the movement of their wages and hours and conditions of work.

NOTES TO CHAPTER 3

1. An early link between trade unionism and the agitation raised by the short-time committees may be seen in the following resolution passed by the Grand General Union of the Operative Cotton Spinners in 1829; 'That each district now present lay before their respective bodies the necessity of an early application to Parliament for an amended Act relative to the hours of labour of young persons employed in cotton factories and that the provisions of the existing laws should be extended to persons of 21 years of age.' Qd. in Cole & Filson, op. cit., p. 251.

2. There are a number of articles on the keelmen in the eighteenth and early nineteenth centuries by Fewster, J. M., in *Durham University Journal*, n.s., xix and xxiv. See also Rowe, D. J., 'The strikes of the Tyneside keelmen in 1809 and 1819', *International Review of Social History*, xiii (1968) and 'The decline of the Tyneside keelmen in the nineteenth century', *Northern History*, iv (1969), from which the following information is drawn.

3. The spout was attached to a staith on the river bank and from it coal could be shot directly into the hold of a collier. Later a 'drop' was added, by which coal wagons were lowered into the hold of the ship, thus reducing breakage of the coal.

4. P.R.O., H.O. 42/146, Lord Sidmouth to the Duke of Northumberland, 25 Oct. 1815; 79/3, H. Hobhouse to W. Marriott, 19 Aug. 1818; and 42/196, H. Hobhouse to A. Reed, 7 Oct. 1819. See also Aspinall, op. cit., xxi.

5. Barker and Harris, op. cit., p. 246.

6. This was a strongly held view locally and was well put by the *Newcastle Courant* (2 Oct. 1819). The keelmen were requesting 'the coal owner or shipowner to substitute an expensive manual labour for a cheap machinery which is already erected and in operation; a demand wholly incompatible with all the acknowledged principles of freedom in trade'.

7. This view is put always lucidly and stimulatingly, if not always convincingly, by Thompson, E. P., *The Making of the English Working Class* (1963).

8. My italics.

9. The material on this strike is drawn from McCord, N., 'The Seamen's Strike of 1815 in North-East England', *Econ. Hist. Rev.*, XXI, 1 (1968).

10. P.R.O., H.O. 41/4, 10 Oct. 1818.

11. See Rowe, D. J., 'Unionization among the North-East coast seamen in 1825', to be published in the *Economic History Review*. The shipwrights and seamen of the Tyne and Wear had been active in the agitation for the repeal of the Combination Acts. Francis Place wrote, 'Soon after the pro-

ceedings in 1825 were closed the seamen of the Tyne and Wear sent me a handsome silver vase, paid for by a penny-a-week subscription.' Quoted in Wallas, G., *The Life of Francis Place* (rev. edn., 1918), p. 240. The combinations of the seamen and shipwrights were considered so serious that the Government added clauses to the 1825 Ships' Registry Bill suspending the Navigation Laws for two years to allow the employment of foreign seamen and the repairing of British ships at foreign ports.

12. *Articles of Agreement between the members of the Seamen's Loyal Standard Association of the ports of Bridlington, Scarborough and Whitby* (North Shields, 1825). Copy in Northumberland County Record Office [N.C.R.O.], Bell (Alnwick) Colln. 404/435.

13. The South Shields Seamen's Loyal Standard Association, for example, was quite large with 1,700 members. In the year September 1825-September 1826 it spent more than £1,000 on sickness and unemployment benefit, while managing to increase its capital by a further £1,000.

14. P.R.O., H.O. 40/18, 25 July 1825.

15. Ibid, Sunderland Magistrates to R. Peel, 5 August 1825. It is interesting to note that John Davison, the magistrate accompanying the troops, was a shipowner. He came off very lightly both at the inquest and from the Home Office. Henry Hobhouse wrote to the Sunderland magistrates on behalf of Robert Peel, the Home Secretary, 'that Mr Davison was fully justified by the consideration of his own personal safety, and of that of the peace officers and troops who accompanied him, in resisting as he did the violence offered to them, and that under the trying circumstances under which Mr Davison was placed, he acted with coolness and resolution, and with as much forbearance as was consistent with the security of himself and of those who were acting under his orders.' P.R.O., H.O. 41/7, 10 Aug. 1825. This letter was also quoted in an editorial in the *Newcastle Chronicle*, 27 Aug.

16. Copy in P.R.O., H.O. 40/18.

17. P.R.O., H.O. 41/7, 18 July 1826.

18. Barker and Harris, op. cit., p. 264.

19. P.R.O., H.O. 40/29, 4 April 1831.

20. At this time it was noted by the authorities that 'radical leaders from Manchester' had been in the area in communication with the pitmen. Since there is little evidence that the pitmen were interested in reform these may well have been leaders of the Lancashire miners' union. There certainly seems to have been a considerable increase in violent action following their visit.

21. P.R.O., H.O. 52/14.

22. Ibid.

23. Ibid.

24. Ibid. The name of the ship was actually *Samarang*.

25. P.R.O., H.O. 52/14, 26 May 1831. It is interesting to note that on no occasion during 1831-2 is there any reflection in the Home Office correspondence of the fear of 1819 that the unions and radical reformers might join forces. There is no evidence to show that the pitmen as a body took any interest in political reform.

26. Ibid.

27. P.R.O., H.O. 52/19, Archibald Reed to the Duke of Northumberland, 4 May 1832.

28. Ibid, 41/11.

29. Ibid, 52/17, Edward Dale to Lord Melbourne, 2 July 1832.

30. P.R.O., H.O. 52/14.

31. P.R.O., ADM 1/1868, 1 Aug. 1831.

32. N.C.R.O., 404/435.

33. There were contemporary reports of a salary of £1,000, but see Challinor, R. and Ripley, B., *The Miners' Association—A Trade Union in the Age of the Chartists* (1968), pp. 84-7.

34. Barker & Harris, op. cit., p. 268.

35. The most recent account of the strike is contained in Challinor and Ripley, op. cit., pp. 126-55.

36. P.R.O., H.O. 41/18.

37. Ibid, S. M. Phillipps to Sir Thomas Arbuthnot, 14 June 1844.

38. Major-General Brotherton informed the Home Office, 'I must say that there being no apparent disposition on the part of the coal owners ... to submit the points at issue to fair arbitration does not seem a very equitable spirit on their part.'

39. Scott, H., 'The Miners' Bond', *Proceedings of the Society of Antiquaries of Newcastle upon Tyne*, 1947.

40. There was a short-lived revival of the union in Northumberland in 1849. See Challinor and Ripley, op. cit., pp. 237-9.

41. P.R.O., H.O. 87/2, 24 Dec. 1850. This correspondence includes an item which is symptomatic of the thoughtfulness frequently shown by Home Office officials. Mr Jobling, the viewer at Jarrow Colliery, wrote to the Home Office requesting a copy of the memorial sent by his pitmen. The Home Office requested Dunn to provide Jobling with a copy but commented, 'It is not necessary that copies of the signatories should be attached to it'. Ibid, 5 Feb. 1851.

42. These figures and most of the remaining section of this chapter are drawn from Clarke, J. F., 'Labour Relations in Engineering and Shipbuilding on the North-East Coast in the Second Half of the Nineteenth Century' (University of Newcastle upon Tyne, M.A. thesis, 1966).

43. Although there was no national union of shipwrights the unions of the north-east had links with other unions of shipwrights throughout the country for consultative purposes.

44. *Thomas Burt, an Autobiography* (1924), p. 155.

45. Burt, op. cit., pp. 174-81.

46. This was a not uncommon form of payment in engineering. For an early example at the Soho works of Boulton and Watt, see Roll, E., *An Early Experiment in Industrial Organization* (1930), pp. 200-2.

47. On merely one aspect of this concern, drunkenness and the divisions which occurred among the ranks of the reformers, see Harrison, B., 'Two Roads to Social Reform: Francis Place and the "Drunken Committee" of 1834', *Historical Journal*, xi, 2 (1968), pp. 272-300.

48. It seems unlikely that the Tees-side branch of the union was reflecting the attitude of the union's national leadership. In 1871 the union's reaction was remarkably cool and aloof. See below pp. 128-31.

49. P.R.O., H.O. 42/146, Lord Sidmouth to Rev. R. Gray, 25 Oct. 1815.

CHAPTER FOUR

The 1871 Strike—Preliminaries

THE prolonged strike among the engineering workers of Tyneside in 1871 was one of the most significant industrial disputes of nineteenth-century Britain.[1] It succeeded in enforcing a reduction of the basic working week in that industry, and marked an important stage in the long struggle for the limitation of hours of work. Yet a study of this dispute discloses many elements which were not new, and which could easily be paralleled from examples of other industrial disputes in the north-east and elsewhere, stretching back over a hundred years and more. Such features as the nature and quality of the leadership evolved by the workers involved, and their ability to mount an effective appeal to a very wide range of uncommitted public opinion, had occurred in the past. So had the intransigence and lack of flexibility revealed by the employers directly involved in the dispute. It would be wrong then to suppose that the 1871 strike presented a completely new pattern of industrial action, although this particular dispute came fortuitously to possess a wider significance than any earlier industrial dispute in the area had aroused.

As has already been shown, the engineering workers of the north-east were far from being the first in the field in the campaign for the reduction of hours of work. If, however, their actions cannot be seen as pioneering efforts in this struggle, it nevertheless remains true that the Tyneside success in 1871 gave a tremendous fillip to such endeavours, for the example set was speedily followed by engineering workers elsewhere, and also by many other groups of workers. Moreover, the 1871 strike has a more general significance in the history of industrial relations in Britain, for it was taken on every hand as something more than a local industrial dispute about hours of work. Instead it came to be regarded as a major confrontation of national importance, involving such basic opposed conceptions as the right of the employers to untrammelled freedom of action in the conduct of their businesses, and the right of the workers to ensure that their interests received due consideration in the decisions taken by employers in the conduct of their businesses.

Rumblings of discontent among various groups of workers at the length of the working week had appeared in many places during the 1850's and 1860's, their success depending very much upon the prevailing economic condition of the trades concerned. When trade and profits were booming, and when the threat of strike action was especially unwelcome to employers, concessions might be won, but when trade was slack and the prospect for profits seemed bleak, employers tended to be in no mood to yield. The immediate background to the 1871 dispute exemplified these trends. In the prosperous years leading up to the mid-1860's pressure from the engineering workers in the north-east for improved terms mounted, only to be engulfed in the recession which succeeded in the latter years of that decade. These years saw commercial setbacks and some notable bankruptcies among local firms, wage cuts and unemployment for local workers. In 1870, however, there were marked signs of recovery, and an immediate recurrence of pressure from workers for concessions. The first fruit of these altered conditions was secured by a movement initiated in the summer of 1870 for the payment of wages in the Tyneside engineering works on a weekly rather than on a fortnightly basis, a demand which had been substantially successful by the early months of 1871. The north-east engineering industry had been lagging behind other areas in this matter, and the concession of weekly payments was a practical gain of real value to the workers, many of whom had previously relied heavily on credit during the weeks which did not include a pay-day. The victory had side effects too, for if it strengthened the confidence of the workers and their determination to press for further concessions it also alarmed many employers, conscious of the need to protect their prerogatives from repeated interference from the workers they employed.

This preliminary victory was followed by moves designed to obtain a reduction in the basic working week in the north-east engineering trade. The existing basic week was 59 hours, and the engineering workers took up the movement for a nine hours' working day, aimed at cutting an hour off each of the five full working days, Monday to Friday, and thereby reducing the basic working week to 54 hours. Before the campaign for weekly pay had ended successfully on Tyneside, the Wearside engineering workers had already moved for the nine hours' demand, and the dispute over hours there provided a curtain-raiser for the more significant and prolonged struggle on Tyneside later in 1871. The engineering industry on Wearside was of more recent growth than its Tyneside equivalent, the employers on Wearside were less securely established, both from the point of view of financial strength and readiness for harmonious co-operation, while the engineering workers on Wearside possessed a ready-made leader for such a campaign in Andrew Gourley.

The movement on Wearside opened with a meeting at the Golden Lion Hotel, Sunderland, on 22nd March, attended by representatives of the men employed in the various local engineering firms. No precise demand had been formulated before this meeting, the object of which was stated generally to be a discussion on wages and conditions of work, although it was abundantly clear that some attempt was to be made to exploit the improved commercial conditions to extract concessions from the employers. Two alternative policies were considered at this meeting, either to press simply for a substantial advance in wages, or to take the favourable opportunity to demand a reduction in the basic working week from 59 hours to the 54 hour week which had already been obtained by groups of workers in other trades, notably in the building industry. The latter alternative was decided upon, and it is worth considering what factors lay behind this decision. A simple wage concession could almost certainly have been won in the existing circumstances, but there were very sound reasons for the decision to press the hours' issue instead. In order to conduct a successful struggle against the employers, it was very desirable for the men to fix upon an issue for which they could successfully appeal for sympathy and, if necessary, concrete support from groups which were not immediately concerned in the dispute. This was the more compelling in view of the fact that only a small minority of the local workers in engineering were enrolled in any formal trade union organization possessing the financial resources to back a strike if one should prove necessary. For the purpose of successfully appealing to public opinion the nine hours' movement was an admirable choice in contemporary terms, for the campaign could be based on the declared desire of the men concerned to enjoy a shorter working week in order to employ the additional time made available to them in a variety of highly edifying ways. The picture was painted in glowing colours of the self-helping worker utilizing these extra five hours to forward the education, culture and health of himself and his family.

It may, however, be reasonably conjectured that the astute men who led the nine hours' movement on Wearside and later on Tyneside realized full well that this idyllic picture could not be the whole story, and that many of their followers might well use the shorter basic week as an opportunity to work much the same hours as before, but with a correspondingly greater proportion of their time at higher overtime rates. Moreover, recent experience had shown how easily wage gains made in good times could be eroded in times of recession, and it was at least possible that a shorter basic week might prove less easily revocable than a wage advance. There was in addition one indisputably important tactical advantage in fighting for a shorter week rather than a straight wage advance. A reduction in the basic working week was a boon which would apply to all trades and all grades of labour employed in the engineering industry, and a fight on these lines avoided the fratricidal conflicts between men in different trades, and between skilled and unskilled labour, which so often bedevilled attempts to obtain alterations in the complex wage structure of the industry.[2] Tactically then the nine hours' movement was a most sagacious choice. Here was an appealing moral case, genuinely containing a boon to those workers who really desired a shorter working week, while at the same time the existing economic conditions made it reasonably certain that a shorter basic week would also in reality provide an unobtrusive and concealed method of ensuring that the men could earn more in practice from longer periods at overtime rates.

Both on Wearside and on Tyneside the nine hours' struggle of 1871 provides interesting examples of contemporary working-class leadership. Only about a quarter of the skilled engineering workers on Wearside was organized in trade unions—though this small proportion was itself greater than the corresponding figure for Tyneside.[3] The most prominent leaders in the 1871 strikes were themselves members of organized trade unions, but their influence and authority with their fellow-workers did not derive primarily from the possession of trade union office, but rather from their own individual prestige and qualities of leadership. Then, as now, groups of men working together were not simply amorphous masses, but rather societies with their own structures of eminence and leadership. The existence of men with authority among their fellow workers did not wait upon the organization of formal trade unionism. The engineering industry in the north-east had mushroomed into importance in a comparatively short period, and had by and large enjoyed considerable prosperity; formal trade union organization in the industry remained very weak, and in such circumstances authority among the workers depended much more on the individual possession of informal prestige than on the tenure of trade union office.

During the nine hours' struggle on Wearside in March and April 1871, Andrew Gourley was the most important leader of the men.

He was a trade unionist himself, and since his arrival in Sunderland
a few years earlier he had worked hard to build up the position of
trade unionism among the engineering workers there. Gourley was
a member of the Amalgamated Society of Engineers, and his efforts
had been largely responsible for the growth of the Sunderland branch
of that union from 140 members in 1866 to 330 in 1870[4]—still,
however, only a small proportion of those eligible to join. During
the strike on Wearside in the spring of 1871 it is very clear that
Gourley exercised much more influence among union men and non-
union men alike than any of the national officials of the A.S.E., and
that Gourley's eminence was very much the product of his own personal standing among his fellow workers.

Gourley had worked on Tyneside until the mid-1860's. In 1866
he had already appeared, together with John Burnett, who figures
prominently later in this story, as a delegate representing the men
of Palmer's works at Jarrow in negotiations aimed at securing the
nine hour day there. His previous activity on this matter may well
have played a decisive influence in choosing the hours' issue as the
objective to pursue on Wearside in 1871. The earlier efforts on Tyneside in the mid-1860's had come to nothing in deteriorating economic
circumstances, and both Gourley and Burnett had found it expedient
to move from Palmer's to other works. Burnett had found a new
billet in the great Armstrong works at Elswick, while Gourley had
moved to Wearside, to emerge in March 1871 as the leader of the
nine hours' movement there, and president of the *ad hoc* committee
formed to conduct this campaign.

The preliminary meeting at the Golden Lion at Sunderland on
22nd March had decided to make the hours' demand the campaign
issue, and summoned a much larger and more fully representative
meeting to endorse this decision and take steps to organize the
workers' side of the struggle. This main foundation meeting was
attended by some eight hundred workers:

> Engineers, blacksmiths, iron moulders, boilermakers, brass founders
> and finishers, patternmakers, coppersmiths, plumbers and all
> persons connected with engineering.

The predominance of the skilled trades in these proceedings is
notable; the meeting duly endorsed the decision to take up the hours'
issue, and entrusted the leadership of the campaign to a committee
appointed at the meeting and carefully chosen to include leading
individuals and also representation of the different trades and different

firms involved.

The committee immediately took up its task, drafting in very respectful terms a petition to the employers, asking that the basic working week should be reduced from 59 to 54 hours. On the last day of March this request was answered with a firm refusal on the part of the masters, who supported this refusal with the argument that to concede such a claim would be fatal to the competitive position of the Wearside engineering industry. The men's committee at once summoned a mass meeting of their followers, attended by about a thousand workers, which voted for strike action by an overwhelming majority, and early in April most of the Wearside engineering works lay idle.

Despite the brave front of resistance presented at first by the Wearside masters, they faced practical disadvantages. They had little real cohesion, and included in their ranks no men possessing prestige equivalent to that enjoyed on Tyneside by such major figures as Armstrong and Palmer. When the Wearside strike began the masters affected made immediate overtures to their Tyneside brethren, asking for support in resisting the nine hours' demand. In response the Tyneside engineering employers held a meeting on 8th April, at which they promised 'substantial support', and agreed to refuse employment to men on strike from the Wearside factories. It seems very unlikely, however, that any substantial support did in fact come from the northern river to the Wearside masters during this comparatively short-lived dispute.

The strikers on Wearside also sent out messages to their fellows elsewhere appealing for help in the struggle, and the workers seem to have received a more realistic support. Before the Wearside strike was a week old engineering workers on Clydeside had begun to send money to supplement the meagre strike funds, and urgent consultations were put in hand by the Wearside leaders to enlist the active co-operation of the Tyneside engineering workers. On the Tyne too the men were already bestirring themselves to take advantage of the improved economic climate to press for concessions, and there too the choice was faced between a simple wage claim and a campaign fought on the hours' issue. At the time the Wearside dispute began the Tyneside men had shown a tendency to press for a wage increase,[5] but in April opinion swung towards imitating the Wearside example. The key decision was taken at a meeting held in Newcastle on the afternoon of Saturday, 22nd April. It was reported then that a limited amount of money had already been despatched to Sunderland to augment strike funds there, and the meeting decided that the nine hours' day should become the target of the Tyneside engineering workers too.

By the time this decision was taken the resistance of the Wearside employers was crumbling. They had received little except encouragement from their fellow employers elsewhere, and were not in a strong enough position to mount a prolonged resistance which would have meant the loss of important orders at a time of expansion in the engineering trade generally. The attempt on Wearside to maintain a common employers' front proved a dismal failure. Breakaway concessions by individual firms paved the way for a general surrender before the end of April, which resulted in a return to work by 5th May with an assured reduction of the basic working week from 59 to 54 hours. The professional journal, *Engineering*, estimated that the actual cost to the masters concerned would amount to 5 per cent on contracts already entered into.[6]

This result represented a rapid and conclusive victory for Gourley and his colleagues, and it is very clear that the *ad hoc* committee had remained firmly in control of the men during this strike. There had been an attempt by William Allan and Robert Austin of the Amalgamated Society of Engineers' headquarters to vindicate control over their followers during the strike, but their intervention had been hotly resented on Wearside and proved wholly ineffective. The leadership of Gourley and his associates, deriving immediately from local considerations and local circumstances, prevailed throughout.

The centre of interest now shifted to Tyneside, where a much greater struggle impended. Here too the spring of 1871 had witnessed growing prosperity in the engineering industry, and by early May *Engineering* was complacently noting that 'In all parts of the North of England engineers are very busy' and 'It is a long time since engineers generally have been so busy as they are now throughout the North of England'. The complacency was, however, tempered by the expression of well-justified fears of what might happen if the workers sought to exploit this changed climate to press for major concessions from the masters.[7]

The Newcastle meeting of 22nd April, held in the town's Lecture Room, has already been mentioned as the first occasion on which the nine hours' movement on Tyneside gathered steam. Most of the speeches and resolutions at that meeting were couched in terms of conciliation and respect for the engineering employers, and there was clear expression of willingness to see the claim for a 54 hour week go to arbitration in the hope of avoiding a head-on conflict and strike action. A respectful hearing was given to a well-known local working man, McKendrick, who emphasised the merits of the settlement of industrial disputes by arbitration, and advocated the application of co-operative organization in industry. Local newspapers of these years show that such topics were very much in the air among more moderate workers and their middle-class sympathizers. This was not, however, the only note sounded at the meeting on 22nd April, though conciliatory attitudes clearly predominated. A more militant element was certainly present, as one of the other speakers demonstrated: [8]

> He remarked that he did not like to hear the word employer mentioned, and thought that working men should be in such a position as to be their own employers. (Hear, hear and applause.) He had been born as respectably as any man, and he did not see why he should have to go down on his knees and say to any man 'Will you give me leave to earn a crust and live in the world?' The working men were the wealth of the world, they ought to take their proper position, and not be at the caprice of any man for a livelihood.

In the week which followed this meeting further discussions took place, resulting in the formation of an *ad hoc* representative committee on Tyneside similar to that which Gourley had led on Wearside in previous weeks. The committee included delegates from the men in the principal engineering works on Tyneside, representing again a genuine leadership which already existed naturally on the shop floor.

On Saturday, 29th April, these moves were formalized at a meeting summoned to the Westgate Inn, Newcastle—which was to remain the headquarters of the campaign during the ensuing months. Here a very full gathering of representatives from different trades and different works approved of the creation of a Nine Hours' League— a title with echoes of the campaigns for repeal of the Corn Laws and Parliamentary Reform—to be headed by the *ad hoc* committee which had already come into existence and was to govern the campaign throughout its course. The committee operated under the style of The Acting Committee of the Nine Hours' League—'Acting' here being used in its contemporary sense as meaning 'active' or 'managing' rather than 'provisional'—and provided remarkably able collective leadership for the men involved in this prolonged struggle. Information about these men is, not surprisingly, tantalizingly scanty in most cases; the names of many of them are not known, and others are known only by name, or by press reports of a few speeches, yet they undoubtedly represent a genuine working-class leadership always present to some degree, but now for a few months emerging more fully into the limelight. It is reasonable to conjecture that before 1871 and the rise of the Nine Hours' League these men already occupied positions of influence among the various groups of workers employed in the local engineering works, yet it is only the focussing of the illumination of public interest during this struggle in 1871 that has even given us the names of men like Pletts, Gillender, Parkinson, Short and Henderson among those who formed the Acting Committee of the League.

In one instance, however, it is possible to fill in a little more detail, and fortunately the man concerned was the main spokesman and principal leader of the campaign.[9] John Burnett was born at Alnwick on 21st June 1842, and educated in the Duke's School in that town. Both his parents died when he was twelve, and he left Alnwick to live with an uncle on Tyneside. For his first two years there he worked as an errand boy, and then at fourteen he was apprenticed in a local engineering works. In early manhood he rapidly secured for himself a reputation for high intelligence and capacity for leadership. We have a description of Burnett as an engineering worker at Palmer's Jarrow establishment from a fellow-worker there who remembered Burnett as he was in the 1860's: [10]

> In the very prime of manhood—a stalwart, muscular figure. He was then noted for his genial, unruffled temper, and quiet, impressive deportment, suggestive of a reserve of mental energy and strength of character in the background. These qualities, however, were never obtrusively displayed, for he was one of the most modest of men.

By the 1860's Burnett was already recognized as one of the leading influences among the workers at Palmer's, and moreover he was better known outside the confines of the engineering industry than any of the other men who were to work with him in the Nine Hours' League. Burnett was one of the most prominent members of the Newcastle Mechanics' Institute in Blackett Street, where his talents as a debater had already clearly emerged. The topics debated there covered a wide range of subjects; Burnett is recorded as taking part in a debate on the question 'Did the Wars of the Roses forward the Cause of English Liberty?'—he thought they did. In January 1867, with reform and the rights of the working men very much in the air Burnett appeared on a wider stage, when the Newcastle Town Hall

was the scene of a public speaking contest patronised by local digni-
taries and employers. The selected theme was 'Strikes and how to
prevent them, showing their disadvantages to nations and individuals'.
Among the most able performers Burnett devoted what the *Newcastle
Chronicle* called his 'excellent address' to a forcible exposition of
the ill-effects of strikes and the virtues of co-operative enterprises
in industry.[11] Burnett appeared as a respected working-class reformer
during the campaign for parliamentary reform in the 1860's, activity
which must certainly have brought him contacts with men in higher
positions in local society which were to prove useful in 1871.

Burnett stands out as a very good example of a kind of working-
class leader which has made a crucially important contribution to
the way in which modern British society has evolved. Intelligent,
perceptive, and a man of very marked gifts as leader and organizer,
he possessed a very high sense of the abilities and the rights of
British workers, and yet he always preferred methods of negotiation
and conciliation to outright conflict in industrial disputes. While
very well aware of the injustices and inequalities which abounded in
contemporary society, he sought to remedy them not by revolutionary
subversion, but by making the maximum possible use of the opportunities for improvement made available in practice by the existing
structure of society. He believed, with some justification, that it was
possible to move significantly towards a more just and equal society
by a policy of co-operation with the more enlightened elements among
the contemporary privileged and influential groups. He believed that
any attempt at violent revolution would be less healthy and less
fruitful for the workers than the more cautious policy of seeking to
induce those who possessed power already to share it more generously and use their power to ameliorate the condition of the less
fortunate elements in society. He was in 1871 about to embark upon
a very tough and prolonged struggle, but it was a struggle fought
in the context of a society which had only a few years earlier conceded that many working men had good claims to political rights,
and a society in which revolutionary political groups were marked
principally for their impotence and irrelevance to the major developments of the day. Burnett was not a unique figure in the British
working class of his day; in North-East England his views were very
similar to those held by Thomas Burt and William Crawford, two
of the most eminent miners' leaders of this period, and it is not surprising that the north-east miners were to contribute generously to
the nine hours' movement led by Burnett.

With the creation of the Nine Hours' League at the end of April,

Burnett became its president, and he drafted the message in which the League committee first placed its objective before the Tyneside engineering masters on 2nd May:

The Nine Hours' Movement.—Gentlemen,—'Coming events so often cast their shadows before,' that the events which have taken place in Sunderland, within the last few weeks, must have prepared you for the request, which we, as the appointed representatives of your workmen, now respectfully prefer, viz.: That you will kindly consent to the reduction of the hours of labour from ten to nine hours per day—or, more properly speaking, from 59 to 54 hours per week; a concession, we believe, that might be made with little or no injury to your own interests, and with great advantage to ours. The various arguments in favour of a reduction of the hours of labour have been so often successfully advanced of late that we will not trouble you with a repetition of them, but content ourselves with assuring you, in all sincerity, that it is our desire to settle this matter, if possible, in a friendly and peaceable manner, and without having recourse to extreme measures. In conclusion, gentlemen, we venture to express a hope that you will not utterly ignore our claims to consideration, by treating this with that silence which looks so like contempt, and which so often helps to precipitate masters and men into a struggle which cannot be otherwise than hurtful to the best interests of both.

Trusting that you will, in reply to this, view the matter in a similar spirit of good will and, anxiously expecting an answer not later than Friday, 12th inst., we remain, gentlemen, yours respectfully,

THE ACTING COMMITTEE OF THE NINE HOURS' LEAGUE.

N.B.—Please address—Secretary of Nine Hours' League, Westgate Inn, Westgate, Newcastle-on-Tyne.

The employers had anticipated the demand, and were determined to resist it. On Tyneside the majority of the engineering employers proved capable of a greater degree of co-operation and cohesion than their counterparts on Wearside had contrived in March and April. Moreover, the Tyneside masters possessed in Sir William Armstrong a leader notable for his personal prestige in the engineering world and for his personal qualities of strong-mindedness and determination. In his firm opposition to the demand made by the Nine Hours' League, Armstrong found vigorous supporters among his fellow employers. It is possible that the story of this dispute might have been different if the two Hawthorn brothers had continued to direct the destinies of the engineering firm they had built up, R. and W. Hawthorn. There had been a change of control there, however, when in 1870 new proprietors took over. The Hawthorn brothers had been enlightened in their labour relations, and personally popular among their workpeople. Robert Hawthorn died in 1867, and his brother sold out in 1870. The two men in control of that firm in 1871 were less experienced in that capacity, concerned to vindicate their authority, and very anxious for the continuance of profitable working, for the purchase of the works had only been made possible by substantial bank credits.[12] The new senior partner was Benjamin Browne, a civil engineer, 32 years of age in 1871, who had sunk all his personal resources into his new enterprise, as well as borrowing heavily from the Newcastle bank of Hodgkin, Barnett & Co. Browne had a growing family, whose prosperity now depended upon the success of the new team at Hawthorn's.[13]

His principal partner was F. C. Marshall, an interesting figure in the dispute in that he had worked his way up from the shop floor to the position of partner in Hawthorn's. His father had been an engineering worker, from a family which had for generations worked as smiths in a Northumberland village. F. C. Marshall had begun his working career at the age of 14 in 1845 as an apprentice fitter at Hawthorn's, moving to the drawing office there five years later. After a time as chief draughtsman at the Spring Garden Engine Works of Thomson & Wood in the early 1860's he had been appointed manager of the engine works at Palmer's Hebburn establishment, moving in 1870 to join Browne in the new partnership at Hawthorn's.[14] Marshall, the man from the shop floor, was to prove even more reluctant than Armstrong to yield to the demands of the League in 1871.

Another employer prominent in resistance to the nine hours' demand was George Crawshay, of the Gateshead works of Hawks, Crawshay & Co. He had a long record of support for radical political movements of various kinds on Tyneside, but this did not make him more disposed to yield to the workmen's demand for a shorter working week.

The refusal of men like these to submit to the pressure of the Nine Hours' League is entirely intelligible, especially when it is borne in mind that the Tyneside engineering industry had expanded with remarkable speed in a few decades, and that no combination as formidable as the League had arisen before to challenge these employers. To the engineering masters the demand for a shorter basic working week was dangerous in itself as it threatened to place the Tyneside masters at a disadvantage compared with their industrial competitors at home and abroad. More than this, however, to surrender to organized labour on such an issue was to jeopardize the prerogatives of the employer to run his enterprise as he thought fit. A master like Armstrong could recognize willingly enough that when skilled labour was in short supply the worker might well be able to obtain better wages from employers competing for his services, but this was a very different matter from a league of workmen presuming to lay down rules as to the number of hours the machinery of a factory should work.

The Britain of 1871 was very different from its successor a century later. The kind of influence for which John Burnett and his fellow-workers were striving was not something generally accepted by contemporary society, but something which was still being fought for and which was not to be won quickly or easily. To someone like Sir William Armstrong, possessed of a well-founded sense of the importance of his own position, resistance to the League was natural. In a quarter of a century he had seen the Elswick works grow under his direction to become one of the greatest engineering enterprises of the day, already giving employment to nearly four thousand men. It was natural that Armstrong should arrogate the credit for this magnificent achievement primarily to his own enterprise, managerial skill and capacity for technical innovation. It was equally natural that he should strongly resent dictation from those whose attainments were so patently inferior, and who, to him, were primarily the beneficiaries of his own abilities and achievements.

Armstrong was willing to take the lead in resisting the demands of the League, and the work of organizing the employers' resistance was largely undertaken by the skilled team of managers associated with Elswick, including the Rendel brothers, George and Stuart, and Captain Andrew Noble. The majority of the other engineering employers on Tyneside were only too willing to follow the firm lead given by Armstrong, and joined as the Associated Employers in co-operative opposition to the Nine Hours' League.

The first task facing the employers was to draft a reply to the respectfully couched letter received from the League's Committee on 2nd May. The form taken by this reply demonstrated the masters' intention of standing firm:

72, Pilgrim Street, Newcastle-upon-Tyne, 6th May, 1871.
To the Secretary of the Nine Hours' League, Westgate Inn, Westgate Street, Newcastle.

Sir,—We are instructed by the Manufacturing Engineers in Newcastle-upon-Tyne and Gateshead to forward to you the following resolution in reply to your circular addressed to them, viz.— 'At a meeting of the Manufacturing Engineers of the Newcastle-upon-Tyne and Gateshead District held at the Station Hotel, on Saturday, 6th May, 1871, Sir Wm. George Armstrong in the chair, a circular having been read from the Acting Committee of the Nine Hours' League, requesting a reduction of the hours of labour, from 59 to 54 hours per week. It was unanimously resolved that the above application be declined, and further, that a copy of this resolution be forwarded to the Secretary of the Nine Hours' League.'

We are, Sir, your obedient servants,

STANTON AND ATKINSON.

This document was not only entirely negative in its content, but also offensive in its manner, a fact of which the employers can scarcely have been unaware. Instead of agreeing to discuss the hours' question with the men, or even addressing the League directly, the associated employers chose to reply through the medium of a firm of solicitors, and that a firm notoriously associated with the Conservative party in local politics. In the past history of industrial relations on Tyneside, the men had repeatedly attached great importance to their being treated openly and directly by their employers, and shrewd employers had been fully aware of the importance of this point.[15] The method of communication now resorted to by the masters could not fail to exacerbate the situation, and throughout the dispute the men and their sympathizers repeatedly criticized the employers for acting in this way.

Events in two major Tyneside engineering works which stayed clear of the strike of 1871 demonstrated that there were important employers in the area whose approach to industrial relations was more conciliatory and skilful. Charles Mark Palmer was not willing to concede the nine hours' demand, but at least he met his own workmen face to face in a specially convened meeting at Jarrow where his own formidable personality and prestige could be deployed effectively. At this mass meeting of his men, he made the offer that he would accept the nine hours' day if and when it was generally accepted by the local engineering firms, and this promise, duly honoured in the outcome, kept the Jarrow men at work during the prolonged strike which was to follow.

Another great Tyneside name which held aloof from the main dispute was that of Stephenson, where the enterprise founded by George and Robert Stephenson was still controlled by their descendant, George Robert Stephenson. G. R. Stephenson had already established a reputation as a sagacious and generous employer, who preferred to take his own independent line in matters of industrial relations. He had invariably refused to take part in any joint organization of employers to resist the demands of labour, preferring to keep his relations with his workmen in his own hands. In 1871 Stephenson, too, was unwilling to concede the nine hours' day, but like Palmer he had the wisdom to deal openly and directly with his workmen. Stephenson was away from Tyneside when the dispute opened, but he sent a long personal letter to be communicated to his men at the Gateshead works, explaining just why he was unwilling to make this concession. He made it very clear that he was always willing to discuss such questions with the representatives of his own men, and stated explicitly his intention of continuing to hold aloof from any combination of employers. Stephenson's workmen reciprocated by deciding not to join the Nine Hours' League, and remained at work throughout the strike which followed. Stephenson promptly conceded the nine hours' day, as soon as the League's victory had forced this concession on the remainder of the Tyneside engineering firms. Nevertheless if the names of Palmer and Stephenson were two notable absentees, the list of engineering employers aligned with Armstrong in a policy of stubborn resistance to the League was a formidable one, and included the majority of the large engineering firms on Tyneside.

The leaders of the League were in no way over-awed by the form of the associated employers' reply, and summoned a mass meeting of their followers for Saturday, 12th May, to consider what action should now be taken. Predictably, at that meeting there was bitter criticism of the form taken by the employers' message, but despite this natural resentment the meeting accepted the advice of the leaders of the League to maintain a tone of sweet reasonableness and to try another attempt to settle the dispute by peaceful negotiation. A resolution was passed in favour of selecting six delegates to seek a conference with a delegation from the employers in order 'to try to come to some understanding'. It was stipulated that any terms arranged would have to be submitted for ratification to the mass of the men involved. A respectful letter was despatched to the employers, asking for such a conference to be arranged.

However, on the following Tuesday a dramatic turn of events made any such conference impossible. From the beginning of the dispute

Burnett and the other League leaders had emphasized the paramount need for restraint by their followers, but these exhortations were now thrown over by the too zealous workmen employed by one of the associated employers, the firm of Clark, Watson & Gurney, where the men now came out on strike contrary to the wishes of the League leaders. There was perhaps some little excuse for this precipitate action, since in that particular firm there was in practice no giving or requiring of notice before terminating employment. By jumping the gun in this way, however, the men concerned impaired the public image of restraint and moderation for which the League's leaders were striving patiently, and this impulsive action seemed to give some excuse for the blank refusal of the masters to yield to the League's pressure. Certainly Armstrong and his colleagues used this event as their justification in the second communication they made to the League, despatched through the same offensive channel—

72, Pilgrim Street, Newcastle-upon-Tyne, May 18th 1871.
NINE HOURS' MOVEMENT.—SIR,—We are instructed to inform you that at a Meeting of the Employers of Engineering Labour, held today at the Station Hotel, after your last letter to us had been read, it was unanimously resolved 'that the Employers see no advantage in the interview proposed by the Nine Hours' League. They (the Employers) would have suggested a written communication from the League, in preference to a meeting, but for the fact that a strike had already taken place. Under the circumstances the Employers feel that no course is now open to them but to refer the Nine Hours' League to their former communication, dated the 6th inst., and to request them to consider it final.'
Your obedient servants.
STANTON AND ATKINSON.
Mr James Parkinson, Secretary Nine Hours' League, Westgate Inn, Westgate Street, Newcastle-on-Tyne.

On Saturday, 20th May, the League held a meeting to consider what to do next. There was some sharp criticism of the precipitate action taken by the men at Clark, Watson & Gurney, and then a resolution was moved calling for immediate strike action to secure the 54 hours' week. This was met by an amendment calling for a further attempt at negotiation with the employers, but this was defeated by a substantial majority, and the substantive resolution for strike action was then overwhelmingly carried. Further resolutions then accepted that the League's committee must be in complete control of the

campaign throughout the dispute, and agreed upon an address to
be published as widely as possible in the North-East and elsewhere:

NINE HOURS' MOVEMENT IN THE NORTH OF ENGLAND

To the Working Men of Great Britain.—After a strike
of three or four weeks' duration, the Employers of Engineering
Labour in Sunderland, on the 2nd of May, yielded to the demands
of their workmen, in regard to a reduction of the hours of labour
from fifty-nine to fifty-four per week.

The men of Newcastle and Gateshead, inspired by the success
of the Sunderland men, have resolved to come out on strike, in order
to attain the same object, and, as the position of the Employers
in these Towns is almost the same as that occupied by the Sunderland Employers before the strike, we have every hope of success.

We have not come to this resolution rashly, or with undue haste,
but have tried every means to gain our object without having
recourse to the last dread resource of a strike. Our Employers, however, have treated all our advances with contempt, and have left
us no alternative but a strike. And as a strike cannot be carried on
without funds, we apply to you for pecuniary assistance.

Our object is not a merely selfish one, for if it is attained by us
it will be rendered more easy of attainment by you, and indeed by
the working men of Britain generally, so that, in fact, we feel that
as we are out on strike, not only for ourselves but for the whole
working population of this kingdom, we have a claim upon your
sympathy and support, which we are confident you will not refuse
to acknowledge.

Our need is urgent, as we will have ten thousand men out on
strike on June 1st, not the 12th part of that number being members
of any Trade Society.

Trusting that you will contribute to our support as liberally as
ever possible,

We remain, Gentlemen, yours respectfully,
THE ACTING COMMITTEE OF THE NINE HOURS' LEAGUE.
Newcastle-on-Tyne, 22nd May, 1871.

Money orders payable to the President—Mr John Burnett.
All communications addressed to the Secretary—Mr James
Parkinson, Secretary of the Nine Hours' League, Westgate Inn,
Westgate Street, Newcastle-on-Tyne.

Already those who conducted the League's affairs were showing their ability to devise cogent and impressive appeals to uncommitted public opinion. There is, however, no reason to doubt that for the majority of the League's leaders at least, the decision to strike was not taken eagerly. It seems clear that they would have much preferred a settlement by negotiation. Nevertheless, once the issue was joined in this way, the leadership of the League was steadfast in its determination to fight the battle through to a successful conclusion.

On Monday, 22nd May, the followers of the League handed in their notices. Twelve engineering firms were affected, and a local newspaper tabulated the number of men involved in the strike as follows—[16]

Armstrong's	2700	Clark, Watson & Gurney	300
Hawthorn's	1200	T. Clark	300
Abbott	1000	Joicey	100
Thompson & Boyd	700	Wylie	90
Hawks & Crawshay	500	Pattinson & Atkinson	40
Black & Hawthorn	500	Donnison	12

The total of men involved in the dispute, at some 7,500, made the League appear a formidable instrument, but the problems faced by its leaders were very great. Only a small minority of their followers was organized in any form of trade union. Some others might have savings or friendly society benefits to fall back on, but the difficulty of raising the money to support the men on strike and their dependants was a formidable one indeed.

In their campaign, however, the men were not without valuable allies. Support of very considerable value came from Joseph Cowen, junior, and his *Newcastle Chronicle*. In a whole variety of ways Cowen's help was of immense use to the League leaders. He was himself a local industrialist of some note, a man of considerable talents and considerable wealth, possessing an influential position in local politics. Throughout the nine hours' strike Cowen was constantly at the elbow of the leaders of the League, advising and in addition proffering direct financial support, and conveying to Burnett any useful information he had gleaned from his own multifarious contacts. Under his skilful personal guidance the *Newcastle Chronicle* was now approaching the peak of its influence. In 1871 its circulation was about thirty thousand daily, while the panache and ingenuity with which it was conducted earned it a place as one of the genuinely influential provincial newspapers.[17] With the *Chronicle* firmly committed to the League's side, the strenuous opposition of the other local newspapers was of little account.

In the very beginning of the nine hours' dispute, the *Chronicle* did not take a firm line. On 24th April its report of the crucial meeting held by the men two days earlier mis-reported Burnett as Bennett, and as late as 8th May an editorial was still uncertain as to how far the League leaders were genuinely representative of the engineering workers of Tyneside. Even before the strike itself broke out, however, Cowen had imprinted a more definite policy on its pages, and any such doubts speedily disappeared from the *Chronicle*'s columns. On Monday, 22nd May, as the men's notices went in, the *Chronicle* made it clear that:

> Compared with the men engaged in many of the turn-outs of earlier times, these men know what they are about ... The demand of the men is perfectly legitimate and even reasonable.

A close co-operation emerged between the leaders of the League and the owner and the staff of this, the most influential of local newspapers in North-East England. Cowen had carefully recruited for his paper a band of able and enthusiastic journalists of liberal sympathies, and it may well be that the League's sure touch with propaganda owed something to this source. One of the *Chronicle* reporters, a bright young man named Hugh Dellow, recalled many years later an experience during the earlier part of the 1871 strike.[18] He was reporting the proceedings at a League open air meeting at which rain began to fall, blurring the reporters' notebooks as they tried to record the proceedings. At the same time the crowded audience was pressing close around the centre of the meeting where the speakers were placed, and the crowd was making things more difficult for the journalists by jostling them as they tried to write. Burnett was only a little distance away from Dellow and the reporter called out to him that it would be useful if the reporters could have a little more room. Without turning, Burnett, probably more than a little wet himself, answered 'Perhaps you'd like me to send for a table and writing desk for you.' Dellow retorted with spirit 'You needn't be so beastly supercilious. If any of you fellows had a piece of work on a lathe and were being jostled as we are, you wouldn't be long in crying out.' At this Burnett turned, and taking in the situation at once he apologized to Dellow, saying that his mind had been busy with something else when the reporter first interrupted him. Then he induced the nearer part of the crowd to move back to give the reporters more room, and at future League meetings Burnett made a point of ensuring that the reporters were given proper facilities to do their work. Dellow and Burnett became firm friends, and remained so for very many years after 1871. The tight alliance between League and *Chronicle* was a strong card in the hand held by the nine hours' movement.

The League also benefited from the outstanding quality of leadership provided by John Burnett. He and his fellows on the League committee never seemed to put a foot wrong during the prolonged contest. They were always careful to present a public image of conspicuous restraint and moderation, in contrast to what seemed the continuing intransigence of Armstrong and his allies. This careful consideration and cultivation of opinion was not directed only at outsiders, but applied also to the leadership's relationship with the mass of the strikers. Throughout the dispute the League leaders drew only the minimum sums necessary for expenses, and made very certain that their followers were made well aware of this. When Cowen offered Burnett a personal gift of money during the strike, the League's President refused any individual present of this kind: [19]

he told him he was almost afraid to go out in the suit then on his back, because, during a strike, men grew so suspicious that they would say almost anything against a leader who was too well dressed.

As the men's notices went in on 22nd May the gloves were off. This fighting action by the men resulted in an attempt at intimidating the strikers the next day, when a meeting of local millers and flour merchants decided that no credit would be available from that quarter to provide food for strikers and their families during a stoppage. This declaration was posted throughout the area, but failed to move the men. The associated employers stood equally firm, and on 23rd May George Rendel of Armstrong's reported the situation to his brother Stuart, away on a business trip—[20]

The Masters held a meeting today and after agreeing unanimously to hold out and to make no concessions without the consent of our association adjourned till Friday next to allow the movement time to develop.

The demands of the men are very great & must be resisted if we are to see the whole of the district continue to flourish. A weak opposition and a quick concession would lead to further demands that would ruin the district not to speak of the immediate loss it would inflict on employers on their existing contracts.

> We are in for a severe contest but it cannot be helped ...

In another letter the following day Rendel expressed the belief, to which the employers were to recur from time to time, that the League leaders were not representative, and that the strike was taking place:

> only against the grain evidently with the majority of the men who are coerced by a minority.

It is impossible at this distance to establish whether or not there was very much truth in this convenient belief; what is, however, perfectly clear is that the League's committee remained very firmly in the saddle during the remainder of the dispute, and there is very little evidence to suggest that this control met with active opposition from more than a small minority of the engineering workers.

Even before the strike actually took place, attempts at mediation began. The threatened stoppage in one of the area's major economic resources naturally aroused apprehension among other groups concerned with the trade of Tyneside. After discussion in the Newcastle Chamber of Commerce, an open letter from 'Merchants, Bankers, Members of Professions, and others, Inhabitants of Newcastle' appealed to the Mayor of Newcastle to intervene to procure a peaceful settlement of the dispute. This document, signed by some of the most influential Tynesiders unconnected with the immediate struggle, was in fact asking the Mayor to take the same kind of conciliatory action as his predecessors in that office had embarked upon in many past industrial disputes in the area. The Mayor in office was well suited for such a role. Richard Burdon Sanderson (1821-76) was a moderate Liberal in politics, and closely connected with a wide variety of local economic interests. He at once agreed to make an attempt at mediation. His formal written acceptance of the invitation to intervene was in Cowen's hands on the evening of 24th May, ready for publication in the next morning's *Chronicle*. On that same evening Cowen held a discussion with some of the League's leaders, with the result that when the Mayor's letter appeared in the *Chronicle* of 25th May, it was accompanied by the following skilfully worded statement from the League:

LETTER FROM THE SECRETARY OF THE NINE HOURS' LEAGUE.
To the Editor of the *Newcastle Daily Chronicle*.
DEAR SIR,—In answer to your suggestion in the *Chronicle* of today that there should be a meeting to allow the Engineers to put

their case before the public; or that the Mayor or some other independent gentleman should endeavour to negotiate the matter in dispute, I beg to say that the members of our committee are, and always have been, willing to discuss the question with either our employers or any disinterested person.

We offered to meet the employers several days ago, and would have done so gladly. They refused to meet us, and to this refusal chiefly the present unfortunate position of affairs is attributable.

No one knows the evils that arise from strikes better than workmen, and I have to say, on behalf of my colleagues and myself, that we would only be too glad to arrive at any solution of this dispute with our honour and interests.

Yours truly,
JAMES PARKINSON,
Hon. Secretary of the Nine Hours' League.

Westgate Inn, Wednesday night, May 24, 1871.

Other voices were being raised at the same time in favour of an agreed settlement; the weekly periodical *Engineering* repeatedly advocated a settlement by arbitration, which can scarcely have endeared it to the Tyneside masters.

The League was prompt to appoint a delegation to confer with the Mayor, and seven of its most prominent members had a long discussion with Burdon Sanderson on the morning of Thursday, 25th May, immediately after the publication of his willingness to accept the role of peacemaker. Proceedings at the meeting began with one of the League delegates offering:

a few words of acknowledgement for the courtesy, for the kindness of heart, and for the self-denial which the Mayor had exhibited in this matter ... They knew that in many cases the office of peacemaker was a thankless one, but they had advanced so far that they said 'Blessed are the peace-makers'. He believed the feelings of the working men of this town towards his worship for the step he had now taken would be feelings of unmixed gratitude, more especially if a happy solution of the difficulty should arise.

The Mayor may have thought that this was rather on the fulsome side, but more was to follow. The League delegation's next step was to read to the Mayor a very long prepared statement, obviously designed for public consumption. This manifesto is too long to be reproduced in its entirety here, but its first page will give a good

idea of the nature and quality of the arguments adduced by the
League in its propaganda:

> Political economy defines labour as the voluntary exertion of mental
> or bodily faculties for the purpose of production, or as the action
> of the human frame directed to the manufacture of useful articles;
> and as labour seems to be the lot of the greater portion of mankind,
> it would perhaps be as well to inquire into some of the conditions
> necessary to the efficient discharge of our duties in the work of pro-
> duction. In the first place, we require strength and energy, aptitude
> and skill to subdue matter and to overcome the many obstacles
> which nature presents us. It is no new discovery, although it has
> of late years attracted considerable attention, that not only is it
> necessary to be possessed of strength and energy, but likewise
> that to these should be added some knowledge of scientific prin-
> ciples—at least, of those which apply to our own particular trades.
> But if all our time is to be taken up with work—if we are always
> to be either toiling 'from morn till noon, from noon till dewy eve',
> or resting our wearied frames that we may be fitted for the leng-
> thened toil of another day, how are we to avail ourselves of the
> means of technical, or indeed of any other sort of education which
> are placed within our reach? Indeed, we recollect a case of one
> employer of labour in Newcastle, who, at a public meeting held in
> the Mechanic's Institute for the purpose of considering the best
> means of diffusing technical education among working men, ex-
> pressed his astonishment that more of them did not avail them-
> selves of the means of technical education, which had then been
> provided, and seemed altogether to forget the fact that in his own
> extensive establishment the majority of his workmen were working
> overtime regularly and systematically—some $12\frac{1}{2}$ and $14\frac{1}{2}$ hours
> per day—so that their chance of attending night schools or science
> classes must have indeed been small, to say nothing of their avail-
> ing themselves of means of relaxation or bodily exercise, whereby
> they might revive their worn-out physical energies. We do not say,
> nor do we for an instant pretend, that we working men, as a class,
> are all that we should or might be. There is a vast amount of
> ignorance amongst us, and a vast amount of drunkenness in our
> midst; but we contend that one of the most powerful preservatives
> of ignorance and one of the most seductive agencies of drunkenness,
> has been the long duration of the hours of labour, and its conse-
> quent effect in the almost total exhaustion which it has produced
> upon the vital energies of the working man; for physical and

mental weariness would have a strong tendency to keep him from the night-school or the science-class, while the desire for some stimulant, the craving for some artificial and easily-attainable means of excitement, would have a powerful effect in leading him to the public-house, and, as many a man put it, to refresh himself after his hard day's work. We know that many working men go to the science class as it is, and distinguish themselves there, and we say, more honour to them for triumphing over the many obstacles placed in their way, and if many have succeeded in this way under existing circumstances, many more will be likely to succeed if the hours of labour are shortened, to say nothing of the improvements in the state of the pupil's mind as regards receiving instruction; for a wearied body generally contains a weary mind, and if the body is not wearied by long hours of work the mind will be fresher and more vigorous to surmount difficulties, to receive impressions, and to originate ideas. So much, then, for mental education after work hours: but we would like to say a few words about physical education as well. Now, as to the workman himself nothing is more necessary than the possession of energy, steadiness, and skill, so to the employer the possession of these qualities in the workman is equally indispensable; the interest, therefore, of the employer and his workman is one and the same, and it is the interest of both to see that it is the truest economy, the most farseeing policy, to preserve, for as long a time as possible, the energy and skill which are of so much importance to both; and as few things are more injurious to a steam engine or to machines of any sort than to task them beyond their powers, so with the human machine. Long hours of work in an impure atmosphere of a factory are more hurtful to it than anything else that we know of, and we believe that to this cause is entirely due the large percentage of deaths which occur in our trade from consumption; the average number from that fell disease being about 30 per cent., and the average age of its victims but little over 30.

Further similar arguments went on to point out that in seeking greater opportunities for the engineering workers to take health-giving physical exercise, the League was engaged on a course deserving the active support of every patriot who cared for the physical well-being of the nation. These arguments were all very well for public consumption, but after this very long address had been recited there ensued a prolonged and more hard-headed discussion between the Mayor and the League delegates about the technical problems involved in the claim for a 54 hour week. During these exchanges the delegates exhibited very considerable and detailed knowledge of the position of the local engineering firms and their current commercial prospects. They pointed out to the Mayor that in many cases the local engineering workers were paid by contract prices rather than on a time basis, so that a concession of a shorter working week need not involve a comparable rise in labour costs, as the employers themselves continued to claim.

In reply the Mayor made no commitment himself, but tried hard to induce the delegates to agree to a withdrawal of the notices already handed in, or their extension, on the grounds that they were now due to take effect in two days time, which left inadequate time for a genuine attempt at conciliation. While profuse in their appreciation of the Mayor's helpfulness, Burnett and his colleagues flatly refused to budge on this, unless the Mayor could offer them some genuine and substantial concession from the associated employers. The delegates averred that even if they themselves should agree to such an extension of the notices, they would certainly see their action repudiated by the great mass of their followers. With some justice the League men pointed out that if in the beginning the employers had acted with courtesy and consideration towards the workers there might have been an atmosphere in which a delay in the strike could have been conceded. As it was the men felt such resentment at the cavalier way in which their respectful approaches had been rejected that there was no chance of an extension of the notices being agreed to unless there was clear evidence that the employers had moved to a less intransigent position. The delegates added too that the employers had already had ample time to consider the demand the men were putting forward for a shorter working week. With this blank answer the Mayor undertook to consult with the employers on the basis of the case expounded to him by the League delegates.

After this prolonged meeting on the morning of 25th May the Mayor went immediately to the Station Hotel, where a meeting of the associated employers was awaiting him. He reported upon his discussions with the men, and as he had promised put forward the League's repeated request for direct negotiations between delegations representing the two parties. Armstrong, in the chair at this meeting, argued against accepting this proposal, in the absence of any intimation that the League would accept anything short of their full demand for a 54 hour week. The Mayor was asked to retire while the employers considered their formal reply, and on his return to

the meeting he was given the following resolution which the masters
had agreed upon:

> That as he (the Mayor) was not authorized to convey any definite
> proposition from the men, except the unconditional concession to
> the nine hours, the meeting is of opinion that there is no reason for
> rescinding their previous decision. The employers will at all times
> be ready to receive and carefully consider any written communica-
> from the men.

This renewal of the employers' bleak refusal to meet the leaders of
the men in direct negotiations helped the picture which the League
was trying to present of entirely moderate and conciliatory men
faced by unmoving and totally inflexible masters, and the employers'
refusal to talk was made much of by the *Chronicle* and the League's
other supporters. It now seemed certain that the strike would take
place. The men's notices expired on Saturday, 27th May, and it
already seemed probable that the struggle would be a protracted one.

Before dealing with the account of the 1871 strike itself, it would
be convenient to mention a local development which aroused a good
deal of interest and which exercised a peripheral influence on the
course of the nine hours' dispute. On Tyneside, as elsewhere, discussions as to the practicability of applying co-operative techniques to
industry had frequently taken place in the 1860's, and had evoked
support from thoughtful working men and from some well known
local liberals. At the time the strike broke out plans were afoot to
bring these ideas to the test of reality, and in early June 1871 the
Ouseburn Engine Works, vacant because of the bankruptcy of a
previous owner, became the centre of an attempt to establish an
engineering works on co-operative lines. Dr J. H. Rutherford, a well
known local liberal and philanthropist, was prominent in this scheme,
which depended to a considerable extent on financial support from
established co-operative societies. Some trade unions also helped
financially, and many of the shareholders in the enterprise were Tyneside workers. The project naturally flourished during the prolonged
nine hours' strike of 1871, but its success continued thereafter only
for as long as economic conditions were healthy. Business in the
engineering trade began to decline in the years after 1873, while
co-operative ownership did not succeed in establishing immunity
from strikes and industrial disputes in the enterprise. In 1875 the
project was ended, with heavy losses to many of those who had
invested their savings in it; the Ouseburn works were kept going for
a few years longer by established co-operative societies. During the

1871 strike, however, the temporary success of the co-operatively
owned Ouseburn works was a source of gratification to the workmen,
and cannot have contributed to the satisfaction of the engineering
employers.

NOTES TO CHAPTER 4

1. The principal sources used in this account are John Burnett's *Nine
Hours Movement. A History of the Engineers' Strike in Newcastle and
Gateshead* (Newcastle, 1872), and J. F. Clarke's dissertation on *Labour
Relations in Engineering and Shipbuilding on the North East Coast in the
Second Half of the 19th century.* (Newcastle University; M.A. in Economic
Studies, 1966.) The letters between Sir William Armstrong, Andrew Noble,
and George and Stuart Rendel, are in the Newcastle City Archives.
2. Many examples of this difficulty are cited in Clarke, op. cit.
3. Ibid., pp. 164-5.
4. Ibid., p. 164
5. Meetings of engineering workers during March, reported in the local
press, talk of agitation for wage increases.
6. 5-5-1871. The account of the Wearside strike given by Clegg, Fox and
Thompson in Vol. 1 of their *A History of British Trade Unions since 1889*,
rather exaggerates its importance.
7. 5 and 12-5-1871.
8. Speech by Mr Gibson, *Newcastle Daily Chronicle*, 24-4-1871.
9. Most of the information about Burnett is gleaned from obituaries published in 1914. The information given in *Newcastle Daily Chronicle* and
Newcastle Weekly Chronicle during February 1914 is especially useful, for
several of Burnett's friends and associates contributed their own recollec-
tions after the appearance of the main obituary notices.
10. Letter from J. Embleton Smith in *Newcastle Weekly Chronicle*,
21-2-1914.
11. *Newcastle Courant*, 31-1-1867.
12. *Life and Letters of Thomas Hodgkin*, by Louise Creighton (London,
1917), pp. 116-7.
13. *Selected Papers of Benjamin Chapman Browne*, edited by E. M.
Browne and H. M. Browne (Cambridge, 1918), p. xi.
14. Obituary of F. C. Marshall in *Engineering*, 27-2-1903.
15. A good early example of such awareness is repeated emphasis on this
point in the diaries of the prominent Newcastle Whig, James Losh, edited
for the Surtees Society by Edward Hughes; Vol. I, 1962, Vol. II, 1963.
16. *Newcastle Weekly Chronicle*, 8-7-1871.
17. For an assessment of the *Chronicle*'s importance see Milne, J. M., *The
Press in Northumberland and Durham, 1855-1906* (Newcastle University,
M. Litt. 1969), and Milne, J. M., *Newspapers of Northumberland and Durham*
(Newcastle upon Tyne, 1971).
18. *Newcastle Daily Chronicle*, 3-2-1914, read in conjunction with *Life
of Joseph Cowen*, by William Duncan (London & Newcastle, 1904) p. 174.
19. Duncan, op. cit., pp. 27-8.
20. Armstrong Papers, Newcastle City Archives.

CHAPTER FIVE

The 1871 Strike on Tyneside

THE notices handed in by the supporters of the Nine Hours' League expired on Saturday, 27th May, and the struggle then began in earnest, although no one then could have supposed that the dispute would drag on for twenty weeks. At Armstrong's, the bulk of the engineering workers were included among the strikers, and Sir William demonstrated his readiness for a fight by locking out the remainder. On the other hand by 31st May it was clear that the men at Stephenson's would not be coming out, as a result of both employer and workmen opting out of the two opposing line-ups, following on G. R. Stephenson's conciliatory methods of communicating with his men. At Palmer's too, a more sensible approach by an employer kept his machines at work. The engineering workers employed in the North Eastern Railway's depot at Gateshead also remained at work during the strike. The workmen there asked their employers for the concession of the nine hours' day, but the request was refused. The leaders of the men there were in close touch with the leaders of the Nine Hours' League, and with the approval of the League the engineering workers in the railway shops remained at work during the dispute. The continuing operation of the railway depot scarcely detracted from the effectiveness of the strike in the other Tyneside engineering works, while the continuing wages of the men there were an important source of contributions for the maintenance of the strikers and their families. Although the men continuing at work at Stephenson's also made some contribution, the railway shop men helped much more by a steady subvention to the League of one day's pay each fortnight, amounting in all to at least £1,000, a significant item in the League's budget. The employers in some of the unaffected establishments, including Stephenson's and the railway shop management, tried to prevent these continuing subscriptions, but reprisals were avoided by the League's adoption of the device of acknowledging such contributions under assumed names in their meticulously detailed and regularly published accounts.[1]

Early in June one or two small engineering firms gave up the struggle and re-opened on the basis of the 54 hour basic week. On both sides, however, the major groups remained immovable. The League made its first issue of strike pay on 6th June. This payment, of three shillings to each man, was confined to the men at Clark, Watson & Gurney, whose impetuosity had led to their being out of work longest, and whose needs were most urgent. A week later the first general distribution was made, but the League's fund-raising activities were only beginning to get under way, and the money available only admitted of a payment of one shilling and ninepence to each of the strikers. The financial question was one of the greatest problems facing the leaders of the League, and their strong position as genuine representatives of the men could well be imperilled if they were unable to do more to support the strikers and their dependants. From the beginning the League leaders adopted a method of distribution calculated to make the best use of the available money. The League committee, whenever a distribution of strike pay took place, made block grants, based on the number of men on its lists, to the delegates representing the men from each firm. On the one hand this enabled individual variations to be taken into account in the actual share-out, while it is unlikely that the astute men leading the League were unaware of how this method would enhance the importance of the delegates themselves and sustain the influence of the League.

The first weeks of the strike were in some ways the most critical for the League, for the resources it disposed of at first were very slender. One of the major preoccupations of its leaders was to raise somehow or other the money needed to support their followers and keep the strike alive. From the beginning, however, there were useful donations from sympathizers from the propertied classes. Preeminent among these was Joseph Cowen, who made it clear to the League leaders that he was prepared to guarantee from his own resources the continued payment of strike pay. In addition to individual support, some trade union groups were quick to promise help in significant amounts. The well-organized Northumberland Miners' Association granted a regular subsidy of £20 each week, raised to £40 during the last weeks of the strike. The Durham miners were less quick off the mark and less generous than their better-organized Northumberland brethren, but in the latter part of the summer they too were making a regular grant to the coffers of the League.[2]

No example of the balance sheets issued by the League has come to light, but their regular issue and thoroughness are attested by references to them in contemporary sources.[3] The League was careful to render to those who gave money a scrupulous account of how it had been expended.

By 20th June the financial situation was already improving, and the League was then able to make a general distribution of three shillings for each man, with an additional payment of sixpence for each dependent child. Skilful management of money, and dexterity in raising funds from a wide variety of sources, was one of the outstanding achievements of the League during its short existence.

During these first critical weeks most of the energies of Burnett and the other League leaders were devoted to the twin allied tasks of enlisting outside support and thereby collecting the necessary money, but they realized too that some obvious public demonstrations must be organized. There were two main reasons for this. One was to maintain the fighting spirit of their own followers, and the other was to give unequivocal evidence to others of the unity and determination of the men. The *Chronicle* could certainly be relied upon to emphasize the representative character of Burnett and his colleagues, but most of the other local newspapers were from the beginning hostile to the strike. A favourite gibe of the *Newcastle Journal*, for example, was the claim that the League committee consisted only of a few trouble-makers who did not really represent the men they claimed to lead. The League therefore held a mass meeting on the Newcastle Town Moor on 19th June; at that meeting, and at similar gatherings later, every effort was made to emphasize the orderly and cohesive nature of the strikers, and to vindicate the truly representative nature of the strike's leadership.

Mid-June also saw a second attempt at mediation from an outside source. In 1870 the national Social Science Congress had been held at Newcastle. Questions of industrial relations had figured in its proceedings, which had aroused a good deal of local interest. Now in June 1871 some of those who had taken a leading part in these discussions tried to bring about a practical application of their theoretical views by seeking to bring the strike to an agreed settlement. The leader of the group involved was Walter Morrison, M.P. for Plymouth, and he and his colleagues spent several days in Newcastle in June, discussing the problem with both sides of the dispute. They found it impossible to budge either party from the entrenched positions they had taken up, though needless to say the League leaders were profuse in their tributes to the good intentions of these would-be peacemakers.

Before June ended the League's financial problems were beginning to ease somewhat. This was not due solely to increased contributions from well-wishers, but also in great measure caused by the facility with which many of the strikers were able to obtain alternative employment in the north-east or elsewhere. Attempts were made by the engineering masters to bring about some general front of employers to support their opposition to the strike by a general refusal to employ strikers, but these attempts clearly had only very limited success, and many employers seem to have been only too pleased in existing economic circumstances to seize the chance to snatch up skilled labour made available in this way. Burnett described some time later how: [4]

> from the very first day of the stoppage of work strike hands began to move off to situations in other places in large numbers. Men were constantly being sent for by employers in all parts of the country.

By mid-June about half of the strikers had ceased to be dependent on the League's funds for support, and between 20th June and 10th October a third of those remaining found alternative sources of support. When the strike ended less than two thousand men remained listed as dependants in the League's accounts.

The end of June brought Race Week, the principal local holiday season. The League held another mass demonstration on the Town Moor on the first day of July; here the strikers were encouraged by an enthusiastic speech from a labour leader with a national reputation, George Odger, who was visiting Tyneside at the time. The first week of July saw a temporary set-back in the amount of strike pay disbursed by the League—the payment for that week amounted only to two shillings and ninepence for each man, with sixpence for each dependent child. Thereafter, however, as the number of mouths to be fed continued to drop, while the League's income grew, the League's financial position markedly improved, as can readily be seen from the following table of the strike payments issued throughout the strike. [5]

Although there are gaps in the information available, a clear picture emerges of growing financial security, and when it is considered that the League raised and expended some £20,000 overall, these figures represent a remarkable achievement on the part of the leaders of this *ad hoc* working-class organization.

One odd feature of the history of the dispute was the tardiness with which the Amalgamated Society of Engineers exerted itself in support of the engineering workers. Although its interest in the dispute at first sight seems an obvious and immediate one, it was not

Table 3

Date	Number of men	Amount s.	d.	Number of children	Amount s.	d.
20 June	3200	3	0	—		6
27 June	—	3	0	—		6
4 July	3046	2	9	—		6
11 July	3400	3	8	—		9
18 July	2817	3	8	—		9
25 July	2770	4	0	—	1	0
1 Aug.	2566	4	6	—	1	0
8 Aug.	2460	5	6	3118	1	0
15 Aug.	2341	5	6	—	1	0
22 Aug.	2272	6	0	2978	1	0
29 Aug.	2181	6	0	2828	1	0
5 Sep.	2114	—		—	1	0
12 Sep.	2074	—		2714	1	0
19 Sep.	1986	8	0	2534	1	0
26 Sep.	1968	11	0	2567	1	0
3 Oct.	1950	12	0	2572	1	0
10 Oct.	1996	12	0	2619	1	0

until July 22nd that the following circular issued from that union's headquarters—

General Office, 90, Blackfriars' Road, July 22, 1871.

Fellow Members,—Up till the issuing of the last monthly report the Council in its corporate capacity, had remained silent to the society upon the great conflict that had taken place betwixt the workmen engaged in the engineering trade at Newcastle-on-Tyne and their employers about a reduction of the hours of labour. This silence is not to be construed into indifference on the part of the Council to the great principles and results involved in the question at issue, but rather to their position in respect to making a levy, as was fully explained in the July monthly report.

In order that there be no misunderstanding upon this point we now issue this circular, and also to stimulate all branches to greater activity in raising timely and substantial support to our friends in the North.

To accomplish this the Council would suggest that each branch should exercise complete influence over its own district, by the appointment of collectors for the various workshops to obtain subscriptions, and, in doing so, let the solicitation extend to every working man, whether he belongs to our society and trade, or otherwise. In recommending this course of action, it must be remembered that the shortening of the hours of labour is a common boon, in which all are interested; and if in the effort to obtain this result the struggles in the North should be crowned with success, it must ultimately prevail throughout the entire kingdom. It is utterly impossible for men of feeling to stand as idle spectators, gazing listlessly on the present unequal contest. The justness of the workmen's request forbids any lukewarmness in this matter; our common interest should incite us to merge diversity of opinion in one common effort to sustain the weak against the strong, and that which is right against wrong.

Let all the members of our society, then, display towards this cause that activity by which they were formerly characterized, and by their subscriptions and personal advocacy aid a movement so deserving of support and success, and they will have the satisfaction of knowing that they have done their duty to their fellow-workmen in the North of England, by promoting one of the most deserving objects in connection with the interests of the working classes, viz., the shortening of the hours of labour.—By order.

(Signed) W. ALLAN, Gen. Sec.

The A.S.E. monthly bulletin of July repeated the advice to branches, while noting that the union's rules made it impossible for the union itself to institute a formal levy in support of the Tyneside strike. Moreover, it was not until the strike had been under way for fourteen weeks that the Tyneside A.S.E. members involved in the strike began to obtain any regular subventions from the union's central funds. This dilatoriness on the part of the national A.S.E. leadership has been the target of much subsequent criticism, including a sharp passage in the pioneering history of trade unions by the Webbs.[6] It may be that William Allan and his colleagues of the A.S.E. leadership disapproved of the strike or its leaders, and remembered the earlier Sunderland rebuff resentfully. It may be that the great problems involved in intervening in a major dispute in which the overwhelming majority of participants were non-union men acted as a brake. The hesitancy at head office, however, was not typical of the A.S.E. as a whole, and some individual branches had shown themselves to be more helpful; the Oldham branch, for instance, had been one of the very first trade union bodies to proffer financial support to the League.[7]

The criticism directed against the A.S.E. leadership may, however, be tempered in the light of another feature of the 1871 strike on Tyneside. Throughout that dispute, as indeed throughout the preceding Wearside conflict over hours, the strike leadership was at pains to avoid the impression that this was a trade union movement. Revelations of recent trade union outrages at Sheffield and elsewhere had not helped the public image of unionism, and during the 1871 strike the press was still frequently outspoken on the subject of such 'trade outrages'.[8] Even the *Newcastle Chronicle* had raised its voice to the same tune. Moreover the League leaders were themselves very well aware of how few of their followers were members of organized trade unions. In contemporary terms there were sound tactical reasons for seeking to demonstrate that the nine hours' movement in the northeast was simply a general movement of the men concerned to extract this concession from their own employers, rather than a manifestation of insidious trade union pressures. Needless to say, this did not preclude the grateful acceptance of financial support from trade union sources, but it did mean that the League leaders were not anxious for established trade union leadership to take a prominent part in the dispute. It certainly remains true that such participation by trade union elements as did take place can in no way detract from the remarkable achievements of the locally-inspired leadership of the League.

The employers had hoped that with the end of the local holiday season the strike might come to an end. When this hope proved illusory, Armstrong and his associates set about the preparation of more far-reaching plans to break the strike. Preparations were made for the recruitment and importation of large numbers of blackleg workers both from other parts of Britain and from abroad. This would certainly be a complicated and expensive operation, and the engineering employers sought at the same time to fortify their position, and obtain substantial help in the task, by trying to bring about a wider co-operation of employing groups throughout the country in face of the unexpectedly prolonged and formidable challenge mounted by the League to the prerogatives of employers. Before these plans fully took shape, however, a third attempt at mediation took place, the agent on this occasion being Charles Mark Palmer.

Palmer's dexterous handling of his own men at Jarrow had kept his enterprise fully working on the basis of his promise that he would concede the 54 hours' basic week if and when it was adopted by the other local engineering works. In mid-July Palmer sought to use his relatively uncommitted position, and his considerable personal prestige, to intervene in the hope of bringing about a renewal of negotiations which might end the existing deadlock. The details of his intervention are not altogether clear, but it seems that Palmer first made private inquiries among his fellow-employers, and then on 19th July he held a long conference with a delegation from the League in his Newcastle home. Burnett and his colleagues re-iterated their proposals for direct negotiations between representatives of both the League and the associated employers, sweetened now by an undertaking that if, as a result of such discussions, the masters offered 'any fair terms of compromise' the League leaders would certainly put them forward in good faith to the mass of their followers for a clear decision on the offer. Palmer seems to have mistaken the extent to which he had secured the cordial co-operation of the associated employers in his peace-making endeavours. On the evening of Tuesday, 20th July, Palmer and a group of delegates met as arranged to initiate negotiations, but through some misunderstanding no representative of the associated employers arrived. Renewed efforts by Palmer actually brought the two sides together at a meeting held two days later in the Newcastle Council Chamber, but the whole attempt at a peaceful solution became hopelessly bogged down in procedural wrangling. The masters were most reluctant to recognize that the League leaders were in reality the authorized representatives of the men, and insisted that before they would embark upon any discussions as to hours of work there must be a clear prior commitment on the part of Burnett and his colleagues that whatever offer the employers might make would be submitted to the mass of the men in a secret ballot. Armstrong and his fellow-employers seem to have hoped that by this device a modest compromise offer on their part might be accepted and the influence of the League leaders over the men broken. The leaders of the League were too shrewd to swallow this demand. They refused to admit that the employers had any right whatever to dictate to the men the manner in which they should reach their decisions; Burnett pointed out that the men were not seeking to interfere in any way with the masters' right to conduct their own side of the dispute, but it may be that the League leaders had better reasons for their refusal to submit to this dictation. Evidence from a friendly source suggests that there may have been elements among the strikers willing to contemplate a breakaway movement.[9]

On this preliminary procedural issue both sides proved adamant, though as usual the League leaders avoided the appearance of complete intransigence. They declared that while they themselves thoroughly approved of taking such decisions by secret ballot, they knew full well that if they accepted such a dictatorial demand from the employers the mass of their followers would strenuously repudiate such an act of surrender. This wrangle brought the discussions to an end without any reference being made to the main issues involved in the strike.

Although maintaining an unbroken front of defiance in public, the employers were in private very considerably worried by the continuing stoppage; while Palmer was trying to bring both sides together one of Armstrong's senior colleagues at Elswick, Andrew Noble, was writing to Stuart Rendel that 'Every day this week we have had long masters' meetings'.[10] These anxious discussions, however, ended in a renewed determination to soldier on, and there was no question yet on the masters' side of surrender.

The League leaders held a meeting of their followers on 22nd July to report on the recent exchanges following on Palmer's intervention. Burnett, who throughout remained a strenuous advocate of direct negotiations, persuaded this meeting to authorize him to put forward an offer intended to break the deadlock. If the employers would withdraw their attempt to dictate the means by which the men should decide on any offer made by the masters, and would put forward concrete proposals for settlement of the hours' dispute, the League would agree that the Mayor of Newcastle should lay down the method by which the opinion of the mass of the strikers should be elicited. When this proposal was conveyed to the associated employers they refused to budge on this preliminary point, contriving thereby to add to their own reputation for inflexibility, in contrast to the willingness of the League to strive for an agreed solution.

The compromise terms contemplated at this point by the employers were never placed before the League leaders, but an idea of their form can be gathered from the next move made by the employers. Characteristically, they still refused direct contact with the League as such. Instead at the beginning of August printed notices addressed simply 'To the workmen' and signed by the employers affected by the strike were distributed about the district. In this manifesto the employers stated that on Thursday 3rd August the factory gates would be re-opened, and employment offered on the basis of a general concession of a 57 hours' basic week, already normal in the Clydeside engineering industry, instead of the 54 hours demanded by the League.

As soon as the news of this move spread, the League leaders summoned a meeting of all delegates to the Westgate Inn; the meeting grew as more and more men arrived to learn what was going on, and the League meeting was adjourned to the nearby open space of the Leazes. A long discussion ensued as to the best course to follow. Burnett and the other League leaders argued strongly in favour of the rejection of the compromise offered, while stipulating carefully that it would have to be accepted if a majority voted in its favour. The delegates agreed to summon a general meeting of strikers to the Leazes, and in this setting the advice of the leaders was overwhelmingly accepted, and it was determined to reject the offer now made by the associated employers.

The employers made all preparations for 3rd August. An application to the local authorities had secured the services of bodies of police at the various works to protect returning workers from the unwelcome attentions of any of their fellows who remained recalcitrant. Their services proved to be largely unnecessary; on 4th August the *Chronicle* reported that no men had returned to work at most of the strike-bound works, and that the total number enticed back to work by the employers' blandishments had only totalled about twenty. Some of the employers, at least, had not expected any very different result. Armstrong had written a few days earlier that 'We shall very shortly make an effort to open but I expect little success till we get foreign labour'.[11]

With the failure of this effort, and from the employers' point of view with the spurning by the misguided workmen of a genuinely generous offer, the associated employers now determined to implement the more far-reaching strike-breaking schemes they had already been considering. Armstrong took the lead in organizing these plans, writing that:[12]

We are now determined to break this strike by importing Foreign Labour ... We have had a long and anxious meeting of Employers this morning and numerous Committees are appointed for various duties ... Altogether the situation is grave ...

Armstrong's able managing team took the lead in seeking to find and import suitable replacement labour. All of their commercial and technical contacts elsewhere were exhorted to bestir themselves in the recruiting campaign.[13] One of these contacts wrote to Stuart Rendel on 7th August to tell him that

I have written privately to a man, in whom I have complete confidence, in Dublin to ascertain what amount of labour, skilled and unskilled, is to be had in Dublin.

Representatives were sent to various centres in Britain and on the Continent, offering generous terms and free transport to induce workmen to come to Tyneside to take the place of the strikers. These importations might set the strike-bound firms to work again, and in addition the arrival of replacements in large numbers might break the nerve of the Tyneside engineering workers.

These intentions of the employers were already well known to the League, and Cowen had already given publicity to them in the *Chronicle*. Burnett and his colleagues were quick off the mark to defeat these new moves by the masters. Burnett visited the headquarters in London of the International Working Men's Association —the First International—in order to enlist the continental contacts of that organization in efforts to dissuade foreign workmen from enlisting as blacklegs. The International was very keen to help, but its actual influence at home and abroad was very limited. Its own secretary, Cohn, a Dane, was sent to the Continent to combat the employers' recruiting campaign there. Belgium was the main theatre of these activities, but after Cohn had been active there for some weeks with modest success, the Belgian authorities expelled him, and put an end to his attempts to interfere with the free recruitment of workers.

The employers were determined to break the strike if they possibly could, and eventually imported more than a thousand workmen from the Continent, from Belgium, Germany, Denmark, Norway and Sweden. In addition recruiting teams were sent to other British centres. At Dundee some two hundred men were induced to sign on for work on Tyneside in return for a five shilling bounty and the promise of good wages and a free passage. Only about half of these Dundee recruits actually turned up to sail, and when they reached Tyneside, agents of the League succeeded in persuading most of them to return home at the League's expense. Apparently the recruiting agents of the employers had not made it clear just what kind of situation the men were being introduced to, and as we shall see strike-breaking on Tyneside in these weeks was no bed of roses. After his expulsion from Belgium, Cohn came to Tyneside to use his talents in persuading foreign workmen to return home. Trade union groups also co-operated whole-heartedly in these anti-blackleg activities

When the A.S.E. finally began to bestir itself in earnest, the persuasion and repatriation of foreign workmen was one activity in which it took part. Joseph Cowen very willingly advanced ready money to the A.S.E. agents to enable them to set about this task quickly.[14]

With the arrival of the blacklegs in force, retaliatory tactics by the local workmen became more strenuous. There had already been a small number of minor disturbances arising out of the strike, but these increased in number and seriousness in July and August. The Newcastle and Gateshead Police Courts, in particular, were frequently involved in hearing cases arising out of the strike. In the very early stages of the dispute the firm first affected, Clark, Watson & Gurney, had made an attempt to break the resistance of their workers by bringing prosecutions for breach of contract against four of their men in the Gateshead Police Court. This suit had failed, partly because of the absence of any recognized system of giving notice to quit work in that firm, partly because the League leaders persuaded the men concerned to offer to return to finish any uncompleted work on which they were engaged at the time of the stoppage. For the time being, there was no further attempt on the part of the masters to resort to the courts in this way.

The courts were kept busy, however, because the strike led to a certain amount of disorder, arising mainly from the employers' increasing use of blackleg labour, and the hostility to these workers on the part of the strikers and their sympathizers. On 11th July the *Chronicle* published reports of proceedings in the police courts of Newcastle and Gateshead arising out of a fracas the previous day at the works of T. Clark & Co., one of the engineering works affected by the strike. There the employers brought in a group of labourers from Sunderland to remove some completed boilers from the factory, and this move led to interference from a large crowd of strikers and their sympathizers; stones were thrown, and there were a number of assaults on the Sunderland men. At Newcastle Police Court a man was sentenced to two months' imprisonment for attacking one of the labourers involved in the removal of the boilers. A parallel case at Gateshead has added interest; there a lad of seventeen was sentenced to fourteen days' imprisonment for throwing stones and shouting slogans like 'The Commune, sink the d — d blacklegs'. The presiding magistrate remarked that:

> To imagine that persons in this country could shout for the Commune, and obstruct their neighbours with impunity, was to imagine something much too preposterous to be tolerated.

It transpired during this trial that the youth involved was not himself an engineering worker, but merely a militant sympathizer. It cannot be seriously supposed that in expressing enthusiasm for the Paris Commune he was in any way truly representative of working-class opinion in Britain. During recent months both national and local newspapers had been full of the detailed story of the Commune, and its bloody repression accompanied by atrocities on both sides. It is clear enough that the overwhelming majority of the working classes in Britain evinced no desire to re-enact in this country the activities of the Parisian communards, and indeed in view of the history of the Commune it required a singularly robust act of faith to believe that it offered a more attractive or effective device for ameliorating the condition of the working classes than the studied restraint of the Nine Hours' League. Certainly in the proceedings of the League itself there is no trace of revolutionary fervour, and instead a studious avoidance of wider political questions and deliberate concentration on matters immediately relevant to the strike.

Nevertheless the disorder on Tyneside during the summer of 1871 was on a sufficient scale to present the local authorities with serious problems, at a time when their police resources were faced with other problems too.[15] During 1870 and 1871 there were grave internal dissensions in the Newcastle Borough Police Force, caused partly by difficulties over pay and conditions, but also because of the activities of the stern and overbearing Chief Constable. The total strength of that force was about 160; during 1870 half of its members had left its ranks, and in November 1871 there was a further massive block resignation of 87 constables. Throughout these years the Watch Committee and the Town Council were faced with frequent complaints about conditions from members of the force, paralleled by another series of accusations of insubordination levelled by the Chief Constable. As Mayor, Burdon Sanderson took the line that, as far as the engineers' strike was concerned:

His duty was not to interfere in the dispute one way or another, but to see to it that the men who had entered into contracts were enabled to carry them out in peace.

In implementing this policy, however, he was faced not only by the internal troubles of the borough police, but also by vigorous criticism from Joseph Cowen and other radical members of the Town Council, who objected to the diversion of the borough police from their proper functions in order to protect blackleg workers. Reinforcements for the borough force had to be brought in from the Northumberland and Durham county forces, at the expense of Newcastle ratepayers, and Cowen stressed the injustice of inflicting this expense for the purpose of helping the engineering employers in their efforts to break the strike. Moreover the engineering strike, though the largest, was not the only industrial dispute facing Tyneside in 1871; joiners and bakery workers were among other labour groups taking strike action in these months, and the prolonged strike of the joiners in particular added its own quota of assaults on blacklegs and similar disturbances to the problems facing the police. The Newcastle Borough Force took what action it could to cope with a very difficult situation. A special flying squad of six mounted constables under Inspector Martin was formed to tackle disorders arising from industrial disputes, but there was far too much of this kind of small-scale activity against blacklegs taking place during these months for such police measures to be anything like completely effective.

Sometimes the defensive reactions of the local working classes could be tolerably mild in character. Sir William Armstrong had been the key figure in the determination of the employers to seek to break the engineering strike by the importation of blackleg labour. His earlier efforts at recruitment elsewhere were frustrated to a considerable extent by the success of the League's agents in persuading many of his new recruits to recant and return home. After these experiences Armstrong instituted a régime of protective custody for his imported workers. Special accommodation was contrived for them in and around the Elswick works, and as far as possible the immigrant workmen were sealed off from the dangerous contagion of local society. On 11th August a large contingent of recruits arrived from London and, after running the gauntlet of a jeering crowd on landing, these men were promptly incarcerated in the new Elswick billets. The League responded by holding a mass meeting in the immediate vicinity, partly on the southern shore of the Tyne immediately opposite Elswick, and partly on King's Meadows, a large grassy island in the river, even closer to the Armstrong works. Burnett subsequently described how:

Comparisons were freely instituted between Armstrong's Factory and a common lodging-house, and sarcastic remarks were made upon the violation of the factory rules, to say nothing of the excise laws, by the employers, who had large quantities of beer and tobacco taken into the factories for the use of the imprisoned knobsticks. This meeting was the severest trial of temper to which

the Newcastle men were subjected, during the strike, and they
came through it manfully—not the slightest disposition to molest
the south countrymen being manifested.

On 12th August the report of this affair in the *Chronicle* gave additional picturesque detail:

> Many questions were asked on how they liked their imprison-
> ment, and not a few insinuations were thrown out concerning their
> previous histories; but, with the exception of the chaff and laughter
> which greeted these sallies, there was no disturbance of any kind
> created.

Gratifying as such evidences of restraint may have seemed to
contemporary society, at a time when newspapers frequently emphasized 'trade union outrages' elsewhere, this was not the whole story.
There were more violent activities, and the engineering strikers and
their friends very often did manifest a strong disposition to molest
the imported workmen, whether native or foreign. Life for a blackleg
on Tyneside in these months could often be neither safe nor pleasant,
despite the efforts of the local police resources to protect men at
work. Many instances could be cited, but the following example is
a typical one, taken from the columns of the League's principal press
supporter, the *Newcastle Chronicle*, of 11th August:

> Yesterday evening, between six and seven o'clock, as a workman
> employed at Hawthorn's factory was going along Clayton Street,
> he was surrounded by a number of persons, who commenced hoot-
> ing him, and a crowd soon gathered. He was followed some dis-
> tance, and to escape further annoyance he went into a public-house.
> Some policemen shortly afterwards came and escorted him along
> to the Westgate Police Station for protection from the crowd. On
> the way he was again hooted and a lad was taken into custody for
> annoying him. The man was kept in the station until the crowd
> was dispersed, and then he was conducted to his lodgings.

In 1871 Gladstone's first government had legislated to provide
legal protection to workmen wishing to work against the unwelcome
attentions of hostile picketing.[16] Questions of molestation and intimidation, however, are difficult to legislate on with precision, and the
definitions attempted in the 1871 Act still left ample room for varying interpretations. Police courts on Tyneside, hearing a long series

of molestation cases in July and August 1871, did not find the legal situation particularly clear, and decisions varied markedly. There were a number of acquittals, including one splendidly Gilbertian judgement delivered by B. J. Prockter, Esq., J.P.: [17]

> The Bench are not satisfied that there is sufficient evidence to convict the defendants, and they are dismissed. And now, my men, take care and don't do it again.

It seems clear that in an imprecise legal situation the personal sympathies of individual magistrates, which varied, had considerable effect on the outcome of these cases. In any event, if some of the magistrates were, as one of them put it, 'determined to put down the grinding tyranny of one man against another', the sentences of imprisonment inflicted on conviction were far from draconian. Certainly, the forces of authority did not succeed in providing enough police resources or legal reprisals to dissuade the local strikers and their sympathizers from their unwelcome attentions to the imported workmen.

Apart from these more serious manifestations, the imported recruits were the target of a good deal of ridicule: many contemporary squibs and jokes were levelled against them on the streets, in public-houses and music-halls, and in the publications sympathetic towards the strike. Here is one example of a local comic song of the period on these lines:

THE
GERMAN'S GROAN!
OR
I'M VATCH'D ON DE TYNE.

AIR.—'*The Watch on the Rhine.*'

Dis soul pe svell'd so pig mit fear,
Me often tink vat prought me here—
De promeese, leetil work, pig pay;
Me tearly vant to run away.

    Oh! Vaterland, so dear to me;
    Oh! Vaterland, me vant to see;

Oh! Vaterland, dat dearest land of mine,
Not like ven I'm Vatch'd on de Tyne.

At work, de masters on de vatch,
Dey tink dey vill me not vork catch;
Vatch, vatching, vatching, all de day,
Vork, vorking, vorking, mit no play.
        Oh! Vaterland, &c.

Dey vatch me in, dey vatch me out,
Dey 'Plackleg! Plackleg!' to me shout;
Von tam'd pig lee, dese legs if seen,
Pe vite like dairs if dairs pe clean.
        Oh! Vaterland, &c.

Dair pluemen valk on py my side,
Or ven dey don't, on horse-top ride;
Dey vatch me here, dey vatch me dair,
Far more tam'd vatching nor me care.
        Oh! Vaterland, &c.

Dair's plenty peer, dair's lots of shmoke,
Dese Inglees pe von funny foke;
Treat Vaterlanders vorking hours,
And Inglees vorkman get the sours.
        Oh! Vaterland, &c.

Dese Inglees pe von shtriking foke,
Dey shtrike, and shtrike, just for de joke.
Dey shtrike von shtrike, mit hands pig size,
And pung poor Vaterlanders' eyes!
        Oh! Vaterland, &c.

Me vish me never sign'd me name,
Me vish dair pond vas one pig flame,
Me vish me only vas at home,
Dis Vaterlander no more roam.
        Oh! Vaterland, &c.

Polonies pig, polonies shweet,
Polonies home so nice to eat;
Oh! vould me could vatch on de Rhine,

And not be vatch'd upon the Tyne.
                    Oh! Vaterland, so dear to me;
                    Oh! Vaterland, me vant to see;
                    Oh! Vaterland, dat dearest land of mine,
                    Not like ven I'm Vatch'd on de Tyne.

The attitude of the leadership of the League to the actions of their followers against the blacklegs is important. Characteristically, the public declarations of the League 'deny most strenuously that any of their members are guilty of intentional intimidation'. It is also true that many of those prosecuted for such offences in these months were not themselves engineering workers, but rather, like the young sympathizer with the Commune, militant supporters from outside the ranks of the League. Moreover, there is direct evidence of the attitude taken by Burnett himself, in a later recollection from a police officer who served in 1871 as a member of Newcastle's special flying squad.[18] This man, Robert Anderson, came to know Burnett well during the strike and recorded that 'I remember well how anxious he was to have the strike carried on in a peaceful way, as far as possible'. Anderson recalled one incident in particular, when he had been an eye-witness to a particularly brutal assault on a German workman. Anderson's evidence had been largely responsible for the conviction of one of the men leading the assault. The conviction and prison sentence imposed had angered the friends of the assailant, who sought to raise an agitation against the conviction and to bring pressure on Newcastle Watch Committee to secure Anderson's dismissal from the borough police force. Burnett took the matter up, and conducted his own enquiry into the affair, after which he told Anderson frankly that he was perfectly satisfied that the man convicted had been guilty, adding that in his opinion there were others involved who were fortunate not to be in the same position.

This attitude adopted by Burnett as a strenuous defender of order was one with many precedents in the history of local industrial relations, and it need not be supposed that it was actuated by any particular sympathy for blacklegs, or that this virtuous attitude had much effect in practice in hindering the operations of the more militant strikers and their sympathizers.[19] What was of paramount importance to the Nine Hours' League, however, was the need to stress in every possible way the moderation and sense of responsibility possessed on the workers' side of this dispute, in order to appeal, and appeal successfully, to a wide spectrum of public opinion, only too likely to be alienated by a parade of violence. It is not necessary to suppose that men as able and acute as Burnett and his associates in the League leadership were ignorant of what was going on in the streets of Tyneside in these months, or that they were particularly incensed by it, provided that the League's public image was not tarnished by too obtrusive actions. There is a tantalizingly vague hint which suggests that on occasion the League leaders had to take a strong line with dissidents among their own following. A biography of Joseph Cowen, written by a close associate and admirer, contains the following intriguing passage: [20]

> On one occasion Mr Burnett met Mr Cowen in the street and was incidentally told of a meeting to be held in a committee-room of the Mechanics' Institute. It had been arranged for that night, by a party of workmen with outside friends, and its object was to concert plans for a return to work. Thanks to the friendly hint, some of the nine-hours leaders attended the meeting—which was designed to break up their movement—and owing to the representations then made, were able to prevent any serious results.

It seems then that the employers may have had some basis at least for their belief that the leadership of the League did not speak for all of the engineering workmen involved in the strike; this instance of threatened disunity seems to have been kept quiet at the time, though it would be most interesting to know just what 'representations' were made to the potential mutineers.

It would be ingenuous indeed to accept at face value all the assurances given by Leaguers that their activities were invariably peaceful. The combination of a skilful and conspicuously non-violent leadership equipped with a large supply of emollient phrases, together with a good deal of successful intimidation in practice, was a singularly successful one. Certainly the picture of the strike's activities painted by the League leaders was the one which overwhelmingly prevailed. A good example of the impression created in this way is contained in an Appendix describing the strike included in a report of the U.S. Consul in Newcastle, Evan R. Jones, which was published in Newcastle in 1873; in this assessment by an uncommitted observer the peaceful and non-violent character of the strikers is strongly emphasized.

The financial cost of the large-scale import of replacement workers was a heavy one to the Tyneside engineering employers. Believing that they were not merely fighting a local industrial conflict, but defending the necessary rights of employers everywhere, Armstrong and his associates sought to appeal to their fellow-employers elsewhere for financial contributions to sustain the employers' side of the struggle. On August 14th they issued an appeal which proclaimed that:

> The engineering firms who are now struck against are, in fact, fighting the battle for all employers of labour, and their yielding would be a signal for a claim for a similar reduction in the hours of labour all over the country. If the reduction of the working hours were obtained, the men would no doubt continue to make other exorbitant demands, with the result of a complete disturbance of every branch of trade, and probably of a conflict between capital and labour disastrous alike to employers and employed.

There was a good deal of truth in the assessment by the engineering masters of the results which would probably follow any surrender on their part, at least as far as the widening of the campaign for the reduction in hours of work was concerned. In their appeal the employers involved in the Tyneside dispute asked fellow-employers elsewhere for a cash contribution on the basis of five shillings for every man or boy employed in order to help to meet the cost of the present stoppage, and the very high cost, some £20,000, involved in the great recruitment and importation of substitute labour. The result of this appeal was in practice very disappointing. Little money was contributed, and employers elsewhere certainly did not unite to refuse employment to Tyneside strikers. This failure to present a united front of capitalism was helped by the widespread sympathy which the League's skilful presentation of their case evoked for the men, and by the remarkably bad public image which the Tyneside engineering employers had themselves contrived to engender.

For this latter circumstance there were many reasons. Some of the tactics employed by the masters were ill-conceived from the point of view of creating a favourable public impression. Armstrong, for example, had closed the schools attached to the Elswick works in order to use them to house blacklegs, and had issued a pointed warning that when the schools re-opened they would be available only to the children of those then employed at the Elswick works. Such tactics went a great deal further than this, and on 10th August the *Chronicle* published a strong attack on the pressure which had induced the authorities of the Newcastle Lying-in Hospital to refuse their facilities to the wives of strikers. Making war through children and pregnant women was not a popular line to adopt, and the sheer ineptitude of such tactics is as remarkable as their unpleasantness. The prospect of a group of wealthy capitalists seeking to defeat thousands of British workmen, who appeared to be striving only for greater opportunities to enjoy constructive and improving leisure, by the use of these brutal tactics, or by the importation of hundreds of foreign workmen, struck most contemporaries as essentially unjust and somehow un-English. The attacks on the engineering employers were not by any means confined to proletarian sources. The Newcastle Council meeting on 6th September saw a concerted attack on the use of local police forces at public expense to help the employers by defending imported workmen, and the attack was led not only by Joseph Cowen, but also by another popular Tyneside figure, C. F. Hamond, a leading local Conservative and a future M.P. for Newcastle.

As the strike prolonged its course national interest in the dispute grew markedly, and a survey of influential elements in the contemporary press easily demonstrates the success of the League's presentation of the men's case, and the clumsiness by comparison of the tactics adopted by the associated employers. The *Newcastle Chronicle* remained trenchant in its unflagging support of the League; here, as examples, are two passages from editorials of early September. On 2nd September the tactics of the employers were described in these terms:

They aggravate the injury by giving these interlopers a great advance upon the wages they paid to their old hands and they display towards them a degree of consideration which they never showed to those who have grown old and worn in their service. They have made exaggerated demands for police protection and have obtained hoses and sandbags to protect their works. Against whom? The men whose patient and cheap industry for years has built up colossal fortunes for employers.

A week later the message is the same:

Not content with deliberately widening the area of the conflict the employers have begun to carry it on in a fashion which they well know is calculated to produce the sorest irritation in the minds of their late workmen. If their immediate object was to insult and exasperate the men on strike it must be confessed they have taken the likeliest means for accomplishing that object ... they embark a considerable capital in establishing a species of coolie trade.

Such opinions, however, were by no means confined to local radical journals. The *Pall Mall Gazette*, among influential national magazines, had this to say of the men's case: [21]

> In itself this demand is perfectly reasonable. Nine hours' continuous labour in the engineering trade is probably as much as can be maintained without a degree of exhaustion which is physically and morally injurious.

The *Spectator* was even more forthright in its support for the League and its spirited denunciation of the employers' tactics; on 16th September it commented:

> Masters who reply cavalierly by lawyers' letters to the demands of their men, refuse personal discussion, and act as nearly as they can like despotic governments against revolutionary bodies can hardly expect their moral claims on the sympathy of the public to be conceded.

Nor were the professional journals of the engineering trade more eager to side with the associated employers. *Engineering* repeatedly urged that the strike should be settled by arbitration. On 14th July it warmly commended the co-operative enterprise at the Ouseburn engineering works; on 11th August it openly doubted whether the import of substitute labour could in practice effectively replace the skilled Tyneside engineering workers. On 1st September this journal fully reported an incident which had caused rejoicing to the League and embarrassment to the employers, when a few days earlier some of Armstrong's imported German workmen had themselves struck for the nine hours' day.

The Engineer was not much better from the employers' point of view. Its columns included several admiring tributes to the skill and dexterity of the League's leadership, and only very muted criticism of the men's case. This journal, however, in two successive numbers on 22nd and 29th September, included some comments on the objectives of the strikers, and the arguments with which their demands had been supported, which are of interest:

> No doubt if the masters are beaten, action will be taken by the men to secure the 54 hours week in other parts of the kingdom ... The men have not yet been educated up to the point of knowing very well how either legitimately to enjoy themselves or instruct

themselves. We shall cure all this, it is to be hoped, by the time the next generation has reached years of discretion, thanks to the operations of our school boards. Meanwhile, however, the nine hours' movement is simply a scheme for obtaining higher wages or for securing the employment of a greater number of hands. This will be indignantly denied, of course.

Had the demands of the men taken the form of a request for more wages, little or nothing would have been heard about the matter by the general public. But the proposal that the length of the working day should be reduced by one-tenth, taken as a *bona fide* proposition was so novel, and involved such great interests, that it was certain to attract attention.... There is reason, however, to believe that, as we have already hinted, the men as a body have no desire to work shorter time. What they really want is more overtime, and consequently higher rates of pay.

Burnett and his colleagues would certainly have denied indignantly this last insinuation, but it may well be that this leading engineering journal was interpreting aright the hopes of at least some of the League's followers.

Overwhelmingly, the tone of the contemporary press was hostile to the engineering employers, and the majority verdict was supported on the 11th September by the magisterial, if not scrupulously accurate, judgement of the *Times*:

For more than three months an embittered conflict between masters and workmen has been paralysing one of the principal industries of the North of England. A movement had been gaining ground for some time past in Northumberland, Durham, and the West Riding of Yorkshire in favour of limiting the hours of work in the skilled occupations. In Sunderland, and partially in some other places, 'the Nine Hours' League,' as it called itself, had succeeded in carrying its point. But the majority of the employers refused to make the reduction in the hours of labour demanded by the men. The large engineering firms, in particular, which have their works in the neighbourhood of Newcastle-on-Tyne and Gateshead, opposed a strenuous resistance to these claims. Sir William Armstrong and the Messrs Hawthorn made up their minds to fight the trades' unionists on their own ground, if they were determined to give battle, and to resort to any expedient rather than yield. It was notified to the remonstrant workmen that if they persisted in their threat to strike unless their claims were satisfied, the employers would spend any amount of pains and money to obtain labour elsewhere, and keep the works open in defiance of the strikers' challenge. The workmen, however, held their ground, and hold it still. The engineers are probably the most prosperous, intelligent, and closely-organized body of working men in the United Kingdom, and they have in consequence enjoyed for several years a comparative immunity from strikes. Employers have rarely attempted to try a fall with them, and the experiment of the North-umberland masters, so far as it has gone, is not likely to encourage future efforts in the same direction. After fourteen weeks of deter-mined resistance on the one side, and energetic endeavours on the other, the workmen still hold out, and the masters are finding one source of supply for their empty workshops cut away after another. London and the dockyard towns have been ransacked for the unemployed artisans with whom they are supposed to be thronged. Holland and Belgium, Germany and Denmark, have been appealed to for immigrant aid, and from these sources, as well as from various manufacturing towns in England and Scotland, numbers of working engineers have been recruited to replace the men on strike. But all these expedients have been of no avail. Whether it is that the engineers' union disposes of the sinews of war lavishly enough to buy off all interlopers, or that the Inter-national is using its widely extended authority to support the claims of the unionists, it is not easy to determine. But whatever may be the nature of the machinery employed, the result is obvious enough. Every contingent of imported workmen complains of being deceived, throws up its contracts with Sir William Armstrong and his confederate employers, and leaves the manufacturers to fight the battle out on the old terms with the men on strike. No efforts have been spared by the employers to obtain labour in the open market rather than concede what the unionists demand. The East-end of London has sent up a good many unemployed workmen to Newcastle and Gateshead, and some have been enlisted in the southern counties. Unfortunately, most of these recruits are in-experienced in engineering work. The Belgians and Danes are in every way workmen of a better class. But the most skilful, able, intelligent, and reputable are undoubtedly the Prussians, who have been brought from Hamburg at considerable cost. If Sir William Armstrong could have retained his Prussian and Danish labourers, he might have laughed at the strike; but Prussians, Danes, and English have all succumbed to the pressure of working-class opinion in the North or to the secret mandates of the International. The foreign hands excuse themselves by declaring that they were entrapped into engagements with the Newcastle and Gateshead firms on false pretences. The employers of course deny the false pretences, but when there are dealings of this delicate nature between English firms and foreign workmen we must not be astonished if occasional misunderstandings arise. In fact, the foreigners are only following the example of the English workmen who were brought to Newcastle before them, and who have since made their escape from their engagements as speedily as possible. A few prosecutions of foreign workmen for breach of contract have been attempted; but this method is scarcely likely to serve the masters in attracting or retaining foreign labour. The engineers on strike have given liberal assistance to the imported labourers who desire to return home, and, though they have now determined to render no further aid of this kind, they have in all probability succeeded in cutting off the main sources of supply for the Tyneside works. Delegates from the English unionists have been sent abroad to warn the workmen in Belgium, Holland, Denmark and Germany against aiding the employers in the North by migration to England, and a large number of Prussian workmen had their passages paid last week to Hamburg and Berlin, in order that they might explain the state of the controversy and its issues to the German working men. We are inclined to consider the conduct of the employers throughout this dispute as imprudent and impolitic. We do not approve the general policy of trades unions, and are decidedly opposed to their methods of action; but we could wish to see some other ground chosen for resisting the aggression of the unions than a bare opposition to the Nine Hours' Movement. It is alleged, and we believe it, that the engineering trade in the North of England is now most prosperous, and that the masters are making very large profits. If it be reasonable that workmen should from time to time obtain a share in the augmented profits of a business, there is certainly no way in which they could more profitably claim this advantage than in a decrease of the hours of labour. On moral and sanitary grounds short hours of work are desirable, and, so far as industrial interests are concerned, it may be taken for granted that they would gain rather than lose by the further limitation of working hours. The measure of man's capacity for continuous labour is sufficiently well ascertained, and the demand of the Nine Hours' League, that skilled workmen shall not be asked to work more than fifty-four hours in the week, is supported by very strong physiological and practical arguments. It is, indeed, very doubtful whether masters gain anything by exacting longer working hours—whether nine hours' active work does not represent the *maximum* of an average workman's daily labour. If the employers in the Tyneside factories can show that a concession of the workmen's claims would reduce their profits so that the works could not be advantageously carried on, the demands of the Nine Hours' League will, of course, be answered. But in any point of view it was a mistake to introduce foreign workmen, whose sympathies, as might have been predicted, were thoroughly with the men on strike. The latter, so far from being disheartened, are now triumphant, and their triumph will render them, it may be, more difficult to deal with at some future time, when the masters may have the right more clearly on their side, and the men may be acting recklessly and ruinously towards the industry by which they subsist.

This attitude of the press, including some of the most notable contemporary publications, and culminating in this broadside from the most influential of them all, goaded Sir William Armstrong himself into embarking on the treacherous currents of warfare carried on in newspaper correspondence, only to discover that in this area of combat he was far outclassed by his principal opponent, the President of the Nine Hours' League. On 11th September George Rendel wrote to Stuart Rendel in a highly optimistic tone: [22]

We are getting on capitally. Since the Germans ran off scarcely a man has left and we now have nearly 1,200 at work—we want only moulders and a few boilersmiths to be in thorough good working order ... Sir Wm. is constant too. He is now commencing to write a sort of history of the strike which is much needed to meet the lies in the press.

The long letter carefully composed by Sir William was duly despatched, and on 12th September the author himself informed Stuart Rendel that 'I have sent a letter to the *Times* in reply to their shameful article'.[23] Armstrong wrote again the following day in something of a flurry of nervousness lest the *Times* should decline to publish his manifesto. He knew that an earlier letter from another of the associated employers, Thompson of Thompson & Boyd, had been refused entry into that newspaper's columns. Stuart Rendel was now given careful instructions that if the letter did not appear in the *Times* he was to see to its insertion in other papers, and call on the editor of the *Times* to complain of such an act of partiality and disrespect.

However, Armstrong's lengthy justification of the employers duly appeared on 14th September in the *Times*, and inaugurated an exchange of published letters with Burnett. These letters are very long, and do not perhaps make the most exhilarating reading, but they are worth reproducing in their entirety as expressing the two contending views, and because the letters themselves played a part in the alignment of public opinion and the course of the remainder of the dispute. Armstrong's first salvo was as follows:

SIR,—The leading article which appeared in the *Times* of yesterday on the subject of the Engineers' Strike in the North of England exhibits so much misapprehension of the facts that we feel constrained to give you a true account of the history and present position of this deplorable struggle.

In the first place, we beg leave to assure you that you have been completely misinformed as to the result of the effort we have made to replace the men who have struck work. We are happy to say that our endeavours to supply our wants by the perfectly legitimate course of procuring labour, both English and foreign, from other places, have been highly successful, considering the short time which has elapsed since we adopted that line of action. We never for a moment supposed that we should be able to hold to their contracts the whole of the men we might bring from a distance. All experience has proved that men on strike invariably succeed in sending back a proportion of those imported to supply their places, but the following figures will show that the proportion of loss sustained is even less than might reasonably have been expected: —

Number of men who went on strike, 6,595; new hands imported, 1,917; deduct number of desertions, 187—1,730; add men returning to work after desertion, 11; total of new hands now at work, 1,741; to this number is to be added old hands who have come back to work or who never left their employment, and new men engaged on the spot, 1,375; making total number engaged in our works 3,116, being nearly half the number employed at the time of the strike.

Every day brings additions, and we only desire to be left alone in order to restore our shops to their former activity.

Having thus disposed of the allegations to zealously circulated as to the present hopeless condition of the employers, we shall proceed to relate as briefly as possible the history of this strike, in order to exonerate ourselves from the charge of unwarrantably

resisting a reasonable demand on the part of the men, and of rejecting a policy of conciliation.

The movement among engineers for a reduction of working time
from fifty-nine to fifty-four hours per week commenced by a strike
at Sunderland, which was successful after a short resistance of five
weeks' duration. A League was then formed in Newcastle for effect-
ing the same object on the Tyne, and the mere fact of a League
being formed showed that it was by means of combination that
the men from the first hoped to attain their object. We on our
part, well knowing what would follow the success of the Sunderland strike, formed ourselves into an association for mutual support. Thus both sides were in a position of antagonism when the
demand was first made. In the beginning of May the League took
action by sending a circular to each firm, requesting that the hours
of labour should be reduced to fifty-four hours per week. The
masters on the 6th of May simply declined to accede. The men on
the 15th of May proposed a conference between six employers and
six delegates, and required an answer to their proposal any day
that week up to Friday, the 19th. In reply, the secretary of our
association stated that some of the masters were out of town, but
that he had summoned a meeting for Thursday, the 18th, when
the communication would be duly considered.

The meeting was held on that day, but in the meantime (viz.,
on the 16th of May) the men at Messrs. Clarke, Watson, and
Gurney's turned out on strike for the 'nine hours', and as no effort
was made by the League to counteract that step, the associated
masters justly considered it as the commencement of coercive
measures. Being thus embarked in the struggle they passed the
following resolution, which was handed to the committee of the
League, and which has ever since been the subject of their hostile
comments : —

'That the employers see no advantage in the interview proposed
by the Nine Hours' League. They (the employers) would have
suggested a written communication from the League, but for the
fact that a strike has already taken place. Under the circumstances
the employers feel that no course is open to them but to refer the
Nine Hours' League to their former communication, dated the
6th inst., and to request them to consider it final.'

It has been repeatedly contended by the members of the League
that this answer was harsh and uncourteous, and that if the masters
had agreed to a conference some arrangement might have been
made and a strike prevented. We reply that the strike, which had

then already commenced at Messrs. Clarke, Watson, and Gurney's, put it out of our power to treat with the League as if friendly relations were existing, and we appeal to the subsequent proceedings of the League in proof that nothing short of unconditional concession of the full demand would have met with acceptance.

On the 20th of May the League met and decided that a week's notice should be given to cease work at all the remaining shops, and such notices were accordingly given. At this meeting a motion was made by one of the delegates to ask the employers to give the nine hours per day in a month or 'to leave the question to arbitration'. This was opposed by the President of the League, who expressed himself, according to the report of the *Newcastle Chronicle*, the organ of the party, in the following words: —

'The masters had given an uncourteous and uncivil refusal to friendly combat, and what else could it mean but "war to the knife"?'

The motion of the more moderate delegate was put to the meeting, and negatived by a majority of 50 votes to 8.

At a second meeting of delegates held three days later (viz., the 23rd of May) the President further expressed himself in these words: —

'They did not want an advance of wages, if they could get the "nine hours" instead. He himself did not think he had too much wages, but the nine hours would be of much more use to him than the 2s. advance. They would not be bribed by an advance, but would have the "nine hours pure and simple". If they wanted to be eternally disgraced, let them sell the movement for a shilling or two a week. If they wanted to keep their name let them stick honestly to what they had come out for.'

It thus appeared that neither arbitration nor a money equivalent for the reduction of time claimed would be entertained, and in fact that nothing short of unconditional surrender would be accepted.

The next event to be noticed was the attempt by the Mayor of Newcastle to bring about a conference. On the 25th of May, being prior to the expiration of the notice, the Mayor put himself in communication with the League, and afterwards had an interview with the masters. He stated that he was not authorised by the League to make any proposition save the concession of the 'nine hours', and that he had failed to induce the men to postpone their notices even for a week. The result of the interview will be seen from the following resolution, which, having been passed by the masters, was handed to the Mayor: —

'The Mayor of Newcastle, having attended this meeting and communicated what had passed between him and the delegates, it was resolved that, as he was not authorised to convey any definite proposition from the men except the unconditional concession of the "nine hours", the meeting is of opinion that there is no reason for rescinding their previous decision. The employers will at all times be ready to receive and carefully consider any written communication from the men.'

The men turned out at the expiration of the notices, as had been previously done, without notice, at Messrs. Clarke, Watson, and Gurney's.

The men at Messrs. Robert Stephenson and Company's works refused to join the League, but privately applied to their employers for a similar concession as to the hours of work. This application was not granted; but Mr George Robert Stephenson, in a letter dated the 30th May, entered into a full and friendly exposition of his reasons for not complying with their request. The letter was published, and his men, apparently convinced of the soundness of his arguments, remained at work.

On the 12th of June a deputation from the Social Science Association waited upon the committee of the League with a view to arranging a termination of the strike by arbitration or otherwise.

The answer conveyed to this deputation was that the men would not then resort to arbitration, the time for which they said had passed. In consequence of this uncompromising reply the deputation did not communicate with the employers.

The next attempt at negotiation was made on the intervention of Mr Charles M. Palmer, and a meeting was held between the masters and the committee of the League, at which the masters offered to take the initiative in proposing terms of settlement, provided the League would allow the acceptance or rejection by the men of the proposal to be ascertained by ballot under the supervision of the Mayor.

This condition was declined, the delegates alleging that, though they approved of the principle of the ballot, they would not adopt it in obedience to the 'dictation of the masters'. At this meeting, also, the same uncompromising spirit was displayed by the delegates.

They stated they had no offer to make, and that they adhered to their former demands.

Being thus thwarted in our efforts to get at an independent

expression of opinion from the large body of our men who, we had reason to believe, disapproved the arbitrary action of the officials of the League, we determined to publish the terms of arrangement upon which we were willing to receive back our men.

We accordingly announced that we would concede a reduction of time from 59 to 57 hours per week, with a liberal arrangement as to overtime.

These concessions were coupled with a stipulation that overtime should not count until the 57 hours per week had first been worked.

This regulation was taken from the code of rules adopted on the Clyde, and was intended to prevent the common abuse of men absenting themselves at ordinary hours, and making up their wages at higher rates by overtime.

The proposed compromise met with unqualified rejection by the League, and was treated as a sign of weakness on the part of the masters.

At a mass meeting convened to discuss the subject, the President is reported by the *Chronicle* of August 3 to have spoken as follows: —

'He would briefly view their position from first to last. When they first came out on strike the employers refused to hear them on any account whatever. They refused to recognize the League. They then softened a bit, and were willing to meet them and offer a compromise but still would not state the terms till they had a guarantee that the men would vote upon it by ballot. The men would not give that guarantee, and thus the employers voluntarily published the terms of the compromise. They had made many fine promises, and broken them all, and that he considered was an indication of their giving way. The men had now got the matter in their own hands. The thin end of the wedge was in, and if they only gave it a good sharp blow they would drive it home, and the "Nine Hours' System" would be an established fact.'

On the 3rd of August the shops were opened on the new rules, but owing to the opposition of the League, only a small number of our old hands returned to work.

Our efforts at conciliation having thus been not only rejected, but turned to account against us as proofs of weakness, we had obviously no alternative but a recourse to imported labour. We adopted that alternative as a necessity, and we venture to say that not even our most violent opponents will dispute our perfect justification in so doing. Ten weeks had elapsed before we commenced this course of action, and by that time about two-thirds of our old hands had obtained employment elsewhere, as was persistently boasted by the League. The result has been to place us in the comparatively easy position which we now occupy, as shown by the figures previously given.

We were amazed to see ourselves described in your article as being in a condition of hopeless difficulty, and we really felt that, if the League themselves had possessed the power of inspiring that article, they could scarcely have used words more calculated to serve their purposes than those in which it is expressed.

The concurrent appearance in the *Spectator* of an article exhibiting the same bias adds to our surprise. We had imagined that a determined effort to wrest concessions from employers by sheer force of combination was not a thing which found favour with the more educated and intelligent classes, whose opinions generally find expression in the columns of the *Times*. As your article has cast a doubt on the existence of the sympathy of these classes with our cause, we feel it incumbent upon us to state the grounds upon which we have so firmly resisted and still intend to resist the demand for the reduction of work to 54 hours per week.

Those grounds are substantially the same as were enunciated by Mr George Robert Stephenson in the temperate and forcible letter which on the 1st of June last was published in all the Newcastle papers.

Had our men applied for an increase of wages instead of a reduction of time the dispute might easily have been adjusted. Wages fluctuate with demand, but shortened hours of work do not alter, and, therefore, there is less objection to increase wages than to decrease time. Shortened time also involves loss of interest on capital; for when men cease work machines stand idle; and the whole establishment becomes unproductive, thus damaging employers without benefitting [*sic*] the men.

The hours of work which were general in our district at the time of our strikes were 59 a week. That number we have reduced to 57, which is the time worked on the Clyde. On the Continent, in places where equal advantages are possessed to those of the North of England in regard to coal, iron, and railway communication, the common hours of work are 66 a week, and the wages are less than in England.

We refuse the demand for 54 hours a week, because we believe that the district in which our factories are located would be laid under permanent and most serious disadvantage in competing with other localities in the kingdom, or if the system were to extend to those other localities, then the whole country would be placed at a like disadvantage in its competition with foreign producers of machinery. The Nine Hours' League avowedly disregard such considerations as these. They say that 'if trade should leave the district they must make up their minds to follow it, and many worse things may be imagined than an English colony in Belgium'.

The men ostensibly base their claims to the 'nine hours' upon the alleged social and educational advantages which would attend the change. But is this really the object they have in view? Is not the chief burden of their speeches their claim to higher wages? and do they not believe that it is their pecuniary, rather than their social, advantage that would follow the attainment of their demands? We unhesitatingly assert that the only effect of the reduction of hours at Sunderland has been to cause the higher rate for overtime to commence one hour earlier than before, and that the actual duration of each day's labour remains at least as great as ever.

In conclusion, we must, in justice to ourselves, recall your attention to the letter from our secretary which appeared in your paper of the 6th of September, and which ought to have effectually disposed of the assertions that deception had been practised by our agents in the hiring of foreign workmen. Since that letter was written several of the men exported by the actions of the League have voluntarily returned to their employment, thereby affording a forcible comment on the accuracy of that letter.

We are, sir, your obedient servants,
THE ASSOCIATED EMPLOYERS,
PER W. G. ARMSTRONG.
Newcastle-upon-Tyne, Sept. 12.

Any satisfaction given to Armstrong and his associates by the appearance of this account of their tribulations must have been substantially impaired by the appearance in the same place of Burnett's account of the strike a few days later—

SIR,—I see in your paper of today a very lengthy defence by Sir W. G. Armstrong of the conduct of the Newcastle employers whose men are now on strike. Perhaps it would be more correct to say, a lengthy accusation of the men who dared to attempt 'to wrest concessions from their employers by force of combination'.

The letter, however, states one side of the case, and, in many instances, betrays either gross ignorance of facts or a culpable suppression of the truth. Sir W. G. Armstrong states in the *Times* the case for the employers, and if you will kindly give this letter insertion it will put before the British public the case of the men who are now on strike for one of the worthiest movements which ever engaged the attention of the working classes of this kingdom.

Sir William, in the first place, gives certain figures (the accuracy of which I very much doubt) to show that the employers have been very successful in importing a large quantity of foreign labour. This I am perfectly willing to admit, but I really do not see how, by so doing, they have bettered their condition, for, despite the assertions of some of the employers to the contrary, there can be no doubt whatever that the foreign workmen so imported are not equal to the performance of anything like the same amount of work as was performed by the old hands. I do not make the statement without a full knowledge of facts, or from a mere desire to under-rate the quality of the foreign workmen, but simply because it is proved to be the truth from the information of our own fellow-countrymen inside the different works. This statement is further borne out by the reports which have lately been made by order of the Government in regard to the state of the foreign workmen. One report by the English Consul at Antwerp states plainly that although the Belgian workmen are content to live in a more moderate manner than English workmen, it must be confessed that the work which they turn out is not equal either in quantity or quality to the work turned out by their English rivals. It is impor-tant that these facts should be borne in mind, for they prove pretty clearly that the arguments used by Sir William in the latter part of his letter, relative to the economic aspect of the question, are not of much avail when we consider how much cheaper it would have been to have conceded the 'nine hours' at once, rather than have gone to the immense expense of importing foreign labour of inferior quality.

The particular item in the figures given by Sir William to which I most strongly object is the one relating to the number of old hands who have gone back to work, or who have never left their employment, or new hands engaged on the spot: 1,375 is the number given, and can only be obtained by counting men of all grades, such as clerks, draughtsmen, and foremen. In Sir William's establishment the latter class is very numerous indeed. However, I am willing to grant the correctness of his figures for the sake of argument, and I proceed at once to criticize the history which he gives of the rise and progress of the Newcastle strike. I think this is of prime importance, for it is in regard to this part of his letter that I have reason to complain of several inaccuracies and omissions.

Sir William states that his object in giving a history of the strike is to exonerate the employers from the charge of rejecting a policy of conciliation. This charge, however, I think, I shall be able to prove, and when our side of the story is told it will be for your readers to determine whether or not on our side the whole truth has been revealed.

It is true that the Newcastle strike originated in a very natural desire on the part of the Newcastle men to place themselves on an equal footing with the men of Sunderland, who had easily obtained the boon for which we have been struggling these last sixteen weeks, but Sir William forgets to state that before the Nine Hours' League was formed by the men the employers of Newcastle set the example of combination. It was recorded in the *Newcastle Journal* (one of the organs of the employers), at least a fortnight previous to the formation of the League, that a meeting of the whole of the employers of the north-eastern district had been held in the Station Hotel, and that a resolution was passed pledging them to support the Sunderland employers by every means in their power in resisting the demands of their workmen. How the Newcastle employers kept their promise is best known to the employers of Sunderland.

Here is the first evidence of a combination of any sort in Newcastle, and it was undeniably a combination of employers. I write with a full knowledge of circumstances when I state that this meeting of our employers had a very strong effect in calling into existence the counter organization called the Nine Hours' League. It is but fair to state that the Sunderland men had been blamed for acting rashly and with undue haste. We, however, determined to act cautiously, and some of us were sanguine enough to imagine that we might possibly gain our object without having to resort to extreme measures. Therefore we addressed to our employers a circular couched in the most courteous terms.

I enclose a copy of the circular, and I think it will be evident from its tone that our desire was for a friendly settlement, if possible. I am sorry I cannot send you a copy of the answer which we received—through a somewhat unusual channel—a firm of solicitors. The document was a fine example of what may be done with pen and ink in skilful hands. It was a large document, but our answer was contained in the last few words; it was very simple—

'We decline to accede to your request.' This was signed by Messrs. Stanton and Atkinson, and it was left to us to find out who these gentlemen were, for we knew that none of the firms under whom we had been employed, bare that title.

Our hopes were considerably dashed on receipt of this answer, but we determined to persevere, feeling that we were in duty bound to make good the position gained by the men of Sunderland, for it will be readily seen that had we not made a determined effort to gain the same terms for ourselves the men of Sunderland would soon have been reduced to their former condition. We, therefore, sent another communication to our employers, which contained an offer which cannot fail to commend itself to the mind of any reasonable man as a fair and just proposal—viz., that six delegates of the men should meet a similar number of the employers and discuss the matter fairly and dispassionately. Strange to say, this moderate offer was likewise rejected by the employers through their solicitors, and the only reason Sir William can give for its rejection is that one shop had already struck.

It is true, Sir, that one shop had struck—one of the smallest; they had struck contrary to the wishes of the League, and it was a subject of considerable discussion with that body as to whether the men who had so struck should be taken under the protection of the League.

The words 'without notice', in reference to the turning out of these men, are in italics; but I may mention that it was a rule in that establishment that no notice whatever was required on either side, so that the italics were really not needed.

Sir William says that the associated masters (associated masters are not a combination, I suppose), justly considered this as the commencement of coercive measures, and handed a resolution to the League which has ever since been the subject of their hostile comments, and, I add, justly so. We had made an almost pitiful request for an interview. We were told 'that had a strike not already occurred they would have suggested a written communication'. You perceive that, in any case, the interview would not have been granted. This document likewise was a formidable affair, and bore the usual signature. About 300 men had, unfortunately, been rather unruly, and yet these gentlemen, who profess to have been anxious for a friendly settlement, determined to visit the sin of 300 upon the heads of the 7,000 or 8,000 who as yet had done nothing.

Up to, and indeed after, this period there was every chance of a peaceful solution of the difficulty had our employers unbent a little.

This last refusal was the straw which broke the camel's back, and we felt that there was nothing left for us but to strike, or for ever after submit to anything. At our next meeting it was resolved that the men of eight shops be recommended to give a legal notice; only one end of Sir William's works were recommended to act in this manner.

Part of the men in the other end, however, did not like to be left in, and gave their notices; but a great many who did not give their notices were kindly informed that, as many men had given notice, their services would be no longer required. The locking-out of 200 or 300 men was such a trifling fact, that it doubtless escaped Sir William's memory. During the week in which we were working our notices I was on night shift, and the remarks attributed to me were made by the party or parties who filled my place. This is of slight importance, however, so I pass to the intervention of the Mayor of Newcastle.

Of the interview between the Mayor and the men's delegates Sir William says nothing, which is rather singular, seeing that a full report of the proceedings appeared in all the papers next day. The whole of those proceedings we reprinted in a pamphlet. One of the passages in this pamphlet was virtually an offer to submit the matter to the arbitration of the Mayor of Newcastle. There seems to have been a great deal of misunderstanding in reference to it. It speaks for itself, however, and ought to convince the most prejudiced that the men did not want to proceed to extremes.

I will say nothing of the manner in which the employers treated the Mayor of Newcastle; suffice it to say, that they rejected the proposal which we had empowered him to make, and all hopes of a friendly settlement were at an end.

Things went on doggedly for some weeks, and nothing of note occurred until Mr Charles Palmer brought about a meeting between men and masters, but the attempt to arrange a conference fell through, because the masters insisted that the men should vote by ballot on the proposal which the masters had to make. Here arises a very important point. The employers had stated that the delegates exercised great influence over the body of the men. The delegates all pledged themselves to use this influence to induce the men to vote by ballot, yet the masters, although professing to believe what we had said, declined to accept our assurance. The Mayor of Newcastle committed himself to a very decided opinion on the subject. He said that the assurance which had been given by the delegates ought to have been sufficient for the employers. They had received and declined an offer which the Mayor of Newcastle said they should have accepted, therefore, in his opinion, the masters were to blame for negotiations falling through at this point. And, indeed, the conduct of our employers during the present strike has convinced me of the truth of a statement I once read, that nine-tenths of all strikes are produced by the arrogance of the employers, who refuse to treat their workmen on terms of anything like equality. Of the concession offered by the employers it is unnecessary to say anything further than that they kept us out on strike ten weeks, and then offered us the same terms as the men on the Clyde have enjoyed, and as were rejected by Mr Stephenson's men at the commencement of the strike. In reference to what Sir William says about Mr Stephenson's letter to his men, it may be observed that our employers never condescended to give us *any reasons whatever* for their refusal. Their conduct looks very black indeed as compared with the action taken by Mr Stephenson. Into the arguments contained in Mr Stephenson's letter it is not my intention to enter. It was the old story of foreign competition. Nothing was said about the fact that the average wages in London are 10s. or 12s. per week higher than in Newcastle, and 6s. or 8s. per week higher in many other parts of the country. I have already trespassed upon your space too far, and must leave in a very imperfect state this record of one of the most determined struggles which ever occurred in the north of England. About the importation of foreigners Sir William says that their most violent opponents cannot deny that they are perfectly justified in following their present course. There may, however, be two opinions as to the conduct of men who endanger the public health of the district by bringing men from countries where cholera was rife, in almost open defiance of sanitary laws.

I may say this, in conclusion, that our employers would be glad if the history of the nine hours in Sunderland could be blotted out, for it shows clearly that firms can be worked as successfully under the nine hours' system as the ten.

Trusting that you will give this insertion, I remain, sir, yours respectfully,

JOHN BURNETT,
President of the Nine Hours' League.
Newcastle-upon-Tyne, Sept. 14.

P.S.—I omitted to notice in the proper place an expression used by Sir William in regard to the turn-out of Clarke, Watson, and

Gurney's men; he says that this conduct on their part put it out of the power of the employers to keep up friendly relations with the League. He further appeals to the subsequent conduct of the League to show that nothing short of unconditional surrender would satisfy them; but I say he has no right to appeal to our subsequent conduct, for it was moulded to a great extent, if not entirely, by the movements of the employers themselves; and if their conduct had been different, so would ours.

Of the issue of this duel of correspondence there was no real doubt, and Burnett's already high prestige was further enhanced by this giant-killing exploit. Demonstrations of public sympathy for the League continued to multiply. On 15th September *Engineering* reported meetings to express support for the League at London, Liverpool, Manchester, Leeds, Birmingham, Sheffield and Glasgow. The same number also mentioned recent events on Tees-side. At Stockton an engineering worker had been sacked for collecting subscriptions for the Tyneside strikers. This dismissal provoked such an indignant response that something like a local general strike was threatened. The matter was composed peacefully however when the employer gave way, but local employers were left in no doubt that large scale strike action would follow on any attempt to repeat such sanctions. Two weeks later the same engineering journal described how:

All the chief towns in the United Kingdom continue to subscribe liberally to the Newcastle men. Batches of foreigners are leaving the works and returning to Rotterdam, Hamburg and Brussels.

Nor can the employers have obtained much comfort from another tactic to which they resorted at this time. Not since the very beginning of the strike had there been any attempt to resort to the courts on grounds of breach of contract by the men, but on 19th September the Gateshead magistrates heard a number of cases brought by one of the strike-bound firms against workmen, under the Master and Servants Act. When the magistrates decided in favour of the employers the defendants expressed a complete willingness to go to prison rather than pay any fines imposed. The League, however, wisely chose to take a different course. The lawyer they had retained to fight these cases gave notice of appeal against the magistrates' decision, and arrangements for bail were made on behalf of the defendants. This move at the very least involved considerable further delay, since it was clear that no final determination could now be expected before December. There were further tribulations awaiting the masters as a result of this further recourse to the law. The Newcastle bench of magistrates heard a parallel series of cases, only to come to a different conclusion. There the Mayor and his colleagues on the bench dismissed the first case on the reasonable grounds that as the men had in fact worked out their proper period of notice, no breach of contract could be established. The remaining seventeen of this batch of cases would certainly have gone the same way, and it was now the employers' turn to ask for a stay of proceedings pending the conclusion of an appeal in the first case.

Still further disadvantages faced the masters as a result of this ill-judged return to the courts. The resort to legal action after so long an interval seemed a clearly vindictive measure, while the episode provided a further boon to League propaganda. Armstrong and his associates had been arguing that their importation of substitute labour bid fair to render them independent of the services of their old workers. The League could now cogently argue that if these claims had been in any way true the employers would scarcely have been striving to bring back their old hands by legal sanctions.

After these events Sir William Armstrong resorted again to the columns of the *Times*, but this time the tone of his letter had markedly changed. His second letter, published on 22nd September, included the following passage.

The heat and passion which unhappily always accompany the proceedings of a strike make conciliation difficult, but the intervention of some third person of undoubted competency and wholly removed from the sphere of the dispute might possibly in the present case facilitate a compromise.

Unfortunately, the question at Newcastle is no longer the simple issue that it was at first—viz., the terms upon which the men should as a body return to their work. Two-thirds of the whole number have gone away and found employment elsewhere, and of the remaining third, probably not more than one-half are men for whom vacancies any longer exist. The masters have been compelled by stern necessity to embark in the enterprise of manning their shops as best they can with strangers, engaged by contract for fixed periods of service. Already more than half the places are filled, and the masters have neither the power nor the will to dismiss from their employment the men who have come to their relief. Still it would be wise for both parties to make the best of the matter as it stands, and no one would more rejoice than I to see the present contest terminated by a dispassionate and rational compromise.

However much the appearance of this letter might be accompanied by repeated assertions of the employers' undiminished fighting spirit, the shift of ground was unmistakable. The employers had indeed been very confident of victory during the earlier periods of the strike, but by late September their position looked distinctly unenviable. On 16th September their leading supporter in the local press, the *Newcastle Journal* had argued in an editorial that:

> From beginning to end it has been nothing more or less than a struggle on the part of the men for mastery, which the employers felt it to be essential to their very existence to resist. If they have spent much money and incurred heavy sacrifices in organizing their resistance, they have at least the satisfaction of believing that it is at best a loss that can be calculated, whereas the evil of yielding to the capricious arrogance of the workmen would have been absolutely incalculable.

It was true that the loss inflicted on the employers by the prolonged strike was calculable, and it was growing increasingly heavy. On the one hand the skilled labour force on which they in reality depended was increasingly absorbed elsewhere, and its recovery increasingly precarious. On the other hand the loss of orders was glaringly obvious. On 28th August, for example, *The Engineer* had already noted this grim development:

> One local steam-shipping firm is stated to have given orders last week to the amount of £21,000 to distant manufacturers.

In these depressing circumstances the evil of yielding came to wear a less forbidding aspect.

The period of the strike was one of very considerable worry and strain for the employers themselves, especially where, like Benjamin Browne of Hawthorn's, their financial position was not very strong and their whole fortune depended on the prosperity of their engineering enterprises. In a memoir written by Browne's daughters they describe this period in these words: [24]

> It was a time of terrible strain and anxiety from every point of

view, and it put an end to his youth once and for all.

Armstrong himself seemed to have lost his earlier confidence of victory as September came with no signs of yielding on the part of the League, but ample evidence of the employers' unpopularity and of a widespread disposition in many quarters to subscribe to the League the resources it needed to keep going. On 7th September he wrote to Stuart Rendel that 'We are fighting away here very hard and see nothing for it but persevering in our present course', words which hardly illustrate optimism. It is not surprising then that his second letter to the *Times* was markedly more conciliatory than the first.

Burnett soon followed up the indications of mellowing apparent in the 22nd September letter from Armstrong. On 28th September the *Times* published a second letter from Burnett, which rebuffed some of the points Armstrong's second letter had tried to make but which also included the following key passage:

Up to the present time they have met with the sympathy and approval of the general public. They do not wish to forfeit that sympathy and approval; and therefore avail themselves gladly of the conciliatory tone of your correspondent's letter. Sir William points out the fact that the 'employers have already conceded two-fifths of the demands of the men, and that the question is now narrowed to three hours instead of five per week', and suggests that we should seek an arrangement in wages as an equivalent for the remainder. Now, Sir, here it seems strange that both parties should be desirous to forfeit money; such, however, is the case. The men of Newcastle have set their hearts upon the nine hours' system. The various arguments in its favour I need not now go over. They have been repeated sufficiently often already, and are deeply imprinted in our minds. It now seems evident to nearly every one that the change *must* come sooner or later; time, there-fore, is on our side, and now that we are so far on the way to success, it would be a pity to turn back, or even to sit down by the way, tired and footsore though we be. Therefore, Sir, we turn to our employers and to the public and say:—'There are three hours which divide us. You say you cannot afford to give us them, then we say we will not press you hard, we will buy them from you, we will give you for them a certain sum per week each man, which shall be fixed either between ourselves or by an arbitrator, so that there may be peace between us; and if the matter is settled in this way,

I am sure it will be a lasting peace.' Sir William says, in concluding his letter, 'that, by thus indicating his views, he runs the risk of having weakness of purpose attributed to himself and colleagues'. On this point I can only say he need be under no apprehension. Both parties have fought with so much determination that neither need shrink from attempting to bring about an honourable peace. As Englishmen we have fought hard, and as Englishmen, I hope, when the battle is over, we will respect each other for the resolution we have displayed.

This expressed willingness to accept a wage cut in return for a shorter working week was one which Burnett had made entirely on his own responsibility, and not surprisingly there were repercussions and differences of opinion among the other leaders of the League. On the same day as Burnett's letter appeared there was a prolonged meeting of League delegates from which the press was excluded, and the only information of value as to what transpired behind these closed doors comes from Burnett's own later account. Burnett admits that his action came in for some serious criticism, but the final decision was to endorse the offer he had made. The *Times*, despite the press exclusion, stated the next day that the decision had been nearly unanimous and had been taken by ballot. In the valuable account of the strike which Burnett published in 1872 he wrote that 'It is not necessary to go into all the arguments used to induce the men to accept the above resolution.' It may, however, be reasonably conjectured that among the arguments with which Burnett justified the initiative he had taken was the paramount need to maintain the League's reputation for statesmanlike restraint and moderation. More telling may have been the point that in the present state of the engineering trade any such reduction in wages could in practice scarcely be real or lasting.

These exchanges coincided with, and probably prompted, another attempt to settle the long drawn out dispute by mediation. The two sides were apparently drawing nearer and this suggested that another intervention by a disinterested outsider might produce new negotiations and an end to the strike. Anthony John Mundella was a distinguished Liberal politician who then sat in the Commons as M.P. for Sheffield. His own experiences and interests seemed to make him an ideal man for this role as mediator. He was himself a successful manufacturer, and had evinced a deep, abiding and enlightened interest in industrial relations. He had founded a conciliation board for the hosiery and glove industry in 1866, a notable effort in establishing machinery for the pacific settlement of industrial disputes. In the general election of 1868 at Sheffield he had defeated the veteran radical J. A. Roebuck, whose strenuous opposition to trade union activities was a principal cause of his losing his seat. Moreover, in the existing Parliament Mundella had won golden opinions from working-class sources for his trenchant opposition to the Criminal Law Amendment Act passed in 1871 by Gladstone's government, which had been enacted in the teeth of strong protests from organized labour, resentful of the attempt to legislate against picketing activities. Mundella was also Vice-President of the Capital and Labour Committee of the Social Science Association, which had met in Newcastle the previous year. When Mundella made it known publicly that he was willing to try to mediate in the Tyneside dispute, his initiative was welcomed by Burnett and his colleagues, who entrusted him with the task of formally conveying to the associated employers their offer to accept a wage cut if that would win the hours concession for which they were striving. Essentially this offer amounted to an expressed willingness to accept a wage cut equivalent to the price of three hours' work, if the employers would move from the 57 hours they had already offered to the League's 54 hours' demand.

Mundella duly conveyed these terms to the employers on 29th September. On the next day, a Saturday, the League supported their case by staging the greatest public display of strength and popular support to appear during the dispute. A great procession, estimated by observers at figures between 15,000 and 25,000, marched behind bands and banners to a mass meeting on the Newcastle Town Moor. The banners presented an interesting collection of working-class symbols, emblems of a kind which possessed a very long history. Banners like some of those borne in 1871 had floated over great Chartist meetings on the same Town Moor in 1839. Some bore apt quotations from Shakespeare, Burns, Goldsmith and Byron; some of the other legends were

NINE HOURS ELSWICK MARINE WORKS: DEFENCE NOT DEFIANCE.
ELSWICK ORDNANCE WORKS: NINE HOURS PURE AND SIMPLE.
HAWTHORN'S BOILERMEN: TIME STRENGTHENS OUR UNITY AND
   DETERMINATION TO WIN.
HAWTHORN'S ENGINEERS: NO SURRENDER IN TIME—JUSTICE TO
   BRITISH INDUSTRY

At this great rally there were some murmurings of criticism against the offer on pay initiated by Burnett, but much more clear was the fighting spirit of the men, and an overall impression of implacable unity and strength.

Two days later, on Monday, 2nd October, the reply of the associated employers reached Mundella in the form of a letter from Armstrong:

Newcastle-on-Tyne, Sept. 30, 1871.

A. J. Mundella, Esq., M.P.

DEAR SIR,—

The resolution of the Nine Hours' League conveyed yesterday to me through you, has been discussed at a special meeting of the employers held today.

We entered upon the discussion with an earnest desire to discover in the proposal the elements of a compromise that might lead to a settlement of the dispute.

We find, however, that upon the vital question of time no concession is offered, and that the proposal to buy a portion of the time by a voluntary reduction of wages, proves on examination illusory. It is not apparent whether the League contemplated a reduction of wages adequate to cover our loss upon plant as well as our loss in time; but we suppose they do, for otherwise we cannot see how the transaction can be regarded in the light of a purchase as treated by Mr Burnett.

However sincere the intentions of the League may be, it is not difficult to show that it is not in their power to give effect to their proposal. Suppose the strike to be terminated upon the basis they have suggested. Our first object would be to get back the best of our old hands, most of whom have gone away and found work elsewhere. But how would we accomplish this at the reduced wages proposed by the League? It is impossible for us to believe that shorter hours would be held to compensate for lower wages, especially if the reduction of pay were greater than the reduction of time, as would be the case if it covered our loss in idle plant; but, at any rate, it is clear that in order to procure and retain the labour we want we must pay at least its market value, and any agreement with the League to the contrary would be a pure illusion.

If the nine hours' movement really means what it professes to mean, its object must be the actual and not merely the apparent reduction of hours of work. Its tendency must therefore be to diminish the supply of labour and so enhance its price. Now the League are proposing incompatible things—contracted supply and diminished price. If, then, by our consent the League obtained their full demand for reduction of hours, they would speedily regain, by the operation of laws beyond either their or our control, the wages now offered to be surrendered, and thus the nine hours 'pure and simple' would be carried.

This is the difficulty which in the opinion of the employers renders the proposal of the League altogether nugatory, and oblige us to decline it.

No such difficulty would apply to the compromise which I suggested in a recent letter to the *Times*, and which, on behalf of the employers, I now formally repeat.

Our proposal is that the question of time should be compromised by the acceptance on the part of the men of two hours out of the five demanded, and that in lieu of the remaining three hours they should take a proportionate increase of wages. The condition of trade justifies, as we have always admitted, an advance of wages, so that the proposed advance, unlike the proposed reduction, does not conflict with the laws of supply and demand. This increase of pay would amount to 5 per cent, and would apply to every kind of skilled labour: adding the value of the two hours conceded in time, it would represent a total advance of $8\frac{1}{2}$ per cent on the wages current when the strike began.

In terms of money, our offer concedes the whole demand of the men, and from every reasonable point of view it gives them more than half the battle. Surely they might accept such terms as these without any sense of defeat, and we earnestly hope that they may yet be induced to do so, or at all events that they will submit the question to the same mode of decision as they applied to the proposal which you have communicated to us.

If the proposition thus formerly made be rejected, and the League continue inflexible in their demand for the full reduction of time, then we say that if the other objections which we deem insuperable were removed there would remain this difficulty that by conceding the demand we should in a great measure involve all other engineering firms in the country in our decision. We cannot take upon ourselves this responsibility. The question is said to have become a national one. If so, it should be treated on a broader basis than that of a local dispute. The strike is but a rude ordeal for directing even a local question, much more so for settling a national one. Viewed in this light we can see but one way out of the difficulty, and that is to convene a Congress, composed of delegates from employers of engineering labour and from their workmen throughout the country not for the purpose of debating the question—for that, we fear, would be fruitless—but for the purpose of getting it decided by an independent Board of Arbitration.

A Local Arbitration is not the proper mode of dealing with a dispute involving such widespread interests, although unobjectionable for setting a question of wages.

As the proposal of the League first appeared in Mr Burnett's recent letter to the *Times*, we shall forward a copy of this correspondence for insertion in that journal.

I am, dear Sir,

Yours faithfully,

W. G. ARMSTRONG.

Mundella accepted this letter as a clear indication of the failure of his attempt to mediate, and left Newcastle, but not before he had used expressions to the League leaders which left them under the not unreasonable impression that he believed them to be in the right. Burnett and his colleagues expressed their very sincere thanks to Mundella for the good intentions and conciliatory spirit which had inspired his intervention. A few days later, after he had returned home, Mundella sent Armstrong a long letter advocating the setting up of a conciliation board for the engineering industry, on which both masters and men would be represented. This document can scarcely have been welcome to Armstrong, though Burnett inserted it in full in his history of the strike published a few months later. In contrast to other local trades like coal mining and shipbuilding, the Tyneside engineering industry was not a sphere in which notable early experiments in the establishment of conciliation machinery occurred.

The hold of the strikers on uncommitted public opinion throughout the country continued, and indeed was enhanced by the latest rejection by the employers of the concession offered by Burnett. The very varied nature of the support enlisted by the League can be illustrated by three dissimilar instances, two local and one from afar.

At the end of August the workmen employed by Messrs. Charlton, a Newcastle firm of plumbers, learned that some of the work then in the hands of the firm had been sent there by one of the engineering works whose own operations were affected by the strike. The plumbers' workmen at once refused to touch the work involved, downed tools and came out on strike themselves. Their employers offered to send the 'black' work back unfinished if their own workers would return; the men concerned consulted the leaders of the League before accepting these terms, and it was only on their advice that they agreed to return to work.

The example of help from afar is provided by a letter published in the *Spectator* of October 7th. The writer was a man of considerable means and an employer; he was a Derbyshire county magistrate coming from a well-established family in that area, and had taken considerable interest in social and educational questions:

THE NEWCASTLE STRIKE.
[TO THE EDITOR OF THE 'SPECTATOR'.]

SIR,—Sir W. Armstrong, in his letter to Mr Mundella, allows that the Nine Hours' Movement has become a national question. To those who were acquainted with the details of this strike from its commencement this fact has been long recognized. In proof of this, we need only look at the weekly balance-sheets issued by the Nine Hours' League. I have several of them now before me, the last being for the week ending September 26th. From this little pamphlet of thirty pages I have extracted the names of some fifty of the principal towns throughout Great Britain which are now sending their weekly contributions to Newcastle. They are as follows:—Aberdeen, Altrincham, Banbury, Bedford, Blackburn, Belfast, Birmingham, Burton-on-Trent, Bury, Chelsea, Chester, Crewe, Darlington, Dewsbury, Derby, Dover, Durham, Dundee, Edinburgh, Glasgow, Grantham, Hull, Hartlepool, Leamington, Leeds, Lincoln, Liverpool, Londonderry, Manchester, Nottingham, Northampton, Oldham, Otley, Oxford, Plymouth, Portsea, Preston, Ripley, Rochdale, Scarborough, Southampton, Stoke, Stratford, Sunderland, Swindon, Wakefield, Wolverhampton, Worcester, York, and every district of the metropolis. It is equally worthy of note to observe how almost every trade contributes towards the general fund. Among the subscribers we find boilermakers, bottle-makers, brassfounders, brewerymen, brushmakers, builders, carpenters, chemical-works men, cabinetmakers, coachbuilders, colliers, drapers, engineers, gunmakers, grocers, ironfounders (and all departments of this trade), joiners, lacemakers, millwrights, machine grinders, painters, plate-glass polishers, patternmakers, printers, plumbers, shoemakers, shipwrights, stonemasons, spinners, tele-graph-works men, tailors, water-works men, wire-works men, and lastly and most important of all, a large number of men from the various departments of our great Railway Companies, who have been stirred up to action by Mr Bass's energetic appeals to the Directors of the Midland Railway Company.

These accounts are kept with the greatest accuracy, and one

remarkable feature about them is the very small sums which are drawn by the leaders of the movement for their expenses as deputations. This country never yet experienced a strike which was carried on with so much method, economy, and precision as is the present one, whilst the growing sympathy with which the cause is being embraced by the general public is clearly shown by the steadily increasing grant which the League is enabled to make to the men on strike. Last week the weekly allowance was eleven shillings per head, now it is twelve, and this is exclusive of an extra grant of one shilling for each child. Now that the masters have put themselves still further in the wrong by refusing to discuss the conciliatory and temperate proposals of the able leader of the men, Mr Burnett, there can be no doubt that those on strike will receive still further support from the public. Sir W. Armstrong now admits, what I stated in your columns a fortnight ago, that the state of trade warrants a rise in wages; surely then it is preposterous that the men should not be allowed to say in what form they prefer to take that advance?

Many employers of labour are already supporting the League, and I ask you to give publicity to these brief remarks, in the hope that many more who regard the human frame as something better than a mere piece of machinery may be induced to aid it in its struggle against capital. If the Newcastle men win, nine hours of manual labour will very shortly be the limit throughout the country. Without this limitation the Education Act will be a farce.—I am, Sir, &c.,

J. CHARLES COX.

Hazelwood, Belper, October 4, 1871.

It is not possible to evaluate with any precision the claim made here that many employers were in fact supporting the League, but it is unlikely that Cox was making an entirely unsubstantiated statement. Certainly the engineering employers cannot have derived much comfort from the very limited help they received from fellow-employers elsewhere.

The second local illustration of the many-sided support for the men is an event which took place on September 18th. Newcastle Town Hall was taken for a great popular concert in aid of the funds of the League. For this occasion a new song was specially written by Joe Wilson, a leading entertainer and song-writer in the north-east at that time. The song was subsequently published widely by a local firm of printers:

THE STRIKE!

A NEW SONG, WRITTEN EXPRESSLY FOR THE

GREAT CONCERT IN THE NEW TOWN HALL,

Monday, September 18th, 1871,

BY JOE WILSON.

———

AIR—'THE GALLOWGATE LAD'.

———

Cum me canny Tynesiders an lissen
    Tiv a sang that aw's sartin ye'll like,
An' aw'll whisper a word kind an' cheerin'
    Te the monny poor fellows on strike.
Let them keep up thor hearts as they hev deun,
    Thor's a day for the true an' the brave,
An' the time 'ill yit cum when greet Maisters
    'Ill find oot a Mechanic's ne slave!

Is Nine Oors an unreasonable movement?
    Is't not plenty for labour te men?
Let them that condemn'd hev a try on't,
    An' see if they'll alter such plan;
An' if lang oors Industry increases,
    Heh they fund it wi' them that they've tried?
Wi' thor capital heh they got labour
    Like *that* frae the men they've defied?

But a day 'ill seun cum when they'll welcum
    The aud hands they've se often imploy'd
Then the Forriners strength 'ill be shaken
    Frae license that they've lang injoy'd,
I' myekin thorsels thor awn maisters
    An' workin' just when they'd a mind;
If the Maisters pretend to be blind tid,
    Whey, its mair te thor shem, that they'll find.

But cheer up, thor's gud friends that support us,
    Aye, an' Ingland depends on us a',
An' we'll prove that wor true te the movement,
    An' Victory shall let the world knaw

> That Tyneside 'ill nivor be konker'd,
> Wi' Maisters that care nowt for them;
> An' if Maisters is meant te be Maisters,
> Let them find thor's Men meant te be Men!

As so often with the genuine popular songs of the period, Joe Wilson was well expressing the feelings of those for whom it was written. The Nine Hours' League was the representative in these months, not of a down-trodden proletariat, but of workers who were justifiably proud of their own technical skills and craftsmanship and well aware of their own importance, and part of a working class which here as elsewhere was enjoying a rich and popular culture of its own, of which Wilson's songs were one manifestation. In many ways British society at that time was neither particularly comfortable nor particularly easy, and society was riddled with continuing injustices and inequalities. Tyneside, like the rest of the country, was no paradise for the working classes. Yet in seeking to maintain against these workers the prerogative of the employer to do exactly as he wanted with his own, the associated engineering employers of Tyneside were challenging forces which were strong enough to beat them, even if the long drawn out struggle to establish the right of workers to have a voice in the way in which their conditions were determined was very far from over after 1871.

The engineering employers were coming to realize by the end of September just what a precarious state their intransigence had brought them to, and before the end of the month there had been the first signs of the adoption of a more compromising spirit in the communications emanating from Armstrong and his associates. The exchanges of September culminating in Mundella's attempt at mediation had very much narrowed down the area of remaining conflict. The employers' new mood was revealed in their now basing their refusal to surrender on the much narrower and more easily negotiable basis of an apprehension that if the 54 hours' week were conceded then the men might refuse to work the hours, including overtime, regarded as necessary for the efficient and profitable working of the factories. In these conditions agreement seemed distinctly more attainable, and this situation was the signal for a final mediation attempt made by two powerful Tyneside figures working together in close concert.

Joseph Cowen was one of the two men responsible for the moves which finally ended the nine hours' strike on Tyneside. His strenuous support for the men's case has frequently been noticed, and it is unlikely that Cowen himself acting alone could have brought the employers to a speedy settlement. Early in October, however, private discussions on the strike took place between Cowen and another leading local figure, hitherto not publicly involved in the strike, who was very well suited for the rôle of mediator, and indeed represented a kind of mediatory influence which had often been brought to bear with good effect in earlier industrial disputes on Tyneside. This key figure was Ralph Park Philipson, Town Clerk of Newcastle upon Tyne.

Philipson had succeeded to that office in 1867, on the retirement of John Clayton, last of a notable dynasty of Newcastle Town Clerks. The new official was a man of very wide connections, influence and prestige. Early in his career he had played a leading rôle in the local campaign for municipal reform in the 1830's, and before becoming Town Clerk he had sat on Newcastle Town Council, first as councillor and then as alderman, for forty-four years. He was acknowledged to be a leading figure in the local Liberal party. The post of Town Clerk had not yet become the full time professional position it later became, and Philipson had wide commercial interests, which he retained after succeeding Clayton as the town's principal officer. For many years he sat on the Tyne Improvement Commission, which controlled the Tyne harbour. He was Clerk to the Peace for County Durham, and solicitor to the Newcastle and Gateshead Gas Company, the Newcastle and Gateshead Water Company and the North Eastern Railway. As one of the proprietors of an important local colliery he was himself an employer on a considerable scale. Although his career had been helped by his being born into a family already firmly entrenched in the urban oligarchy of Newcastle, he had earned his position of distinction and influence by his own talents. A contemporary observer described him in the following terms:[25]

> Mr R. P. Philipson, whose amplitude of talent and scantiness of speech are almost proverbial. One of the most striking properties of Mr Philipson's mind is his power to express his views in the briefest language possible. You cannot well admire his hard, and occasionally somewhat bitter, manner of doing this; but you feel each sentence to be so much to the point, and to contain so much really valuable matter, that you are carried along in admiration and surprise, as if new lights were constantly flashing upon your mind, until he suddenly ceases, and leaves you wondering that you never before thought of what he has said. He is remarkable for giving a new feature, and often a new direction, to a discussion. He has the

THE 1871 STRIKE ON TYNESIDE

judgment never to speak unless he has something pertinent to say, and which is always well worth the little trouble it appears to cost him to say it. Sometimes, when a question appears to be nearly exhausted, and one speaker is merely repeating the observations of another, Mr Philipson will interpose a few words—rather magisterially it may be—which, starting, perhaps, quite a new view of the subject, either give rise to a long debate, or suddenly close the discussion from a conviction that he has suggested exactly the course which ought to be pursued.

Philipson's predecessors in the office of Town Clerk had often taken a prominent part in the settlement or attempted settlement of local industrial disputes, and his intervention at this point was a natural one. With the apparent narrowing of the issues involved in the strike, he judged, and judged rightly, that the time had come when he might intervene with real hope of success. Only a few days after the failure of Mundella's attempted mediation, Philipson engaged in a series of confidential discussions with Joseph Cowen, which resulted in the drafting of the terms of a proposed settlement, to be put forward as a joint personal initiative by the two men. Their succinct peace formula was as follows:

Suppose the employers were to concede the fifty-four hours per week, the men would agree to work overtime when and to the extent required by the employers.

The wages, both as to ordinary wages and as to overtime, to remain the same in the different factories as existed prior to the strike.

The wages to be reckoned by the hour and quarter hour, and paid weekly at 12.15 p.m. on Saturday.

The agreement to be for twelve months, with power to either party to determine it at the end of six months by giving one month's previous notice.

The men to go to work on the arrangement now existing in the shops (57 hours), and the new terms (54 hours) to take date from January 1, 1872.

The two self-appointed mediators then proceeded separately to secure the consent of the two parties to their proposals. Naturally Cowen approached his friends of the League, while Philipson tackled the associated employers. It is noticeable that Burnett's wage offer was not included in the draft terms. Nevertheless when Philipson approached Armstrong, Sir William at once expressed his own willingness to assent to the terms now put forward, and promised that he would lay the terms before his associates at the first practicable opportunity with a view to securing their acceptance.

Cowen for his part took the peace formula to a regular meeting of the League delegates at the Westgate Inn on the evening of Thursday, 5th October. Burnett was away in Edinburgh on League business, but he was at once telegraphed for, returning in time to join in adjourned discussion the following morning. With Burnett's powerful support, the leaders of the League agreed to accept the proffered terms, subject to ratification of this decision at a mass meeting of their followers summoned the same evening. At the evening meeting a great majority of those present voted to accept the peace formula, though a few more militant voices were raised in favour of standing out for the immediate concession of the 54 hours' week, rather than accept its delayed implementation in January 1871. Burnett and the other leaders, however, were very glad to accept the very great concessions already won. The onset of winter, with the end of seasonal employment and the arrival of heating costs, might well have increased their financial problems, while the terms now offered gave them almost everything they had striven for. At the mass meeting of the League the following resolution was adopted:

> That this meeting of the men on strike accepts the terms offered by Mr Philipson on behalf of the Associated Employers and respectfully requests the employers to appoint a committee of six of their body to meet a similar number of the men to arrange matters of detail.

However 'respectfully' this resolution was couched, there may be a hint of irony in it, in view of the repeated and obstinate earlier refusal of the employers to meet a League delegation face to face.

There was no doubt who had won the prolonged engagement, and the employers had swallowed a bitter draught. On 9th October Andrew Noble of Armstrong's wrote to his colleague Stuart Rendel:

> We have made the best of a hard job but you must not forget my dear Stuart that we pay a fearful price for it. The wages are practically raised 11.6% and this is very heavy.

The settlement gave the workmen gains on both the wages' and the hours' fronts. The labour costs of the engineering firms were significantly increased, but this was reflected not in declining business but in the charging of much higher prices for their products. The principal owner of Hawthorn's engineering works later wrote:[26]

> When the strike began, the price of engines was about £45 per nominal horsepower, and very soon after the strike was over—it lasted a little over four months—the price had risen to nearly £60 per horsepower.

The settlement of the 'matters of detail' still involved some hard bargaining, and even some continued acrimony. Even when surrender had been agreed the most intransigent employers could not give in with good grace. Noble described to Stuart Rendel how the new proprietors of Hawthorn's came near to upsetting the applecart during the final negotiations:

> I write a line to say that the strike is at an end. Our friends Marshall and Browne have distinguished themselves to the end. Marshall got into conversation with the delegates & raised one or two awkward points such as saying that we would not take on members of the League. Of course the point would not have been raised had he not been so indiscreet.

The employers were in no position to attempt such reprisals, and the men made it quite clear that this kind of victimization must not happen. Elsewhere in this letter Noble talks of F. C. Marshall in terms which suggest that this employer risen from the shop floor had played a major part in bolstering up for so long the intransigence of the employers—'In fact Marshall has ruined us.'

The Philipson-Cowen peace formula needed precise interpretation on a number of points. The employers stipulated that overtime rates should not come into operation until the man involved had actually worked the basic 54 hours' week—there was to be no taking ordinary time off and working overtime hours instead. Bargaining followed between the two delegations; the masters made a number of minor concessions, excluding from this ruling time lost for idle machinery, or time off taken with the foreman's permission, and the men then agreed to this stipulation. By Monday, 9th October the detailed settlement had been agreed, and it was decided that a large scale resumption of work should begin on 12th October. Even then, however, some difficulties cropped up. Some of the more militant strikers objected to working alongside men who they regarded as blacklegs, while there were other demands that all the strikers should be re-employed simultaneously. The men finally accepted arrangements for a return to work phased over a few weeks, as work became available in the factories for the men of different trades. The employers then tried to stipulate that their men must make individual personal applications for reinstatement, but on this the men were adamant in refusing any opportunity for victimization. There was an almost general acceptance that all the old hands would be re-employed within a very few weeks. Within four weeks of the settlement only about a hundred men appeared on the League's books as dependants, and for them the League continued for the time being an allowance of ten shillings per week, with a shilling weekly for each dependent child.

The nine hours having been won, the major firms which had held aloof from the conflict, Palmer's and Stephenson's, came into line. Palmer accepted the terms set out in the main agreement, while G. R. Stephenson characteristically went his own way, in accepting the suggestion from his manager, Douglas, that in his works the 54 hours' week should begin on 1st November 1871, instead of waiting until 1st January 1872 as the main settlement laid down. Stephenson's workers responded to this generous arrangement by staging a demonstration of rejoicing and gratitude of their own, but it is scarcely surprising that Burnett's account of this celebration should end with the somewhat bitter reflection that 'many of them did little or nothing to help the movement'. At Palmer's the bringing in of the 54 hours' week did not go entirely smoothly. In early 1872 disagreements as to the detailed implementation of the new system there sparked off a short-lived strike, demonstrating that the Jarrow men's passivity during the nine hours' strike had not been due to supineness. Once again Palmer acted effectively. He called a special meeting of the men, met them face to face to discuss the problems, and his personal intervention brought the 1872 stoppage to a speedy finish and restored smooth working. Before these events the League had organized its own formal victory celebration in January 1872, as the main settlement came into operation. And so, the great nine hours' strike was over. On Tyneside a mock mourning card circulated in commemoration of the strike's demise:

In strange remembrance of Tyney Strike, son of Sir Capital and Lady Labour de Tyne, who, despite of parental care, magisterial nursing, official day and night watching, and tenderest hopes of all its friends, expired on the 7th October, 1871, aged twenty weeks.

The loved one came! our hopes were budding thick!
He lived, and often played a prankish trick,
As we who lived *well* (?) know,
That ha(r)ppy touch gave Tyney's windpipe rick—
The little darling did the bucket kick—
PRO BONO PUBLICO.

NOTES TO CHAPTER 5

1. Burnett, op. cit., p. 29.
2. *Newcastle Chronicle*, 13-9-1871.
3. See above p. 172.
4. Clarke, op. cit., p. 273.
5. Ibid, p. 276.
6. Webb, S. & B., *The History of Trade Unionism* (1920 edn., 1950 reprint), p. 318.
7. Mutual help between Tyneside and the textile districts had a long history. The accounts of the local seamen's union for 1825-6 included a sum of £50 donated to the artisans at Bradford. (P.R.O., H.O., 40/21.)
8. A good example in *Engineering*, 7-7-1871; article on 'Trade outrages'.
9. See below p. 143.
10. 21-7-1871, Armstrong Papers, Newcastle City Archives.
11. 31-7-1871, ibid.
12. Ibid.
13. N. Palliser/Rendel, ibid.
14. Duncan, op. cit., pp. 28-31.
15. Account of police troubles based on Newcastle Council and Watch Committee minutes in Newcastle City Archives.
16. Criminal Law Amendment Act, 34 & 35 Vict. cap. 32.
17. *Newcastle Chronicle*, 19-8-1871.
18. *Newcastle Weekly Chronicle*, 14-2-1914.
19. Henry Woodroffe, President of the local seamen's union, and leader of their strike in 1831-2, presents a very good analogy, best illustrated by a group of letters from Commander Glascock, R.N. in P.R.O. Adm. 1/1868.
20. Duncan, op. cit., p. 28.
21. Quoted in *Newcastle Weekly Chronicle*, 23-9-1871.
22. Armstrong Papers, Newcastle City Archives.
23. Ibid.
24. Browne, op. cit., p. xi.
25. Welford, R., *Men of Mark 'twixt Tyne and Tweed*, Vol. III, p. 264 et seq.
26. Browne, op. cit., p. 167.

CHAPTER SIX

Conclusion

IT might generally be expected that in a campaign for the gaining of a shorter working day from employers a leading part would be taken by either a government or a trade union, or both. The remarkable thing about the Nine Hours' Movement amongst the engineers on Tyneside in 1871 is that neither government nor union comes significantly into the picture: the Government not at all, and the union, in this case the A.S.E., only slightly, almost irrelevantly and certainly in a belated, almost casual, manner that might be reasonably interpreted as implying a mild, or even possibly more than a mild, reproof. Indeed, when the Sunderland engineers were conducting their successful campaign for a reduction in the length of the working day, the Newcastle District Central Committee of the A.S.E. issued a statement condemning 'the hasty action of a few members of the Sunderland Branch which precipitated the strike'. It has been said that when the employers acceded to the full demands of the men, the official union group was nonplussed and shaken: no wonder, for it seems also to be a part of the situation that they had not been disposed to take strike action in the first place and when the strike had commenced were inclined to recommend the acceptance of a partial and compromise solution which the outcome showed to be completely unnecessary. But they should not be written off as callous or lazy, or blind to the need for action such as that which was being taken by the strikers: they were acting consistently in accordance with 'the lights' which had established the 'New Model Unionism' so solidly from the 1850's to the 1870's and contributed in no small measure to the very much wider acceptance of trade union formation and activity which had been evolved. As administrators of a union which like the other craft unions had made friendly society functions a large part of its programme they were almost inevitably preoccupied with the condition of their financial reserves. Quite apart from their general tendency to favour a 'quietist' policy, to avoid strikes, and use them only as a last resort, they were well aware that strikes can be expensive manoeuvres and are apt to run the financial reserves dangerously low. They tended to think and act as trustees of a friendly society rather than as leaders of activist campaigns against the employers. But if in 1871 they had not yet learned the lesson that this sort of bias could stand in the way of active campaigning, they were certainly quicker to learn in the years that followed. The A.S.E. delegates to the T.U.C. in 1890 were instructed to support the case for legislative action to establish an eight hour day and to vote in favour of a motion to this effect.

The rise of John Burnett to high office within the Union may have worked in the same direction. On the death of William Allan, he was chosen to be General Secretary. A number of members of the Executive Committee were opposed to his election and as influential a person within the Union as William Newton expressed himself as being opposed to Burnett's election. Nevertheless Burnett was elected. Despite the opposition that clearly existed, his election suggests that there was already a group in the A.S.E. prepared to adopt tactics which would represent a departure from those of 1851 onwards. However, as we shall see, parts of the A.S.E. membership were to show themselves by the mid-1880's markedly more militant than Burnett. At the end of the 1870's, a movement of the employers to bring about a longer working day evoked the expected response. In 1871, the purpose of securing a nine hour day led to the establishment of the Nine Hours' League: in 1879, the threat of the employers to undo the gain which had then been achieved evoked a similarly protective response in the shape of the Nine Hours' Maintenance League. But there was a difference and it shows the change in attitude and stance which had come about. The support for the Nine Hours' Maintenance League was widespread: the Nine Hours' League of 1871 had been confined to Tyneside. The officials of the A.S.E. had stood aloof from the 1871 campaign. In 1879, the campaign was blessed, sponsored and supported by the union. In a period of rising unemployment when the pressures from the employers' side were growing stronger, the union stood firm in defence of the nine hours' principle. This had been won for them by a largely non-union group of campaigners in 1871 towards whom the union officials of that year had been, at best, unco-operative—or at least for a long time so— and at worst almost hostile. The achievement of John Burnett and his associates in gaining acceptance of the nine hours' day from the employers is enhanced still further, we may think, in that it would seem that not only had they to carry the day against the employers, but they had also to carry it against the moderation of the existing union officials. Economic conditions in 1871 had an important bearing on the course of the strike. A boom was being generated in which the engineering employers were undoubtedly sharing. As has been stated earlier, boom conditions generally tended to make the securing of improvements by labour easier, while recession and outright depression conditions tended to tilt the bargaining strength towards the employers and made it hard for trade unions to resist employers' demands for the withdrawal of gains previously conceded, let alone achieve further gains. A view of the situation that developed on Tyneside might therefore be more clearly illuminated if the question to be asked is how did it come about that the employers were so stubborn in their resistance to the League's demand for the nine hour day. The answer undoubtedly lies, it may be thought, in the firmness with which Sir William Armstrong and his associates confronted the men and the rigidity of the interpretation which he seems to have put upon the League's campaign. He seems to have been convinced that the strikers were using the plea for a reduction in the length of the working day as a mask for their real intention of increasing their earnings. He seems also to have formed and retained the strong idea that success in gaining a nine hour day would be followed, after possibly not too long an interval, by a demand for the eight hour day. He seems also to have regarded the action of the strikers as an affront to his position as industrial leader and easily the outstanding employer in the whole of Tyneside.

Sir William Armstrong moved easily and authoritatively in circles, scientific, technological and political, which were far removed from the provincial pattern of relationships of remote Tyneside. His associates, as has been shown, moved easily between positions of high responsibility in the War Office or Admiralty and positions of high managerial responsibility in his works. It is not difficult to build up the supposition that a busy, crowded life passed in such circles would be likely to create a gulf between the small élite in charge at Elswick and the great mass of working men who made up the labour force. There is perhaps no direct evidence available which would convert such a supposition into a firmly supported hypothesis, but there is undoubtedly a good deal of support for it from his multifarious activities, often in London as much as in Newcastle, and the tactics which he employed in his capacity as leader of the employers' side against the workers in their conduct of the nine hours' campaign.

On the evidence which is set out in earlier pages of this study, there is only one verdict which can be passed on the tactics of the employers: they played their hand extremely badly. They displayed an intransigence and insensitiveness which created a bad public image, and in so doing Sir William Armstrong must himself take a great deal of the blame. He and his associates could possibly have learned something from the attitudes towards their workmen of other employers on Tyneside. Employers, in various trades, had, in the past, often shown greater capacity for flexibility and appreciation of their workers' interests. During the 1871 strike itself, the attitude and consequent experiences of Palmer and Stephenson had shown the advantages which might accrue from more enlightened, or at least more man-to-man, attitudes towards industrial relations. The associated employers, under the stubborn, inflexible leadership of Sir William Armstrong were, in fact, very largely the architects of their own defeat. It may be that the bitter experience of 1871 taught a lesson to some at least of the vanquished though, in the light of accounts over a much later period of prickly and suspicious industrial relations in engineering and shipbuilding on Tyneside, it is not easy to dispel the notion that this confrontation of 1871 created a cold, even hostile, relationship between masters and men which has lingered, in some degree, even to the present time. Whatever may be thought of this notion, it is certainly the case that Lord Armstrong mellowed in some respects as he grew older; he has a secure place in the history of North-East England. There are constant references to his more enlightened attitude towards industrial relations in his later years, when he undoubtedly displayed a keener and more continuous interest in the condition of his workmen. The 'Collected Papers' of Sir Benjamin Browne, who survived until 1917, bear evidence of an increasingly warm and relatively enlightened interest in industrial relations, and it suggests that he, too, may have learned something from his early experiences as an engineering employer. As far as the 1871 strike is concerned, it can reasonably be suggested that they chose a very hard way to learn.

On the men's side, there were three positive factors which can be adduced as causes of their victory. First, the quality of the League's leadership was superb. Never losing sight of the twin needs to maintain an excellent public image, and to raise the necessary sums to support their followers, throughout the long dispute Burnett and his associates never put a foot wrong, and their skill contrasted forcibly with the singular tactical ineptitude displayed by their too confident opponents during the early periods of the conflict. Secondly, the strike must have failed had it not been for the very varied and widespread sympathy and concrete support given to the League by men in all parts of the country and from all ranks and conditions in contemporary society. Nearly forty years later Benjamin Browne was of the opinion that:

> The Engineers' Nine Hours' strike of 1871 and the celebrated Dockers' strike in London are cases where the men probably won chiefly because they had such a very large amount of public sympathy, which took the form both of substantial subscriptions and also of a good deal of side pressure brought to bear on the employers by those whose interests suffered from the continuance of the strike.[1]

This crucial question of public sympathy for the strikers well illustrates how strong the bonds of cohesion and co-operation could be in that society, harsh and unpleasant as many of its aspects might be. Incidents like the nine hours' strike surely demonstrate how difficult it is to analyse the development of modern British society in terms of stark class warfare.

Finally, the victory was won by the stubborn loyalty and determination of the engineering workers themselves, concerned not only to obtain the actual concession they demanded from their employers, but determined also to vindicate their claim to decent treatment and consideration at the hands of those who controlled the enterprises for which they provided their labour. The repeated refusals, couched in unconciliatory forms, to discuss the problems involved in the dispute with the men's leaders, were one of the major errors committed by the associated employers during the strike, for it meant not only a refusal of the men's demands, but a wounding refusal to concede that the men had a right to be heard and considered in the taking of decisions which vitally affected them. Not only did such treatment markedly stiffen the resistance of the Leaguers themselves, it also rallied to their support a great deal of external working-class support as well as support from other elements in society.

Two postscripts may be added to this account, one personal, and one more general. During the strike, Burnett had rightfully earned a considerable reputation for his conduct as the strike's principal leader and spokesman. It was obviously inexpedient for him to return to his old employment at Armstrong's Elswick works. Instead, for the next few years, he worked as one of the staff of Cowen's *Newcastle Chronicle*, supplementing his income by lecturing for Joseph Chamberlain's National Education League. As we have seen, in 1875, on the death of William Allan, Burnett succeeded him as General Secretary of the Amalgamated Society of Engineers. Burnett's tenure of that office was not, however, a happy one, principally because of continued friction between Burnett and some of the more militant members of the union. One of Burnett's personal friends later summed up these difficulties, perhaps in a rather one-sided way:

> Though a thoroughly capable organizer and an out-and-out trade unionist, he was too moderate and cautious for the reckless hot-heads in the union at that time who were pushing to the front and always striving to force the organization into indefensible courses. This uneasiness was especially pronounced during the trouble with the Manchester engineers, in the early eighties.[2]

Fortunately an alternative opportunity came along to rescue Burnett from this uncomfortable situation. In 1886 the Liberal government decided to set up a Labour Bureau under the aegis of the Board of Trade. Although the parliamentary moves for this objective were associated primarily with Bradlaugh, radical M.P. for Northampton, Burnett himself had worked behind the scenes for this official recognition of the importance of labour and the need of government to be well informed about the workers' conditions. By a happy chance, the President of the Board of Trade at the time that the new Bureau was created was Mundella, who retained a very lively respect for Burnett's talents, dating back to the 1871 strike. Burnett, therefore, became the first Labour Correspondent of the Board of Trade; in 1893, with the expansion of the Bureau to form a Labour Department, Burnett moved up to be the first Chief Correspondent, a post he held for more than a decade. These were appointments made by successive Liberal governments; in 1891, the Conservative government appointed Burnett to the Royal Commission on Labour.

Like his opposite number in the Northumberland Miners' Union, Thomas Burt, and William Crawford of the Durham Miners' Union, Burnett was something of a show piece working man of the late Victorian establishment, much referred to as conclusive evidence that in that society a manual worker could rise to a position of considerable respectability and public responsibility. Promotion and influence did not spoil Burnett: he remained modest and kindly throughout his life. Nor did he lose his astuteness. He proved a very able and useful civil servant, but the eruption of this unusual figure into the higher echelons of public service fluttered the dovecotes of Whitehall somewhat. One last typical glimpse of him may be given. His new colleagues in government service insisted on pronouncing his name Bur*nett* instead of the more homely pronunciation to which he was accustomed on Tyneside. A friend recalled his reaction[3] 'he remarked with a shrug of his shoulders "It pleases them and it doesn't hurt me" '. Burnett died suddenly, early in 1914, and his death was marked by obituaries full of praise of his character and his services both to labour and to government, in such places as *The Times*, the *Annual Register*, and not least in the columns of the *Newcastle Chronicle* and its associated papers. *Engineering* had this to say of him in its obituary of 6th February 1914:

> A most sympathetic man, who had gained general respect by his absolute fairness in all matters pertaining to labour ... his straightforwardness, experience and sage judgement ... won recognition from all parties.

It may be, however, that Burnett's first great service to labour, as President of the Nine Hours' League, was his greatest, for as both friends and enemies had predicted, the local victory of the Tyneside engineering workers in 1871 did not remain merely a local victory. In ensuing weeks, engineering workers all over the country emulated the Tyneside men by exerting pressure in favour of the 54 hours' week, which was very generally secured throughout the engineering industry by the end of 1871. The monthly bulletin of the A.S.E. in November 1871 urged engineering workers who had not yet secured the nine hours' day to act for the object immediately, and recommended that, as the League had done, A.S.E. members should cordially co-operate with non-union men in joint efforts to secure the 54 hours' week. During the same month, successive numbers of *Engineering* reported concession of the nine hours' day on Tees-side, at Sheffield and at Halifax.

The somewhat equivocal rôle which the A.S.E. had played during the greater part of the prolonged strike in 1871 had not gone unnoticed. Although in its own publications, the A.S.E. tried hard to gloss over its early inaction, and to arrogate to union efforts rather more credit than was their due,[4] it is noticeable that the 1871 victory did not lead to any mass movement of engineering workers on Tyneside into the union's ranks; the rate of growth of the local A.S.E. branches in the early 1870's was no greater than it had been in the 1860's.

The League's victory, however, had consequences which were not confined to the engineering industry, for it provided a great impetus to efforts by other groups of workers to obtain shorter working hours. In the north-east itself, the latter part of 1871 and the early months of 1872, saw pressure exerted for this purpose by several different groups of workers, including shop assistants and agricultural labourers, and some gains were made.[5]

The effect of the Tyneside victory was thus not merely a local or a sectional one. The very wide publicity and interest which the 1871 strike had evoked meant that the Nine Hours' League marked an important stage in the campaign for restriction of hours of work in this country. It was not long before Sir William Armstrong's predictions of further demands were abundantly justified, and the demand for an eight hours' day appeared in its turn. The 1871 strike, however, has an importance which does not stop there, for it was in addition a clear warning that it would not always be possible for arrogant and inconsiderate employers to ride roughshod over the wishes and the interests of the men they employed. The League's victory was a blow struck for a healthier conception of industrial relations in Britain, even if it was to be a very long time before the lessons to be drawn from this story were generally learned.

NOTES TO CHAPTER 6

1. Browne, op. cit., p. 200.
2. *Newcastle Weekly Chronicle*, 3-2-1914.
3. Ibid.
4. Cole and Filson, op. cit., pp. 598-9.
5. See, for example, *Alnwick Journal* for February and March 1872.

APPENDIX A

NORTH-EAST ENGLAND
POPULATION CHANGE 1801-1901

Date	Increase %	Change in Net Migration %
1801	—	—
1811	9.3	—
1821	16.1	+1.9
1831	16.1	+1.7
1841	20.0	+9.2
1851	20.4	+2.7
1861	24.4	+5.3
1871	26.5	+8.0
1881	24.2	+2.8
1891	16.8	−1.3
1901	17.0	+0.4

Source: Table I. House, J. W., *North Eastern England.*

POPULATION CHANGE IN
URBAN AND INDUSTRIAL TYNESIDE
1841-1901

Year	Upper Tyneside (Thousands)	Lower Tyneside (Thousands)
1841	107	56
1851	134	66
1861	167	80
1871	210	115
1881	254	150
1891	329	192
1901	410	233

In 1841, 17% of the population of North-Eastern England lived in Upper Tyneside and 9% in Lower Tyneside. In 1881, the comparable figures were 17% and 10% respectively.

Source: Tables I and III. House, J.W., ibid.

APPENDIX B

APPROXIMATE STATISTICS OF ENGINEERING MANUFACTURE IN THE NORTH-EASTERN DISTRICT

(TYNESIDE, OR NEAR TYNESIDE FIRMS ONLY)

Name	Address	Date when established	Description of Work	Total Number of persons Employed in 1863
Hawks Crawshay & Co.	Gateshead	1747	Millwork & general machinery Mill, colliery & marine steam engines: bridges	1,500
Murray & Co.	Chester-le-Street	1793	Foundry: boilermaking, hauling engines	200
Losh, Wilson & Bell	Walker	1807	Millwork: steam engines for mills & colliery purposes	250
R. & W. Hawthorn	Newcastle	1817	Millwork & general machinery: mill, colliery, marine & locomotive engines	984
R. Stephenson & Co.	Newcastle	1823	Locomotive, marine & mill engines, bridges	1,500
Marshall & Co.	Willington Quay	1830	Paddle engines: other marine engines	1,000
W. G. Armstrong & Co.	Elswick	1847	Millwork, general machinery, bridges, cranes	800
W. G. Armstrong & Co.	Elswick	—	Guns and ammunition	3,000
J. Renoldson	South Shields	1847	Marine engines	40
Palmer Brothers & Co.	Jarrow	1852	Marine engines & machinery connected thereto	600
Morrison & Co.	Ouseburn	1853	Millwork: general machinery, marine engines, steam hammers	600
Thompson & Co.	Newcastle	1856	Millwork & general machinery: mill & marine engines	400

INDEX

Abbott, (engineer), 115
Addington, Henry, 1st Viscount Sidmouth, 66, 68, 94
Admiralty, 18, 21-3, 60, 65-6, 74-5, 184
Allan, William, 104, 128-31, 183, 186
Alnwick, 106
Amalgamated Society of Engineers, 50, 80, 87, 90, 93-4, 102, 104, 128-31, 135-6, 182-3, 186-8
Anderson, Robert, 142
Annual Register, The, 188
Anti-Poor Law agitation, 40-1
Arkwright, Sir Richard, 35
Armaments, 9, 18-24
Army, use of in police rôle, 61, 62, 66-7, 69, 71, 77-8
Armstrong, W. G. 1st Baron, 9, 19-26, 79, 84-5, 88, 102-3, 108-13, 115, 117, 125, 131, 133-4, 138, 144, 146-8, 150-67, 169-73, 175, 177-8, 184-6, 189, 191
Ashley, Lord, see Cooper, Antony A.
Austin, Robert, 104

Bailey, J. 16
Baines, Edward, 44
Bedlington, 59, 71
Black & Hawthorn, (engineers), 115
Blaydon, 14, 59
Blyth, 82
Board of Trade, 187
Boilermakers' Society, 80, 89-92
Bolckow & Vaughan, (ironmasters), 86
Boulton, Matthew, 30
Bowden, P. J. 12
Bradlaugh, Charles, 187

British Association, 18
Browne, Benjamin (later Sir), 109, 165-6, 179, 185-6
Burnett, John, 91, 93-4, 102, 106-8, 110, 113-17, 122, 127-8, 132-5, 138, 142-3, 147, 151, 153, 155, 157-63, 166-9, 171, 173, 179-80, 183, 185-8
Burt, Thomas, 83, 107, 187
Bussey, Peter, 41
Byker, 13

Cadburys', (chocolate manufacturers), 33
Cartwright, John, 68
Caulfield, Captain, 66
Chamberlain, Joseph, 186
Charlton's, (plumbers), 171
Chartism, 40-2, 75-6, 168
Chester-le-Street, 191
Clark, T. (engineer), 115, 136
Clark, Watson & Gurney, (engineers), 113, 115, 126, 136, 152-4, 160, 162-3
Clayton, John, 176
Clennell, Thomas, 61, 94
Coal and coal mining, 9-12, 16-19, 43, 59-65, 70-84, 126, 171
Cobbett, J. M. 49-50
Cochrane, Alfred, 20
Cohn, —, 135
Combination Acts, 63-4, 68, 70, 94
Conciliation boards, 81-2
Cooper, Antony Ashley, 7th Earl of Shaftesbury, 33, 40, 44-5, 47-9
Co-operative societies, 123
Cowen, Joseph, 83, 91, 115-18, 126, 135-8, 143, 145, 175-8